# 100 THINGS
# BUCKS FANS
# SHOULD KNOW & DO
# BEFORE THEY DIE

Eric Nehm

## TRIUMPH
### BOOKS

Library of Congress Cataloging-in-Publication Data

Names: Nehm, Eric, author.
Title: 100 things Bucks fans should know and do before they die / Eric Nehm.
Other titles: One hundred things Bucks fans should know and do before they
    die | Hundred things Bucks fans should know and do before they die
Description: Chicago, Illinois : Triumph Books LLC, [2018]
Identifiers: LCCN 2018029196 | ISBN 9781629376189
Subjects: LCSH: Milwaukee Bucks (Basketball team)—History. | Milwaukee Bucks
    (Basketball team)—Miscellanea.
Classification: LCC GV885.52.M54 N44 2018 | DDC 796.323/640977595—
dc23 LC record available at https://lccn.loc.gov/2018029196

This book is available in quantity at special discounts for your group or organization. For further information, contact:
    **Triumph Books LLC**
    814 North Franklin Street
    Chicago, Illinois 60610
    (312) 337-0747
    www.triumphbooks.com

Printed in U.S.A.
ISBN: 978-1-62937-618-9
Design by Patricia Frey
Photos courtesy of AP Images unless otherwise indicated

*To my family.*
*Thank you for your support.*

# Contents

# 1 The 1971 NBA Championship

After a loss to the New York Knicks in Game 5 of the 1970 Eastern Conference Finals, Milwaukee Bucks center and New York City native Lew Alcindor (later Kareem Abdul-Jabbar) was serenaded by his fellow New Yorkers. As the 22-year-old rookie left the floor, the Madison Square Garden crowd taunted him with a song: "Good-bye Lewie, good-bye Lewie, good-bye Lewie, we're glad to see you go."

Despite a Rookie of the Year season in which he averaged 28.8 points and 14.5 rebounds per game and helped the Bucks win 29 more games than they had in their previous, inaugural season, Alcindor did not leave New York happy. Instead, the singing left him determined to come back in 1971 and triumph over the mighty Knicks. As he left the floor, he told Bucks general manager John Erickson, "We'll be back, Mr. Erickson."

In the off-season, the NBA added three new teams and the Bucks moved to the Western Conference, which meant Alcindor & Co. would have to wait until the NBA Finals to perhaps enact their revenge against the Knicks.

For that to be possible, the Bucks needed to give Alcindor a true running mate and that is exactly what Erickson and Bucks president Ray Patterson set out to do. They didn't waste any time either, trading for 10-time All-Star and former MVP Oscar Robertson on April 21, 1970, the day after losing to the Knicks.

"When I heard that Oscar was coming to play with the Bucks, I was very happy," Abdul-Jabbar later said. "I thought that really made it easy for us to win because of his abilities on both ends of the court. Getting to work with him every day really helped me see his greatness."

Entering his 11th NBA season, Robertson was no longer in his prime as an athlete, but he still represented a massive upgrade for a Bucks team desperately needing more scoring and dynamism from its guards. Since he was feuding with Cincinnati Royals head coach Bob Cousy at the time, Milwaukee only gave up shooting guard

*The only NBA champions in Milwaukee Bucks history: (clockwise) Bob Dandridge (10), Lew Alcindor (33), Greg Smith, Oscar Robertson (1), head coach Larry Costello, and Jon McGlocklin.*

Flynn Robinson, coming off a career season, and previous seventh-round pick Charlie Paulk to acquire the 10-year-veteran.

The pairing worked out terrifically. Robertson's scoring average dipped in Milwaukee, but it wasn't needed in the same way it was when he was the lead man in Cincinnati. With Alcindor in the middle leading the league in scoring and winning NBA MVP for the first time, Robertson could focus on being a floor general and keeping his teammates involved.

Both Bobby Dandridge and Jon McGlocklin recorded the best shooting percentages of their careers in the 1970–71 season with "The Big O" at the helm. Erickson acquired a little bench help with a trade for Lucius Allen and Bob Boozer shortly before the season and the Bucks turned into a well-oiled machine running the Triangle offense implemented by head coach Larry Costello. Ultimately, the Bucks put together a 66–16 record, good for the first seed in the Western Conference and a franchise record for wins.

The Western Conference didn't pose much of a challenge to Milwaukee as the team needed only five games to vanquish each of its conference foes. In the first round, they blew past Nate Thurmond, Jerry Lucas, and the San Francisco Warriors, with a 106–104 loss in Game 4 serving as their only hiccup. Alcindor outplayed Wilt Chamberlain as the Bucks blew past the Los Angeles Lakers—who were without Elgin Baylor and Jerry West due to injuries—in the Western Conference Finals. The Bucks won their four games over the Lakers by an average of 20 points per game.

And with that, the Bucks awaited their rematch with the Knicks—but it never came. The Knicks fell to the Baltimore Bullets in a seven-game series in the Eastern Conference Finals and the Bucks have not met the Knicks in the playoffs since. But the Bullets paid a price to get through the Knicks, as forward Gus Johnson and guard Earl Monroe got banged up in the series. Each player missed two NBA Finals games, while center Wes Unseld dealt with injuries throughout the playoffs.

A healthy Bullets squad might have made for a tough matchup, but given their injuries they had little chance in this series and the Bucks swept the 1971 NBA Finals. Alcindor was brilliant, posting 27 points, 18.5 rebounds, and 2.8 assists per game in the series and adding a Finals MVP to go along with his regular season MVP. Robertson averaged 23.5 points and 9.5 assists per game, while Dandridge added 20 points per game as well. The Bucks were the better team and they simply took care of business.

"I joined the Bucks," Robertson later said. "I knew we were going to win the championship that year as soon as I got there. Destiny, confidence. I just knew we were going to win."

In just three years, the Bucks went from expansion team to NBA champion and, if you ask those involved, there was never a doubt in their minds.

# Game 6 of the 1974 NBA Finals

"Oscar Robertson throws to Kareem," described Bucks radio announcer Eddie Doucette. "Seven seconds. Finkel. The skyhook is good! Kareem with the big pressure shot!"

Abdul-Jabbar's incredible shot gave the Bucks a 102–101 lead with just three seconds left in double overtime of Game 6 of the 1974 NBA Finals. It would cap what Bucks forward Jon McGlocklin calls "one of the great games in NBA, not just Bucks, history." When taking a closer look at the game, it's obvious why he would come to such a conclusion.

Trailing 3–2 in the series, the Bucks were forced to fight for their playoff lives with a depleted roster in the Boston Garden. Lucius Allen missed the entirety of the playoffs with a knee injury.

A torn calf hampered McGlocklin's movement throughout the series and a torn groin kept Robertson at less than 100 percent. No one felt too bad for the Bucks, since they had three-time MVP Abdul-Jabbar and the league's best record going into the series, but those injuries hampered them throughout the series.

Milwaukee led for much of the game, but Boston chipped away at the deficit and eventually Celtics guard John Havlicek hit a jumper to tie the game at 86–86 with just under a minute left in regulation. On the following possession, the Bucks ran a pick and roll with Robertson and Abdul-Jabbar on the right wing late in the shot clock. Celtics center Dave Cowens switched onto Robertson and capably defended for a few seconds before poking the ball away from "The Big O" with three seconds left on the shot clock. Cowens sprinted after it, dove, and eventually the referees correctly assessed a shot clock violation.

The defensive play would lose some of its luster as the game went on, but it was a perfect encapsulation of the entire series— Cowens with a dogged effort defensively, Robertson unable to take advantage of the switch, a possession ending in a turnover for Milwaukee. Neither the Celtics nor the Bucks scored again, with McGlocklin missing a baseline jumper short off the rim, sending the game to overtime.

Both teams struggled to get much of anything going in the first overtime with a combined eight points between the two teams. The Bucks were so out of sorts that Robertson failed to even get a shot attempt up as time expired and the game moved to a second overtime, tied at 90–90.

The first 90 seconds of the second overtime seemed to be following a similar script as fouls, deflections, and missed shots marred the start of the period. A short baseline jumper for Havlicek, plus a free throw to give the Celtics a 93–92 lead, got the action started as the game transitioned from a messy slog to the late rounds of a marquee heavyweight fight with both fighters connecting on haymakers.

Abdul-Jabbar immediately answers with a hook shot. Bucks lead, 94–93.

Havlicek retaliates with a pull-up baseline jumper over the outstretched right arm of the 7-foot-2 Abdul-Jabbar. Celtics lead, 95–94.

Robertson dribbles down the floor on a cleared-out right side and dribbles into a pull-up jumper over Jo Jo White. Bucks lead, 96–95.

Abdul-Jabbar blocks a Havlicek runner. Out of bounds. Havlicek inbounds. White hits a baseline jumper. Celtics lead, 97–96.

Abdul-Jabbar kicks out of a double team to Robertson, who dribbles into a runner as the shot clock expires. Bucks lead, 98–97.

Outlet to Havlicek, who cans a pull-up jumper from the right elbow. Celtics lead, 99–98.

Cowens picks up his sixth foul on an Abdul-Jabbar postup. Boston subsequently forces a shot clock violation.

After the two teams combined for scores on six straight possessions, sometimes on seemingly impossible shots, the Celtics got a stop and shifted the pressure back to the Bucks, who now trailed 99–98 with 1:02 left on the clock and Boston in possession of the ball.

They would need to make a play defensively and that is exactly what Robertson did. Havlicek caught the ball on the right wing after coming around a few screens, but Robertson stayed in front of the All-Star guard, who eventually dribbled the ball off his foot with 44 seconds left. Milwaukee struggled mightily getting the ball up the floor, but eventually Mickey Davis attempted a contested baseline jumper and hit it with 23 seconds left to grab a 100–99 lead for the Bucks.

The Celtics brought the ball up the floor and coach Tommy Heinsohn called for a timeout as nothing developed, but no one could hear him. His team played on and eventually Havlicek got the ball on the right wing as he ran off a baseline screen. He ripped the ball through low and in front of his body to get a slight advantage on Robertson to the baseline. Abdul-Jabbar once again came from the backside to attempt to block his shot and even ended up hitting Havlicek's right arm with his right arm, but his contest didn't matter. Havlicek made it for his ninth point of the second overtime period and a 101–100 lead for the Celtics with just seven seconds left.

The Garden erupted and the Bucks immediately called a timeout to draw up a play. With the game on the line, things got a

*Kareem Abdul-Jabbar skyhooks the winning basket against the Boston Celtics in Game 6 of the 1974 NBA Finals.*

little chaotic on the Bucks' bench as coach Larry Costello grabbed for his yellow legal pad and started to draw up a play.

"Larry was kind of like, frantic, trying to think up a great play," Abdul-Jabbar later told OnMilwaukee.com. "And, we just couldn't figure it out all the way, who was supposed to get free."

As the team broke the huddle, there was mass confusion.

"I was a player who always knew what I was supposed to do," McGlocklin told Fox Sports Wisconsin. "I knew the plays. I knew my assignments and I did them. So, I'm standing on the free throw line down in front of the Boston bench. Oscar has it out of bounds. Mickey Davis is standing next to me. I said, 'Mickey, I have no idea what I'm supposed to do.' On Larry's legal pad, he had me in three different places. Oscar has the ball yelling, 'Break! Break!' We don't know what to do."

Abdul-Jabbar knew what to do: get the ball and score.

The MVP center got position at the elbow and made sure to go to the basketball. He collected it with Hank Finkel on his back a few feet outside of the lane slightly above the right elbow. He pivoted to look for Davis cutting down the middle of the lane and then attacked with a single dribble to the baseline. Finkel stayed on his left hip, forcing him to dribble parallel to the sideline instead of toward the basket. From about 17 feet out Abdul-Jabbar collected the basketball, even with Don Chaney trying to poke it away after chasing him down from Robertson. Planting off his left foot and extending his right arm high, the game's most dominant player released his patented skyhook and it splashed through the net.

Bucks up 102–101 with three seconds left.

The Celtics would have one last-ditch effort, but White's jumper was no good and the Bucks had won Game 6 of the 1974 NBA Finals to force the series back to Milwaukee for a Game 7. It was one of the greatest Finals games ever played and one few would soon forget.

# 3 The Lew Alcindor Coin Flip

There were no doubts about what was at stake. Phoenix Suns general manager Jerry Colangelo called it a "monumental, once-in-a-lifetime flip of a coin." And that's exactly what it was.

National Basketball Association commissioner J. Walter Kennedy would flip a 1964 Kennedy half-dollar into the air with his right hand, catch it with his right hand, and turn it onto the back of his left hand. The results of the flip would be given to the participating teams over the phone. The winner of the flip would be rewarded with the first pick in the 1969 NBA Draft and the right to draft UCLA Center Lew Alcindor.

The Phoenix Suns and Milwaukee Bucks would be the two participants in the coin flip by virtue of their records during the 1968–69 season. Both teams were new to the NBA as expansion teams and finished with the worst records in their respective divisions.

The Bucks finished last in the Eastern Division with a 27–55 record, while the Suns finished rounded out the Western Division with a 16–66 record. At the time, in the 14-team NBA, the teams in last place in their respective divisions would participate in a coin flip for the first pick of the draft. With the worst record overall, the Suns were given the right to call heads or tails.

To figure out what to call, the Suns held a poll asking their fans to choose either heads or tails. The poll ended with a majority of fans deciding on heads. Then 29-year-old Suns GM Jerry Colangelo decided to roll with the fans' decision and called heads.

It was tails.

In Phoenix, devastation. In Milwaukee, elation.

Wes Pavalon, principal owner of the Bucks, and John Erickson, Bucks vice-president and general manager, were listening to the call together and celebrated the moment they heard that they had won the first pick. In the excitement, Pavalon actually burned his colleague with a lit cigarette he accidentally jammed into Erickson's right ear.

"It stung a little, but I didn't notice it," Erickson told *Sports Illustrated*. "I didn't care, once we had Lew."

Their excitement was totally justified. Alcindor was a once-in-a-lifetime talent. At UCLA, he was changing the game under coach John Wooden—literally. In 1967, the NCAA outlawed the slam dunk and many suggested Alcindor was the reason the rule was added. Some even went as far as calling it the "Alcindor Rule."

In his three-year career at UCLA, the Bruins lost just twice in 90 games and won the national championship in each season. Alcindor was named the NCAA's Final Four Most Outstanding Player each of the three years, a feat that has yet to be matched. And, in his final year, he was awarded the first Naismith Trophy, an award given annually to the nation's top player. Like Wilt Chamberlain and Bill Russell before him, Alcindor was an insanely athletic 7-footer with fluidity and rhythm incredibly rare in players so tall.

"He may be the first of the 7-foot backcourt men," Bucks guard Fred Crawford told *Sports Illustrated* during Alcindor's first year in Milwaukee. "He can dribble and make moves that no big man ever made before. Russell could dribble straight down the floor, but Lew can bring the ball down and handle it and give you fakes, and no one his size could ever do that."

With such prodigious talent, Alcindor's skills were in high demand around the world and the other professional basketball league in the United States, the American Basketball Association (ABA), posed a real threat to the Bucks. The organization had won the first pick of the NBA Draft, but Alcindor had previously expressed a preference to play in Los Angeles or New York.

The ABA's New York Nets could have posed a problem as they would have had the money to pay Alcindor more than the Bucks and they could help place him in New York, but the fledgling NBA could not allow him to go to a different league. To make sure Alcindor would sign with the Bucks, the NBA's 14 team owners banded together and helped the Bucks put together a five-year, $1.4 million deal, the largest amount ever offered a player at the time.

It was enough. They outbid the ABA and secured the rights to a franchise-changing and league-altering rookie. They had signed Lew Alcindor, and nothing would ever be the same in Milwaukee.

For the record, the Suns' consolation prize was Neal Walk, a center from the University of Florida. He played five seasons in Phoenix, averaging 14.7 points per game.

# 4 Herb Kohl Purchases the Bucks

"We want very much for someone in Milwaukee to buy the Bucks, because we feel this is where they belong," Bucks principal owner Jim Fitzgerald said at the news conference announcing his decision to put the team up for sale on February 5, 1985.

Despite Fitzgerald's wishes, he was in a tough spot with the team. They were in one of the NBA's smallest markets. They played in the league's smallest arena, the Milwaukee Arena, which seated only 11,052 fans. To counteract each of those facts and create more revenue, the Bucks created Sportsvue Cable Network, a pay-television venture the team operated with the Milwaukee

Brewers and several other teams, but it didn't work out and ended up losing money as well.

With all of that in play, it would have been easy to understand if Fitzgerald, a Janesville, Wisconsin, native, sold the team to someone who might be interested in finding a more viable location for a team to thrive. Or if he simply couldn't find someone who was willing to keep the team in Milwaukee, a market rife with potential pitfalls for an NBA team.

Fitzgerald, however, would quickly learn there was at least one other person as committed as he was to keeping the team in Milwaukee: Herb Kohl.

Kohl, a local businessman, tried to get a team in Milwaukee before the Bucks existed. In 1967, the American Basketball Association searched across the nation for new markets and a group led by Kohl expressed interest, but ultimately couldn't get everything together fast enough for the league. In December of 1967, a Kohl-led group formally applied for an NBA expansion franchise, but when the league announced Milwaukee would be awarded a franchise, it was given to Marvin Fishman and Wes Pavalon's group.

"I called Walter Kennedy, the commissioner, and went to see him in New York," Kohl later told OnMilwaukee.com. "He said they were going to expand and Milwaukee would be a good place. I came home and cleared dates at the old Arena and met with the expansion committee. Then Kennedy called me and said they were going to award a franchise. He said I could have it but if I didn't want it there was another group, Pavalon's group, and the NBA was fine with them. I was very busy at Kohl's and my dad, he didn't think a basketball team was the way for his son to be in business. So I said no and the rest is history."

When the opportunity came back around in 1985, Kohl's situation had changed. He came to be president of Kohl's, a chain of family-owned grocery stores, department stores, and pharmacies, and eventually sold the business. With the necessary assets to purchase the team, the interest in owning an NBA team, and the time needed to properly serve a team with a complicated future, Kohl stepped up and purchased the team for $18 million.

According to Kohl, Fitzgerald could have received as much as $7 million more for the franchise, but turned down those offers to sell to someone committed to Milwaukee. In his introductory press conference as owner, Kohl made his commitment to the city and state abundantly clear.

"We couldn't afford to lose them," Kohl told the *Milwaukee Journal.* "Psychologically and economically, it would have been a disaster. Fitz [Fitzgerald] knew that, and I didn't think he would sell to outside interests. He wanted to maximize the value to a buyer in Milwaukee, but I knew he would sell for less to a Milwaukee person or group than somebody from outside."

Owning an NBA team in Milwaukee surely fulfilled a dream for Kohl, but it was just the beginning of an uphill struggle. The team would need to find a way to become more viable and that started with a new arena. It may have just been excitement over buying the franchise, but Kohl was convinced Milwaukee would get a new arena.

"I feel now that we can get something done," Kohl said. "I'd bet on it. Things should move forward now on their own momentum."

A few days after purchasing the team, Milwaukee natives Jane and Lloyd Pettit notified him they would donate $90 million toward the construction of a brand-new downtown arena. Maybe it was fate. Maybe it was the power of positive thinking. One thing was for sure, though: Herb Kohl would keep the Bucks in Milwaukee.

# 5 The Big Three

The nickname has been commandeered by many trios over the years, but the Big Three in Milwaukee can only refer to three guys: Ray Allen, Sam Cassell, and Glenn Robinson.

Each player had a unique journey to Milwaukee and during the years after they left, but all three shared three special seasons together playing the best basketball the city of Milwaukee had seen in nearly two decades from 1999 to 2001.

Robinson came first. Drafted by the Bucks first overall in the 1994 NBA Draft, the "Big Dog" exhibited the prodigious scoring talent that made him National Player of the Year at Purdue by scoring 20 points per game from the moment he hit an NBA floor. Allen came next as part of a draft night trade that moved the sweet-shooting No. 5 pick in the 1996 NBA Draft and a future first-round pick from Minnesota to Milwaukee, and No. 4 pick Stephon Marbury to the Timberwolves. Cassell was the final piece, joining the team at the trade deadline during the 1998–99 season, but only appearing in seven games for the Bucks, including a three-game sweep at the hands of the Indiana Pacers in the 1999 Eastern Conference Finals.

With Cassell's ankles healthy and ready to go, the 1999–2000 season would be the first real go-round for the Big Three and everyone around the league was watching. Long-time NBA scribe Sam Smith of the *Chicago Tribune* wondered if three big-time scorers would be able to propel the Bucks to winning the Eastern Conference. *Sports Illustrated*'s Mark Bechtel asked if Cassell would be enough of a distributor to run the show or if his scoring would get in the way of fostering a team environment. The Big Three did not share those same concerns.

*Ray Allen, Sam Cassell, and Glenn Robinson—forever known in Milwaukee as the Big Three—hold a special place in the hearts of Bucks fans despite never reaching their full potential.* (Photo by Jeff Gross/Allsport)

"To be successful in this league, you have to have a little cocki-ness," Cassell told the *Chicago Tribune* before the 1999–2000 season. "What's made George Karl a successful coach is he's cocky in his own little way. I know if I'm healthy, I'm one of the best point guards in the league. The last year I was healthy there was only one point guard who outscored me, and that was Allen Iverson."

For the next two years, the Bucks blurred the line between confidence and cockiness as the Big Three lit up the league. In their first full season together, they were the league's second-most-efficient offense, scoring 108.2 points per 100 possessions. The next season, the offense bumped up to the league's best, with 108.8 points per 100 possessions. The team's success was predicated on the knowledge that any member of the Big Three could hurt you on any given night.

"They didn't bring me here to be Muggsy Bogues," Cassell told *Sports Illustrated* of his role in Milwaukee. "Some nights I'll score big; some nights I won't. But getting assists won't be a problem on this team."

Bucks general manager Ernie Grunfeld was fond of calling Allen and Robinson the best shooting guard–small forward combo in the league and that's part of what made it so easy to find assists. Robinson was able to do some damage on the block, from the elbows, and at the rim. As a sharpshooter from deep, Allen could fill it up from anywhere and Robinson told *Sports Illustrated*, "He's the most natural player I've played with."

The beauty of the Big Three was their inability to be anyone else. From the moment Bucks head coach George Karl got them together, he wanted a more complete threesome. More rebound-ing, better defense, more consistent passing. Eventually Karl's demands for defense led to the trio's divorce, but those three never fundamentally changed their games.

The Big Three were all unabashed gunners. They simply wanted to put the ball in the basket and they did it well. And they did it together. In their three years as teammates, Allen averaged 22 points and 4.1 assists per game, Robinson averaged 21.2 points and 2.7 assists per game, and Cassell averaged 18.8 points and 7.8 assists per game.

They did everything in their power to outscore their opponents and carried themselves with a swagger that suggested they would do just that every single night. Allen, Cassell, and Robinson would not end up winning a championship, but their infectious confidence and high-scoring offense made them some of the most beloved Bucks of all time.

# 6 Wayne Embry

Wayne Embry's basketball career caught him by surprise over and over again.

The 6-foot-8 center put together a successful career at Miami (Ohio) and hoped to play for the Harlem Globetrotters, but ultimately decided on moving on from basketball. As he prepared for graduate school at Miami, he was informed he had been drafted by the NBA's St. Louis Hawks. Soon after the draft, he was traded to the Cincinnati Royals.

After a rookie season of mistakes and learning how to play at the next level, Embry found a niche for himself as a strong, tough-minded center in his second season. After that second season, the Royals drafted University of Cincinnati guard Oscar Robertson and Embry's career took off as he formed a close bond with the future Hall of Famer on and off the floor. Embry went to the next five All-Star Games before his body started to wear down in the

1965–66 season, his eighth NBA season. With his body betraying him, Embry decided to retire.

Embry found a job with Pepsi and prepared to start his life after basketball before once again getting a call that would keep him from leaving the game. This time, it was a call from Boston Celtics player-coach Bill Russell, who wanted Embry, one of the centers that made his life difficult, to be his backup. Embry jumped at the opportunity and won a championship with Russell in the 1967–68 season, his second season in Boston. The NBA would be expanding the next season with two expansion franchises and Embry knew there was a chance he would be claimed, but his friend Russell tried to convince him he would be able to stay with the Celtics.

"As it turned out, on the day of the expansion draft, I'm playing golf with Bill Russell, who had said that he was going to try to do everything to keep me in Boston," Embry told Fox Sports Wisconsin. "I call home to see where I went in the expansion draft and my wife says we're going to Milwaukee. I said, 'Oh my god.' I came back out to Russell and said, 'You said you were going to keep me in Boston. I'm going to Milwaukee, the coldest place in the world!'"

Deep down, Embry knew there was a good chance he would be selected in the draft, but he had hoped Phoenix would be the team to select him and he'd be able to move to a warm weather city. Embry played for the Bucks in their first season before deciding to retire and once again try to start a career outside of the NBA.

He briefly moved back to Boston for a position as a city recreation director before receiving a call from Bucks owner Wes Pavalon. The owner offered Embry a position as a front office assistant and he accepted. Shortly after agreeing on a position, Pavalon told Embry about a project the organization had been working on that the former Cincinnati Royal could help finish: a trade for his former teammate and pick-and-roll partner Robertson.

"I think Oscar had a no-trade contract or approval, and [Pavalon] asked me if I'd pick up the phone and give him a call, and kind of push him our way," Embry told NBA.com. "I told Oscar I was going back and it'd be great for him to win a championship after all these years. And of course I was interested in pushing it along, if I was going to go back there, too."

The Bucks completed the trade for Robertson immediately after the 1969–70 season and went on to win the NBA championship the following season. Embry would spend another year as an assistant to general manager Ray Patterson before getting a call from Pavalon to head over to his office.

"He and two of his board members were in his office. He just looked at me and said, 'You're the new general manager of the Milwaukee Bucks.' It didn't register. I was, what, 34, 35 at the time? There never had been any [black GMs]. I just told them I'd do the best I could in whatever capacity I was in. But to be named the man in charge came as a complete shock."

At 35 years old, Embry would become the first African American general manager in NBA history. Thirteen years after he thought was done with basketball, seven years after he thought he was done playing in the NBA, two years after he was ready to move onto something outside of the NBA, Embry was making NBA history.

"I had mixed feelings because usually you go from player to coach, but not player to general manager," Embry told Fox Sports Wisconsin. "I thought about it for a little bit and said, 'Well, thank you.'"

Embry would serve as the team's general manager for five seasons. The team would remain strong during Embry's first two seasons, even dropping the 1974 NBA Finals in seven games, but ultimately fell off once Kareem Abdul-Jabbar requested a trade out of Milwaukee. The three seasons following the trade would be a struggle for Embry and the Bucks, but that wasn't the only place Embry had struggles.

He also went through many of the same problems as other groundbreaking athletes, receiving hate mail throughout his tenure as general manager. Despite making history and dealing with racism and prejudice throughout his time, Embry remained modest about his accomplishments.

"I was asked at the time if it was significant, and I said only if it was significant to others," Embry said. "I just felt I had a job to do. I put pressure on myself to do the best I could, prepare myself for it, and work harder than everybody else."

Embry stepped down as general manager in 1977 when Jim Fitzgerald took over controlling interest of the team, but remained with the Bucks as a consultant. Eventually, Embry would go on to serve as the Cleveland Cavaliers' general manager and team president, the first African American team president in NBA history. He won Executive of the Year in both 1992 and 1998 with the Cavaliers before moving on to an advisory role with the Toronto Raptors in 2004, which he still serves in to this day.

"He may be underappreciated out there in the big scheme of things, but in the basketball universe, there are very few people that are more respected than Wayne Embry," Bucks broadcasting legend Eddie Doucette told Fox Sports Wisconsin.

The respect for Embry and his sterling career come as a surprise to no one...except maybe Embry himself.

# 7 Nellie's Last Game

Everyone in the Milwaukee locker room knew what was on the line as the Bucks prepared to step on the floor at the Boston Garden for Game 7 of their Eastern Conference semifinals matchup against the Boston Celtics.

Win? Advance to the Eastern Conference Finals to play the Detroit Pistons. Lose? Don Nelson has coached his final game in Milwaukee, ending an 11-year run as head coach.

The drama was surely ratcheted up a few notches because of the setting, the stakes, and the location, but the Bucks had dealt with that for much of the series. Their backs had been against the wall since the moment they dropped Game 4 to the Celtics 138–137 in a double-overtime heartbreaker or, possibly more accurately, the moment after they dropped that game.

After the Game 4 loss, Nelson decided to go public with some of the struggles he had with Bucks owner Herb Kohl. Nelson had been hired by former Bucks owner Jim Fitzgerald, but remained coach when Kohl took over in 1985. In the year and a half Kohl had owned the team, Nelson struggled with the adjustment of working with a new owner and the two had "serious disagreements over such things as the Jack Sikma trade, recent drafts, and the general operation of the franchise," according to the *Chicago Tribune*.

Nelson discussed the slim odds of him returning to Milwaukee and the changing atmosphere and feeling around the team, but the major takeaway was Nelson's most memorable statement: "I feel that I am the Milwaukee Bucks."

Nelson publicly clearing the air might have lit a fire under his team or maybe the Celtics' injuries just became too numerous, but either way, the Bucks fought back from a 3–1 series deficit and forced a Game 7 in Boston.

With 5:52 left in the fourth quarter, the Bucks took a 108–100 lead on a step-back jumper from Jack Sikma, who had gotten a mismatch in the post with Celtics guard Dennis Johnson on him. As Johnson dribbled the ball up the floor, the Celtics' odds looked long.

Guard Danny Ainge had left the game in the third quarter with a sprained knee. Larry Bird was just 8-of-20 at the time with just 23 points. He had been cold in Games 5 and 6 as well, hitting just 4-of-20 shots in the two games combined. Center Robert Parish had missed Game 6 with a sprained ankle and hobbled through Game 7 with limited mobility. Forward Kevin McHale's right foot was fractured as well, but he kept playing through the pain. Nearly the entire Boston roster was injured in some way. The Bucks had an eight-point lead with just under six minutes left and an opportunity to vanquish their most-hated rival.

And then it all fell apart.

With Ainge on the bench, the Bucks sent an extra defender to trap the ball out of Johnson's hands (which also kept the Celtics from posting up Bird) and forced bench guard Jerry Sichting to make a play. And he did, sandwiching jumpers on back-to-back possessions between buckets from McHale and Bird.

Bucks forward Paul Pressey had been killing the Celtics the entire night—28 points, eight assists, four steals, and two blocks—but he picked up his fourth and fifth fouls during this short time period. The first was on a questionable charge call and the second on a reach-in against Johnson. Even with a couple strong minutes from the Celtics, the Bucks still led 113–111, even forcing a missed shot from Parish and a turnover from Bird. But then disaster struck.

While Bird was setting up in the post, Pressey grabbed the All-NBA forward and fouled out of the game with 2:32 left. Bird calmly stepped to the line and sank both free throws to tie the game, and the Bucks' offense spiraled out of control the rest of the way. They would go scoreless for the final three and a half minutes, ultimately losing 118–113 and dropping the series to Boston.

"I lost it after the game, started crying like a baby," Nelson later told ESPN. "Players were coming over to me to console me, which was pretty strange. That's the only time I can remember where I just felt that I let the team down and we should have won."

Kohl and Nelson would be unable to come together and work something out following the season. Nelson resigned from his position two weeks later before eventually becoming the general manager for former Bucks owner Jim Fitzgerald and his new team, the Golden State Warriors. The divorce was complete. The Bucks had fittingly once again lost to the Celtics. And the Nelson Era in Milwaukee was over.

# 8 Drafting Giannis Antetokounmpo

"Hey," Bucks assistant general manager Jeff Weltman said, walking into general manager John Hammond's office in late 2012. "I think we should make a trip. We need to go over to Greece and see this player. He's getting a lot of attention."

That was Hammond's first recollection of the player who changed his career.

His scouting staff was well aware of him because, as Hammond will happily explain to anyone who wants to listen, a team's scouts are always scouring the entire basketball world for players, but Hammond had not yet gotten a chance to watch him play.

With Weltman at his side, Hammond made the trip to Athens, Greece. And they made the drive out to the 500-seat gym of Filathlitikos B.C., a basketball team located in the Athens suburb of

Zografou. And they watched three days of basketball in the club's gym with springless backboards and cracked window panes. And they got their first in-person look at Giannis Adetokunbo. (His official surname is a Greek transcription of his parents' Yoruba language name; this is usually transliterated letter-for-letter back into the Latin alphabet as Antetokounmpo.)

"We sat down in that gym and it didn't take us long to realize that this guy had a chance to be a good player," Hammond later told The Vertical.

The rail-thin 17-year-old they saw in that gym was a scout's dream. Six feet, nine inches tall. Huge hands. Deft ballhandling. Strong court vision. Great footwork, due to a childhood preference for soccer over basketball. It was all there, except the competition.

Despite the NBA skillset, Antetokounmpo was only playing in Greece's second division, a league ill-suited for testing a potential first-round pick's abilities. Any projection of the lanky young forward's abilities for the upcoming 2013 NBA Draft proved difficult. When he played with the club's men's team, it was at small forward, where he averaged nine points and five rebounds per game. With the youth team, Antetokounmpo would shift over to point guard. With a lack of quality opponents, it was difficult to figure out just what he could be at the next level, but that didn't stop the NBA from trying.

Scouts made their way to Greece throughout the season, as did NBA general managers. Oklahoma City's Sam Presti, Atlanta's Danny Ferry, Houston's Daryl Morey, and Toronto's Masai Ujiri all made the trip to the modest, threadbare gym just outside of Athens to get a closer look at Giannis Antetokounmpo.

As NBA personnel folks flocked to Greece, they would look around the gym and see folks they knew, as well as one other group at every game: Antetokounmpo's family. And, in talking with his family, they would find out that there was much more to Antetokounmpo than the game of basketball.

For years, his family struggled. His parents immigrated illegally to Greece in 1991 from Nigeria for a better life, but it was difficult to find. His mother, Veronica, found work as a babysitter, while his father, Charles, became a handyman for an electrical company. While in Greece, they had four children—Thanasis, Giannis, Kostas, and Alex—and each of those children did what they could to help the family.

When Spiros Velliniatis found Antetokounmpo (and his brother Thanasis) in his childhood neighborhood of Sepolia, he had to convince Giannis that playing basketball was a good decision.

*Selecting Giannis Antetokounmpo, a skinny teenager from Greece, in the 2013 NBA Draft was the best decision the Bucks have made in a generation.*

Antetokounmpo insisted that he needed to find a job to help his parents and family, instead of trying to play basketball. Velliniatis explained that basketball could be a way out of poverty for both him and his brother and eventually convinced Antetokounmpo to start playing for Filathlitikos.

Basketball also led to citizenship for Antetokounmpo and his family because NBA scouts were not the only people starting to pay attention to Giannis and Thanasis on the basketball court. The Greek National Team became interested as well, but, in order to play for the country, they would need to be citizens of Greece. On May 9, 2013, both brothers were awarded Greek citizenship, which meant NBA draft graphics and replica draft night jerseys would spell their last name Antetokounmpo.

Even with all of the excitement for Antetokounmpo, no one really knew which team would be given the chance to fit all 13 of those letters across the back of one of its jerseys. Antetokounmpo was, as described by ESPN draft analyst Fran Fraschilla, "the youngest player in the draft and the most mysterious" and surely on the radar of many NBA teams, so it would be impossible to predict exactly where he would go.

Shortly after 8:00 PM in Milwaukee on June 27, 2013, NBA commissioner David Stern stepped to the podium at the Barclays Center in Brooklyn, New York, and said, "With the 15th pick in the 2013 NBA Draft, the Milwaukee Bucks select… Giannis Antetokounmpo from Athens, Greece. He last played for Filathlitikos in Greece."

After the pick, ESPN cameras flashed to a shot of Antetokounmpo in the arena. He slowly rose from his seat and gave a quick fist pump with his right hand before embracing his brother Thanasis, who was sitting to his left with his arms spread wide waving a Greek flag. They were, however, not in the green room with the rest of the draft picks in attendance, but rather cramped into the seats in the lower bowl of the arena, waiting to see if, and when, they would be selected.

"Going into that draft night, we had our rankings on our board at 15 and we had Giannis at 15," Hammond later told NBA.com. "He was our guy at 15."

Dressed in a light blue, patterned suit jacket, Antetokounmpo threw on a green Milwaukee Bucks hat and did his first NBA interview with Hall of Fame broadcaster Craig Sager. His excitement was clear with wide eyes and a smile carrying him through an interview in a second language he wasn't entirely comfortable with at the time.

"It's a wonderful feeling," Antetokounmpo told Sager. "I can't describe how excited I feel. It's a dream come true. From Europe to the NBA, from Division Two of Europe, not even in Division One Europe. From Division Two to the NBA, it's wonderful."

Little did he or anyone know, just how wonderful his time in Milwaukee would be.

# 9 Retired Jerseys: Kareem Abdul-Jabbar's No. 33

Kareem Abdul-Jabbar asked to leave Milwaukee five seasons into his career and left the Bucks after his sixth season. Choosing to leave a franchise is enough for some fanbases and organizations to ostracize a player for the rest of their career, enough to never forgive them. That was never the case with the Bucks and Abdul-Jabbar, though.

"A lot of the things we do in life—sometimes, we might do a great job and never have it appreciated," Abdul-Jabbar said during a pregame ceremony before his last NBA appearance in Milwaukee

*Despite orchestrating a trade to Los Angeles in 1975, Kareem Abdul-Jabbar received a warm reception from Bucks fans when the team retired his jersey number in 1993.*

on December 11, 1988. "I never had to deal with that when I was here. A lot of times you do great work and you don't get paid for it. I never had to deal with that when I was here. So many times, you're just able to pass through a situation and not make any friends and that, to me, is the most important thing I achieved here.

"Because all through the time I have not been here, especially out in Southern California, so many people from Wisconsin and upper Michigan and Minnesota and Iowa and northern Illinois and they all say, 'We used to watch you when you were with the Bucks. You were great. We really loved you.' And I just want to send back some of that love. You people are wonderful. Thank you very much."

The Bucks would not retire Abdul-Jabbar's No. 33 jersey until April 24, 1993, but the words he spoke during his speech in Milwaukee in his final NBA season couldn't ring more true.

Bucks fans truly appreciated the work he did in Milwaukee and there was a lot of it to appreciate. Abdul-Jabbar only played six seasons in Milwaukee, but he still managed to be at the top or near the top in many statistical categories. Points? First, with 14,211. Rebounds? First, with 7,161. Field goals made? First, with 5,902. Field-goal percentage? First, at 54.7 percent. Blocks? Fifth, with 495, even though blocks were only an official stat in his final two seasons in Milwaukee.

His contributions didn't just serve him though; it carried his teams to a place among the best of all time. Abdul-Jabbar led the team to its only NBA championship in 1971, as well as its only other NBA Finals appearance in 1974. During his time in Milwaukee, the Bucks won nearly 70 percent of their regular season games, a number that would have been even more outlandish without the team's struggles in Abdul-Jabbar's final season in Milwaukee. After beating the Bullets in the 1971 NBA Finals in just five games, guard Lucius Allen asked why the team didn't seem more excited and his answer nearly perfectly summed up the Bucks' Abdul-Jabbar era.

"People expect us to win," Allen told *Sports Illustrated*. "Everything we see in the paper says we'll win. It takes some of the excitement away from us. And I guess if you get right to it, we're not a very emotional bunch."

Abdul-Jabbar was also correct in saying he was paid for the work he did in Milwaukee. To start his career, the Bucks needed to work with the NBA to offer him enough money to make sure he was in their league and not the ABA. He would eventually sign a five-year, $1.5 million deal—the largest contract ever offered to a player at the time—to play for the Bucks after being drafted by them in the 1969 NBA Draft.

He ended up being worth every penny and Bucks fans knew it. They were heartbroken when Abdul-Jabbar informed the Bucks he was no longer interested in continuing his career in Milwaukee, but they were always there for him through the good times and the bad.

"Management was always great to me too," Abdul-Jabbar later told OnMilwaukee.com. "Wonderful fans. I have absolutely no bitterness about my stay [in Milwaukee] at all."

Most basketball fans will remember the goggled version of Abdul-Jabbar who won five championships out on the West Coast, but not Milwaukeeans. They will always remember their 22-year-old freak athlete that won 56 games as a rookie in the franchise's second year of existence, their young center who paired with Oscar Robertson to win their first championship, their three-time MVP, and their first superstar.

# 10 Retired Jerseys: Oscar Robertson's No. 1

Fittingly, the first number the Bucks retired was No. 1. After just four years with the franchise, Milwaukee retired Oscar Robertson's jersey on October 18, 1974.

Among the players who wore each of the jerseys in the rafters, Robertson's tenure in Milwaukee was the shortest, but the team's accomplishments in those four years led to the recognition immediately upon his retirement. Robertson's Bucks compiled a 248–80 record (.756 winning percentage) in his four seasons in the Brew City. They went to the playoffs all four years, with trips to the NBA Finals bookending his time in Milwaukee. And, of course, they won the franchise's first and only NBA championship in 1971, the Hall of Fame guard's first season with the team.

Milwaukee's addition of Robertson struck fear into the rest of the league. *Sports Illustrated* put Robertson on the cover of its NBA preview for the 1970–71 season and titled the Midwest Division section, "Here comes the Milwaukee dynasty, and there goes the chance for a four-team division race." There was little discussion of whether the two stars would fit together or if their egos would get in the way, but rather conversations about exactly when they would figure it out.

It didn't take long. The Bucks rattled off a 10-game win streak after splitting their first two games with Robertson and Alcindor on the floor together and they only got stronger from there.

"The Big O was the first guard who took defenders where he wanted to go, using his well-muscled 220 pounds to back them down, his head always up, looking for cutters, wary of double teams, waving teammates to open spots or maybe carving out space to release his deadly jumper, held in one hand, far above his head, virtually unblockable," wrote legendary basketball scribe Jack McCallum in *Sports Illustrated* in 2002.

Robertson's efficiency and command of the floor shined for the Bucks. He took fewer shots and looked to score less, taking just 13 shots per game in Milwaukee instead of the 21 shots per game he was taking in Cincinnati. With a superstar alongside him, Robertson focused on getting his teammates involved and fostering a team effort, rather than just taking turns with Alcindor.

"You must commit to playing together and we did that," Robertson later told Bucks.com. "I know there were a lot of personalities, but we always played together. I sacrificed my offense my last two or three years. I could have shot the ball more, but I knew for us to win, we needed to make everybody on the team productive. And that was my goal."

With Robertson at the helm, the Bucks were the model of efficiency. He controlled the ball, hunted out the best shots, and put his teammates in position to cash in those open looks. In fact, the 1970–71 Bucks were the first team in NBA history to shoot over 50 percent from the field, a number another team wouldn't reach again until the 1977–78 season. It has happened 57 times since the Bucks did it originally, but rarely outside of the easy offense era after the NBA-ABA merger. For the time, it was a total outlier as offenses simply didn't operate with that level of efficiency, and Robertson served as the conductor of the masterful offensive orchestra.

Even while focused on maintaining a well-functioning offense, Robertson managed to make an impact as an individual performer. During his time in Milwaukee, he averaged 16.3 points and 7.5 assists per game, earning selections to the All-Star Game in his first two seasons. As time went on, the veteran guard started to show his age, but that didn't keep him from helping lead the Bucks to the 1974 NBA Finals. Milwaukee ultimately lost to the Celtics in seven games, as injuries piled up for the Bucks and they just couldn't match Boston.

Things got ugly as Robertson's time in Milwaukee came to an end, with both sides getting embroiled in a contract dispute before the 1974–75 season, which ultimately led to the 14-year veteran opting for the broadcast booth. As late as 2002, Robertson contended the organization was trying to send a message to him to retire after the 1973–74 season by holding "Oscar Robertson Night" during halftime of the regular season finale against the Kansas City–Omaha Kings.

Despite the disagreeable ending to their relationship, the Bucks decided to retire his jersey before the next season on October 18, 1974. Even if the honor was given quickly and the relationship was on rocky terms, the organization will likely never regret it. Few people deserve the honor more than Robertson. Without adding one of the all-time greats to a roster with their young superstar, the Bucks may have never won the 1971 NBA championship and thus never secured a title in the organization's 50-plus years of existence. And that's why Robertson was the one and only player to ever wear the No. 1 for the Milwaukee Bucks.

# 11 Larry Costello

He wasn't the Bucks' first or second choice, but he ended up being the right choice.

Bucks owners Marvin Fishman and Wes Pavalon wanted to make a splash with their franchise's first coach, so they went after one of the biggest names in coaching and one of the biggest names in the city of Milwaukee.

"Al McGuire was our first thought because of the reputation he had gained at Marquette," Fishman later told PBS Milwaukee. "We could not reach out for Al without some good feeling on getting him. We sought Al out and Al was in favor of a switch to the NBA. There was a meeting with Al, but we had to get the approval. He had a contract with Marquette."

Surprisingly enough, the meeting went well. The Bucks met with Marquette president Rev. Raymond McAuley who was "more or less in charge of the sports area" at Marquette and he gave Fishman the approval to make an offer to McGuire, despite the adoration the school had for its coach. After hearing of this, some notable Marquette alumni pressured McAuley and ultimately the university decided to retain its coach.

After getting turned away on McGuire, Fishman recalls moving on to Philadelphia 76ers coach Alex Hannum, who had led Wilt Chamberlain and the 76ers to the 1967 NBA championship. Again, they were unable to get their man and had to move on to their third option, a man Hannum had convinced to join his team as a player-assistant coach in the 1966–67 season.

On April 3, 1968, the Bucks would make Larry Costello their first head coach.

Costello played in the NBA for 12 seasons with Syracuse and Philadelphia, making six All-Star Games, before stepping away from the game in 1965. When Hannum took the job with the Sixers for the 1965–66 season, he desperately wanted a tough guard who he could count on and decided to ask Costello, a former player for him in Syracuse, if he would return to the NBA. Costello ultimately paired with Hall of Famer Hal Greer in the backcourt of a team that ultimately put together a 68–13 record, despite Costello tearing his Achilles tendon with the Sixers at 44–4.

Despite only serving as an assistant coach before taking the Bucks job, the organization only heard good things about Costello and his potential as a coach. As a player, Costello obsessed over mental and physical preparation, as well as hard work on the defensive end of the floor and those tendencies carried over to his work as a coach.

"He was straightforward and direct," former Bucks guard Jon McGlocklin told the *Chicago Tribune* when Costello passed away in 2001. "No airs about him. It was the way he played and the way he coached. He never was calculating or conniving. He was just a hardworking guy who loved basketball."

Costello compiled a 410–264 record (.608 winning percentage) in nine seasons as Milwaukee's head coach, but didn't end up receiving a ton of credit for his work. People tend to diminish coaches given the opportunity to coach all-time greats, which is exactly the privilege Costello received in coaching Lew Alcindor and Oscar Robertson. This was even more true when the Bucks won 56 games under Costello in Alcindor's first season and an NBA championship in his second.

No matter how well he coached, people were going to diminish what he did because most assume great players mean little coaching is necessary, but that is not the way Costello approached things. He regularly told anyone who would listen, "If I geared our offense around those two guys and the other three stood around, we'd lose."

There were two things Costello was known for: relentless, thorough preparation and a deep playbook. When asked about it, he would call it simple, but no one that played for him seemed to agree. Jack McKinney, a Bucks assistant coach from 1974 to 1976, remembers the playbook having more than 80 plays, and perfect execution was always demanded.

"I don't think anyone worked harder or knew any more about X's and O's," veteran NBA executive Rod Thorn later told the *Chicago Tribune*. "He knew basketball. He was a basketball junkie."

Costello's demeanor could wear on players—he was exacting and demanded maximum effort from all of his players, especially in practices. But often players came to believe in his methods because they understood that few coaches prepared and obsessed over the game like Costello and they won a lot of basketball games.

"Larry's work ethic, dedication to the integrity of the game, and love for Bucks fans in Milwaukee and throughout Wisconsin helped early to establish Bucks basketball in this community. Larry pioneered many new coaching approaches and techniques. His legacy is Milwaukee's only NBA championship, and an indelible place in our state's history. He will be missed," Bucks vice-president of business operations John Steinmiller told Bucks.com upon Costello's passing.

Not bad for the third choice.

# 12 Edens and Lasry Buy the Bucks

Herb Kohl had been through this before…just from the other side.

He had bought the Bucks in 1985 when he was told Milwaukee was too small of a market, the arena was too old, a new arena would be impossible to build, and the Bucks would end up leaving Milwaukee.

Almost 30 years later, Wes Edens and Marc Lasry heard all of the same things, but they remained unmoved and purchased the franchise for $550 million, an amount more than 30 times the $18 million Kohl paid for the Bucks, on April 16, 2014.

"For Wes and me, it really is a dream come true," Lasry said during the introductory press conference.

While Kohl was a Milwaukee native, both Edens and Lasry were from out of town. Edens was co-founder of Fortress Investment Group LLC, an investment management firm based in New York City; Lasry was the chairman, CEO, and co-founder of

Avenue Capital Group. At the time of the sale, Lasry's personal net worth of $1.5 billion was good for No. 352 on the *Forbes* list of the 400 wealthiest Americans.

Before purchasing the Bucks, both Edens and Lasry had expressed interest in potentially owning a professional sports franchise. Steve Greenberg, the Allen & Co. executive who handled the sale of the Bucks for Kohl, told the *Milwaukee Journal Sentinel* people had thought of Edens as a potential owner for years because of his wealth and love of sports. Lasry, on the other hand, had explored purchasing another sports property a short time before purchasing the Bucks.

Although it was great to have a new basketball-loving ownership group, many Wisconsinites couldn't keep themselves from calling the new owners "New York hedge fund billionaires" and fearing

*Milwaukee Bucks owner Herb Kohl introduces investment firm executives Marc Lasry (center) and Wes Edens (right) at a news conference after reaching a deal to sell the franchise in 2014.*

their team would ultimately leave Wisconsin. Kohl, however, did not share those same fears.

"I believe we're doing the right thing at the right time with the right people and that good things will happen," Kohl told the *Milwaukee Journal Sentinel*. "This is a major step forward in my goal of keeping the Bucks here."

Like Jim Fitzgerald in 1985, Kohl could have made more money selling the team, but opted to make less to help try to keep the team in Milwaukee. The exact number was never discussed, unlike in 1985, but the long-time Bucks owner insisted the team stay in Milwaukee and thus chose to only discuss the sale of a team with interested parties that pledged to keep the team in Milwaukee.

As a part of the sale, both sides offered to put at least $100 million toward a new arena in Milwaukee as a sign of good faith and a way to lower a new arena's cost to the public. It would be a start, but both sides knew they were a significant distance away from a new arena and, as Kohl admitted in an interview with the *Milwaukee Journal Sentinel*, the Bucks would leave Milwaukee without a new arena.

"We have to find a way and we will find a way," Kohl said after the June 2013 press conference announcing the hiring of head coach Larry Drew. "We know we have to find a way to get a new facility and we will. The question is when and how. But we will because that is the future of not only the Bucks…Milwaukee and Wisconsin need a 21st century sports and entertainment complex."

Both parties felt the sale of the team and the $200 million pledge would create momentum for getting the necessary money to build the arena, but the battle over public funding for the arena would be contentious for more than a year. Eventually, though, an agreement was reached. On August 12, 2015, Wisconsin governor Scott Walker signed into law the plan to raise $250 million in public funding to build an arena for the Bucks.

In the end, the new ownership group would see its contribution to the project upped to $150 million, Kohl would donate $100 million, and the public would raise $250 million. The money from the public would come from the state of Wisconsin, Milwaukee County, and the city of Milwaukee.

For years, Kohl had been approached about selling the team and while rumors regularly swirled, he stood resolute in assuring the Bucks' future in Milwaukee. He turned down good offers. He turned away potentially good owners. He turned away anyone who might move the team. All to ensure the Bucks would stay in Milwaukee. With Edens and Lasry, Kohl was able to do the thing he always wanted most: secure the Bucks' future in Milwaukee.

# 13 Retired Jerseys: Sidney Moncrief's No. 4

After 10 seasons with the Bucks, Sidney Moncrief saw his jersey raised to the rafters of the Bradley Center on January 6, 1990. When asked about his star guard in 1985 by *Sports Illustrated*, Bucks head coach Don Nelson put together a description that perfectly explains why the Bucks guard was being honored five years later, but might have only made sense if you were able to regularly watch Moncrief play the game.

"Nothing stands out with Sidney, and everything does," Nelson said. "It's not one minute, it's 48. It's not one play, it's every play."

It's not that Moncrief's contributions didn't stand out. It's just that you couldn't really pick out one single thing to highlight.

In the five seasons between 1981 and 1986, Moncrief averaged 21 points, 5.8 rebounds, 4.7 assists, and 1.5 steals per game. He made five consecutive All-Star appearances. He was named to an

All-NBA team all five seasons, with First Team All-NBA recognition in the 1982–83 season. He was named to the All-Defensive First Team each of the five years except for 1981–82, in which he received All-Defensive Second Team recognition. He won the inaugural Defensive Player of the Year award in that same season and repeated as Defensive Player of the Year in the 1983–84 season.

Simply said, he was one of the league's best players in those five seasons.

Defensively, Moncrief was the perfect leader for a Nelson-led team and Nelson (in the 1980s) would insist starting any description of one of his Bucks players on the defensive end. Moncrief managed to cover anyone and everyone, switching between assignments and wreaking havoc on opposing offenses all over the floor. Nelson felt free to use him against incredible scoring guards like Andrew Toney and Michael Jordan, a tall playmaker like Magic Johnson, or a lanky fill-it-up forward like George Gervin. Moncrief had a specific scouting report and game plan for each player.

Via *Sports Illustrated*:

"Force [Gervin] right. He has many more moves going to his left."

"Take away his right. Don't let [Johnson] shoot a set shot. Make him move when he shoots."

"Keep [Toney] out of the middle, where he can go all the way or hit in-between shots."

"[Jordan] finishes his drives on opposite side of basket. Don't foul him in the air. Actually, you don't play Michael Jordan. You play *at* him."

Offensively, Moncrief used his incredible quickness and athleticism to get to the rack and found teammates when defenders shaded too far in his direction. He did it all and served as the focal point of a multi-faceted attack that tore through defenses throughout the 1980s.

*Sidney Moncrief spent 10 seasons with the Bucks and remains third on the team's all-time scoring list.*

Unfortunately, Moncrief's knee betrayed him as his career progressed. He had struggled with knee problems on and off since his days at the University of Arkansas, but they never forced him to miss extended time until the 1986–87 season. In that season, his eighth in the NBA, Moncrief played in just 39 games—missing 13 straight with a sore right knee and later 23 straight games for tearing tissue below his left knee—and averaged just 25 minutes per game.

"Cutting his minutes is one of the hardest things I've had to do as a coach because he's just like a thoroughbred, he wants to go," Nelson told *The New York Times*. "He has such a big heart, but he just can't do what his heart wants him to."

After the season, Moncrief opted for left knee surgery and missed the start of the 1987–88 season. The surgery didn't fix everything, however, and fewer games and limited minutes became the new norm for the Bucks guard. His knee issues persisted and forced him to retire just two seasons later. Moncrief would try to return with the Atlanta Hawks in the 1990–91 season after retiring for a season, but he was only able to play 15 minutes each night in 72 games before opting to retire again.

In each of Moncrief's 10 seasons in Milwaukee, the Bucks made the playoffs. When he retired, only Kareem Abdul-Jabbar had scored more points as a Buck than Moncrief. (He's now third.) Only Paul Pressey had more assists. Only four Bucks had recorded more rebounds. Only Quinn Buckner had recorded more steals. (Moncrief is still third in steals.)

Knee injuries might end up keeping one of the best players of the 1980s out of the Basketball Hall of Fame, but it didn't keep the Bucks from rewarding one of their all-time greats by raising his jersey to the rafters.

# 14 The Creation of the Bucks

Think of only three things: your God, your family, and the Milwaukee Bucks—in that order.

There might be a slight transcription error in that quote from legendary Packers coach Vince Lombardi, but it may as well be credited to him because the Milwaukee Bucks would not exist without him.

"Actually, Vince Lombardi was responsible, to some degree, for us getting the Bucks because my efforts were initially to get an AFL ballclub for Milwaukee," original Bucks owner Marvin Fishman told PBS Milwaukee. "Lombardi actually flew into Milwaukee on his private plane and met with the county board of supervisors right after I had made a presentation. And his help took the form of an extension of a 10-year lease with exclusive playing of the Packers in County Stadium."

The Bucks originally started as the idea for an American Football League expansion team for the 1967 AFL season. Fishman, a local real estate developer, believed Milwaukee should have its own football team because it seemed strange for the country's 11th-largest city to only see professional sports when the Packers played in County Stadium three times each year.

Before Lombardi came to Milwaukee, Fishman collected the money needed for an expansion franchise with a group of local investors and an oral contract from the AFL confirming he would be able to bring a franchise to Milwaukee if he fulfilled their requirements for an expansion franchise. He had completed each of those steps, but saw the deal die when he could no longer use Milwaukee County Stadium for his team's AFL games.

Turned away by Lombardi and the Packers, Fishman pushed forward undeterred with his dream of bringing a major league team to Milwaukee again. The city had lost the NBA's Hawks to St. Louis in 1955 and Major League Baseball's Braves to Atlanta in 1965.

"I feel like the Packers, with their no games here, make it inconvenient or almost impossible for the youngsters to see games other than on television. My feeling is still the same now [as it was then]: Milwaukee deserves a label of its own," Fishman told PBS Milwaukee while he motioned across his chest to the place a city name occupies on the front of a jersey. "And I think Milwaukee, at that time, would have supported an AFL ballclub."

With Fishman's interest in bringing professional sports back to Milwaukee publicly known, a number of leagues pitched him on their ideas, but his mind had already moved to basketball. The American Basketball Association was in the process of building its league bigger and stronger, but Fishman decided to aim even higher and went after an NBA franchise.

In early December of 1967, Fishman learned NBA commissioner Walter Kennedy would be at a luncheon in Chicago and immediately hopped in his car, drove to the restaurant, and started telling the commissioner about his intention to purchase a franchise. Kennedy had never met Fishman before that moment, but quickly found out the stranger in front of him was deadly serious about bringing an NBA team to Milwaukee.

Like the AFL, Kennedy told Fishman there would be a number of tasks he would have to accomplish before being considered. On the top of the list for Fishman? Finding more investors.

Enter Wes Pavalon.

Pavalon grew up on the north side of Chicago and dropped out of high school in his sophomore year. The only child of a single mother, Pavalon soon started to run with a rough crowd, and hustled to make money anyway he could. Eventually, though, he straightened up when he met Ed Kelly, a local parks supervisor, who soon became Pavalon's basketball coach.

It was through basketball and some tough lessons from Kelly that Pavalon got his life back on track. He took a course in TV repair at 18 years old and then talked himself into a job as an instructor. Six months later, he was running the school. Then, just two years later, he moved to Milwaukee and opened a TV repair school. After that, he moved on to writing textbooks for the school and eventually other technical fields. Ten years later, he was founder and president of Pavalon's Career Academy, "a $200 million-plus international complex of private trade, technical, and home-study schools."

Fishman and Pavalon were introduced shortly after Fishman's meeting with Kennedy and quickly formed a tremendous partnership. Two days after becoming partners, Pavalon had already raised most of the $500,000 initial investment required for anyone looking to buy an NBA franchise.

On December 29, 1967, they had satisfied all of Kennedy's requirements. It had been just three weeks since Fishman had barged into Kennedy's luncheon and a couple weeks since Fishman and Pavalon became partners. Less than a month later, on January 22, 1968, NBA owners approved new franchises for Milwaukee and Phoenix.

With that, basketball was back in Milwaukee.

# 15 Game 6 of the 2001 Eastern Conference Finals

The Bucks had blown their opportunity at going to the 2001 NBA Finals…twice.

Up 2–1 in the Bradley Center for Game 4 of the Eastern Conference Finals, the Bucks were down just three points with three and a half minutes remaining. NBA MVP Allen Iverson was 8-of-28 from the field for only 20 points. Bucks forward Glenn Robinson had the ball on the right wing and attempted to drive past Sixers guard Eric Snow. He was bumped and turned the ball over and the Sixers took it the other way for a layup and a five-point lead. Bucks lose.

The series shifted to Philadelphia for the fifth game and again, the Bucks put themselves in a great position to make Game 6 in Milwaukee a closeout game. Tied at 70–70 after three quarters, the fourth quarter featured five lead changes and two ties. Down 89–88 with 1.8 seconds left, Robinson took an eight-foot jumper on the left baseline on the edge of the lane line. It rimmed out. Bucks guard Ray Allen had a chance at a tip, but it was altered by Sixers center Dikembe Mutombo. Bucks lose.

Between Games 5 and 6, Allen and Bucks coach George Karl were fined a combine $85,000 for their comments about a conspiracy theory: the NBA wanted to get the Sixers into the Finals because they had the league MVP, and did not want a small-market team like Milwaukee in its marquee event. They had amassed a startling number of technicals and flagrant fouls. In short, from the outside, they appeared shook and about to get bounced from the playoffs because of an inability to refocus after two painful losses.

In only took two quarters in Game 6 for them to let everyone know the Bucks were alive and well.

Things started off with a bang as bruising Bucks center/forward Scott Williams threw a forearm shiver at Iverson and caught him under the chin for a flagrant-one foul. Williams wouldn't only make an impact physically, he also came out and scored 10 of the first 14 points for the Bucks to give them a 14–11 lead with 6:11 left in the first quarter.

Over the next seven minutes and 37 seconds, only two players scored, and they weren't really trading buckets. With 10:34 left in the second quarter, the Bucks led 33–15. Iverson had scored four points, while Allen rattled off 19 consecutive points. He started with a short pull-up and a free throw before he really got going. With the Sixers struggling to score, that meant plenty of transition opportunities for the Bucks and lots of space for Allen.

Off a Sixers steal, Allen brought the ball up the right side of the floor and attacked the defense with a pretty right-to-left crossover and a right-handed finger roll in traffic. Next time, Allen brought it up the right wing again, but this time without numbers. No matter—he pulled up for a three over the top of Iverson. Bang.

Then, it was time for a little work in the halfcourt. First, Allen wrapped around a couple screens before fading to the right corner for a catch-and-shoot three. Splash. Next, it was a backside flare when the defenders expected him to curl to the ball. Skip pass over the top of the defense. Bango.

And finally, back out in transition one more time after an Iverson miss on the other end, Allen caught the throw-ahead pass from backup point guard Lindsey Hunter on the left wing, took one dribble, and let a pull-up three go from the left wing. Good.

The Bucks increased their lead all the way out to 60–31 at the half as the defense remained resolute and the offense kept cooking. The Sixers chipped away at the lead throughout the second half, which surely put Bucks fans on edge after Games 4 and 5, but the Bucks were able to hold them off. Especially Allen, who ended the night with 41 points, including 9-of-13 shooting from deep. Eventually, the Bucks pulled out a 110–100 victory.

Game 7 would not go quite as well for the Bucks. Williams was suspended for accumulating too many playoff penalty points when his flagrant-one foul from the first two minutes of the game got upgraded to a flagrant-two by the NBA. The Bucks simply struggled in the winner-take-all game of the series and fell 108–91. Their defense could not contain Iverson (44 points), which might not have been much of a surprise since their defense struggled throughout the Big Three's time in Milwaukee. The offense, though, failed to keep up with Philadelphia and their Game 6 win, a magical moment that turned into an interesting footnote in a disappointing end to a special season.

# 16 Bucks Finally Beat Sixers

"The ghost has been exorcised! Milwaukee has finally beaten Philadelphia," CBS television broadcaster Brent Musburger exclaimed as the final horn sounded in Game 7 of the 1986 Eastern Conference semifinals.

The call may seem a bit over-the-top decades later, but it was a staggering outcome for the Bucks in the moment.

In four of the previous five seasons, the 76ers had eliminated the Bucks from the playoffs. Milwaukee hadn't eliminated Philadelphia from the playoffs since 1970, Kareem Abdul-Jabbar's inaugural trip to the postseason. To that point, the Bucks had lost each of the four Game 7s they had played, including a 1974 NBA Finals heartbreaker to the Celtics and a loss at the hands of the Sixers in the Eastern Conference semifinals.

With the Bucks' desperation and the team's playoff history, there was more than enough bad blood for the series, but ultimately it would be a bad foot that decided how it went. First-team All Defense and All-Star guard Sidney Moncrief suffered through a bout of plantar fasciitis (a stress-related injury to the heel and arch) of his left foot in the Bucks' first-round playoff series against the New Jersey Nets. Milwaukee swept the series in three games, but Moncrief was seriously hampered against the Sixers.

"My biggest problem with the injury is walking and trying to jump," Moncrief told *Sports Illustrated* before thinking about his statement for a second and smiling. "I guess in my occupation that can be a serious problem."

Moncrief felt a stabbing pain every single time he took a step with his left foot, so the Bucks went into the series knowing he could only take so much pain and he would need to sit out every other game they played. Moncrief sat out the first and third games of the series, and the Bucks lost both. He played in the second and fourth games of the series and the Bucks won. With the series split coming back to Milwaukee, the Bucks surprised the Sixers and pulled out a game without Moncrief. Bucks coach Don Nelson opted to sit Moncrief for Game 6 in Philadelphia to give him some extra rest and set the stage for an epic Game 7 performance in Milwaukee.

But that performance would have lacked meaning without some drama leading up to the deciding game and 76ers forward Charles Barkley made sure there was plenty of that. Philadelphia's lightning rod forward made news by, well, opening his mouth and talking trash to Bucks forward Terry Cummings. As the Bucks' second-best player behind Moncrief and a power forward, Cummings was the most likely target, but also a slightly illogical mark for Barkley's derision. The Bucks' talented big man had been an ordained minister for almost 10 years and did not at all seem the type to participate in any sort of Barkley's shenanigans.

After Game 2, Cummings told media members he was tired of "Barkleymania," which inspired Barkley's most discussed line of the series. He told assembled media members to tell Cummings "to go [bleep] himself," before adding "but do it in a religious way." After the Sixers' win in Game 6, Barkley informed the media that both his mother and grandmother had told him they had grown tired of his talking and thus he told everyone, "My speaking career is over."

The two teams had split the first six games, Barkley had helped turn up the drama, and the stage was set. Game 7 was a battle the entire way. The Bucks took their biggest lead at 67–58 after making the first two buckets in the second half, but the Sixers fought back and the two teams traded leads in the fourth quarter. Despite the massive pain in his left foot, Moncrief was able to put together a Willis Reed–type performance by scoring 23 points on the night, including a number of big plays down the stretch.

With three minutes remaining, Bucks point forward Paul Pressey found Moncrief under the basket for a layup on which Moncrief was fouled. His three-point play put the Bucks up 107–106. It was the first of seven lead changes in the final three minutes as the two teams went back and forth. The Bucks always had an answer when they needed it, including Moncrief hitting two free throws to put the Bucks up 111–110 after he was fouled by Sixers forward Julius Erving with 53 seconds remaining. Barkley immediately answered with a quick, bullish move to the basket on Cummings. With some nifty ball movement, Pressey found guard Craig Hodges underneath the basket for a shot which was goaltended by Barkley for a 113–112 lead with 28 seconds remaining.

Philadelphia brought the ball up the floor without calling a timeout, eventually entering the ball to Barkley on the right block. Moncrief doubled from the weak side, which forced Barkley to pass the ball back out to the game's leading scorer, Sedale Threatt.

He drove on the right wing and attempted to make a pass on the baseline to Erving, which was deflected out of bounds by Moncrief.

With seven seconds left in the game and five seconds on the shot clock, Sixers coach Matt Guokas called a timeout to draw up a play. Barkley inbounded the ball to Threatt on the left wing and immediately stepped inbounds to post up. Erving was near the left corner and cleared out to the elbow. His defender, Moncrief, stayed near the corner to help on Threatt and remain in the passing lane to Barkley, which left Erving open at the left elbow.

"When I saw Doc take the last shot, I knew, I was positive, he would make it," Bucks coach Don Nelson said after the game.

The coach's gut feeling of impending doom was warranted because the Sixers had been such a problem for the Bucks over the years, but this time, it went the other way. Erving's shot missed off the right side of the rim, Cummings was able to body Barkley away from the ball, and it fell to the court. The buzzer sounded. The Bucks had finally beaten the Sixers.

Nelson called it the "nicest win I've ever had," while Pressey told the *Los Angeles Times*, "I've been waiting for four years for it to happen."

The win was momentous. It was a spectacular moment for the entire organization, but as often happened throughout the 1980s, another team still stood in the Bucks' way. Beat the Celtics, the Sixers await. Beat the Sixers, the Celtics await. And in 1986, it was one of the best Celtics teams of all time, which had won 67 regular season games. Without a healthy Moncrief, the Bucks just didn't have enough to compete against the Celtics and were swept out of the playoffs in a four-game Eastern Conference Finals.

# 17 The Bradley Center

The Milwaukee Arena—part of the larger Milwaukee Exposition, Convention Center, and Arena complex—was too small. The Milwaukee Bucks and, more importantly, the NBA had outgrown the league's smallest arena, which seated just 11,052 fans, and Bucks owner Jim Fitzgerald knew it. The need for a new arena was one of the principal reasons Fitzgerald put the team up for sale on February 6, 1985.

Eventually, Fitzgerald sold the team to Herb Kohl for roughly $18 million, despite getting offers of around $7 million more from other potential ownership factions. Kohl had committed to keeping the team in Milwaukee and that was important to Fitzgerald. Unfortunately, Kohl hadn't quite figured out how a new arena would go up in Milwaukee.

"How we would get to a new arena was something that was totally unknown," Kohl later told the *Milwaukee BizTimes*. "But I thought, 'Well, I'll buy the team anyhow, we'll worry about that afterward, but let's keep the team in Milwaukee.' I just had faith that things would turn out well."

Kohl purchased the team on a Friday. On Monday morning, he had unexpected visitors at his office and they told him they wanted to pay for his arena. It seemed too good to be true, so he decided to learn a little bit more about his visitors.

The folks visiting his office were representatives of the Pettit Family. Jane Pettit was the daughter of Harry Lynde Bradley. Her father co-founded the Milwaukee-based Allen-Bradley Company in 1903. On February 20, 1985, Rockwell International purchased Allen-Bradley for $1.65 billion, the largest acquisition in Wisconsin history.

Also, in 1985, the Jane Bradley Pettit Foundation was founded. It made numerous donations around Milwaukee, including $20 million to the Lynde and Harry Bradley Technology and Trade School, $9 million for the Pettit National Ice Center, and more than $100,000 to the United Way of Greater Milwaukee and Waukesha County.

"She was motivated by a love of Milwaukee, a sense of her family having been grounded here, being nurtured by Milwaukee and wanting to nurture the city in return," her granddaughter Sarah Zimmerman told the *BizTimes*.

The foundation's biggest gift, though, would be the Bradley Center, a gift made in memory of her late father. Jane and her then husband Lloyd Pettit offered to donate up to $40 million to pay for the construction of the new arena to help Kohl achieve his dream of keeping the Bucks in Milwaukee.

The new arena would be home to the Bucks, the Marquette Warriors, and the Milwaukee Admirals, the IHL hockey team owned by the Pettits. As plans were being drawn up, however, the price of the construction costs rose to $90 million. Despite needing more than double their planned donation, the Pettits never wavered and remained committed to picking up the entire construction tab.

Construction of the arena started on October 20, 1986, and finished up a little less than two years later. The Bradley Center officially opened on October 1, 1988, with a sold-out crowd watching a National Hockey League exhibition game between the Chicago Blackhawks and the Edmonton Oilers.

The "Fortress on Fourth," as the arena came to be nicknamed for its utilitarian, drab exterior and concrete innards, served as the home of the Bucks for 30 years and, despite not always having the best teams, provided a home-court advantage in Milwaukee. When the Bucks did provide high-quality teams, the Bradley Center was always up to the task of bringing the noise. Bucks fans even set the record for loudest indoor crowd with a 106.6-decibel performance in 2008.

In 30 years in the Bradley Center, the Bucks posted a 646–523 record for a winning percentage of .552. Despite the winning record, the team did not enjoy many larger successes in the building the Pettit family helped build. Just one division title (2001 Central Division Champs) and one Eastern Conference Finals appearance in 30 years.

The level of play may not have lived up to the generosity of the donation, but the Bradley Center served as a home to the Bucks for three decades and kept the team in Milwaukee. And that alone is more than enough reason to remember the Bradley Center.

# 18 Jim and Jon

On October 31, 1986, Jim Paschke put on a headset for a Bucks television broadcast with former Bucks guard Jon McGlocklin for the first time. More than 30 years later, every Bucks fans has grown so comfortable with the duo that they're known simply as Jim and Jon.

Everyone knows McGlocklin's story because he's been around the team forever. After spending the final eight seasons of his career in Milwaukee, including winning the 1971 NBA Finals, McGlocklin retired. On the night of his jersey retirement, he announced the formation of the Milwaukee Athletes Against Childhood Cancer (the MACC Fund), a foundation focused on helping children fight cancer, and also joined his good friend Eddie Doucette on Bucks broadcasts. He hasn't gone anywhere else since that moment, which is why people know him as "Mr. Bucks" and "The Original Buck."

Paschke's story is slightly different, but over the years he has become no less beloved by fans. Doucette is a legend to fans for being the Bucks' first broadcaster, but also his incredible command of the English language and his colorful descriptions of the play on the floor. Paschke had his work cut out for him, but he has handled the job with aplomb.

His broadcasting career began in radio and also included time in television as the sports director at WMTV in Madison and WITI in Milwaukee. He's called everything in the state of Wisconsin—University of Wisconsin football and basketball, Milwaukee Brewers baseball, Milwaukee Admirals hockey, and Marquette University basketball games—but Paschke has solidified himself as the level-headed voice alongside McGlocklin.

Sometimes, though, McGlocklin is not so level-headed. "Jonny Mac" often feels the joy of victory and the pain of defeat as though he's still wearing a jersey even though he is now only a member of the broadcast team.

"I'm a Bucks guy before I'm an announcer," McGlocklin told Bucks.com. "I want the team to win. I want to win. If Jim and I are mediocre that night, I'm happy because we won."

At times, that emotion can become too much for McGlocklin to handle, like it did against the Dallas Mavericks on November 29, 2005. The Bucks led the Mavericks 112–108 with 20.9 seconds left in overtime. The Mavericks had the ball and McGlocklin spent the timeout before the play explaining the need to step out to three-point shooters and keep it from being a one-point game. After a couple passes, Mavericks guard Jason Terry hit a three and that didn't sit well with McGlocklin.

"When he made that shot, I took my $600 headset and I slammed it on the table," McGlocklin recounted. "And it went out on the court into multiple pieces."

As McGlocklin tried to collect the pieces of his headset, Paschke connected the pieces of the broadcast without his partner and kept the ship afloat for a few moments. As always, Paschke was there to guide the broadcast and keep it moving, but that doesn't always mean he is calm and unfeeling. He has plenty of exciting calls of buzzer-beating shots:

"In for Dudley, back to Middleton. There was a bump. Oh! It went! The Bucks win! The Bucks win! Khris Middleton!"

"Williams. Three. Yes! For the win! For the win!"

"Let's get this one. Robinson step-back three. Yes! Glenn Robinson! He's an All-Star!"

"In for Jennings. Three. It's good! Brandon Jennings! Brandon Jennings on opening night! A three with seven-tenths on the inbounds play and they'll go home happy in Milwaukee tonight!"

Each of those calls is almost certainly accompanied by McGlocklin's joyful exclamations. Whether a "Yes," "Ahh," "Ooh," or "Whoa," Paschke believes McGlocklin's "sound effects," as he calls them, make his call that much better.

"It's always been great," Paschke told McGlocklin during a Bucks.com interview. "I can work around that. I work over that. That's made it special—those buzzer-beating calls—because of the way you react."

The calls on those buzzer-beaters are a perfect summation of their work. McGlocklin's unbridled joy, even as he's aged, paired with Paschke's superb calls. One could never be without the other. And in the hearts and minds (and eyes and ears) of Bucks fans, they will always be remembered together.

# 19 Redd's 57-Point Night

Nineteen Bucks players have scored 40 or more points in a game 105 times in franchise history. The list of these games is overwhelmingly filled with one name: Kareem Abdul-Jabbar. He scored 40 or more points in 55 games during his six seasons in Milwaukee. But despite dominating the list of 40-point games, he does not own the highest-scoring game in Bucks history.

That honor belongs to Michael Redd and his 57-point game against the Utah Jazz on November 11, 2006.

Redd holding the top spot on that list is a surprise, but even more shocking is just how he got to that number. It was the seventh game of the season for both the Bucks and Jazz. In the early going, both teams were playing the basketball each would play for the entire season, with the Jazz on their way to a 51-win season at 5–1 and the 2–4 Bucks on their way to one of the league's worst records. The first half played out exactly like their records and overall quality would suggest, with the Jazz hopping out to a 62–41 lead.

And then, it happened. Michael Redd went off.

The shooting guard set the tone early in the second half, quickly rattling off seven points in the first 90 seconds of the third quarter with a couple of buckets and three free throws. Redd, known as a three-point bomber, was often at his best when he was also getting to the free throw line, and that was the game plan against the Jazz. In the second half, he got to the line 12 times and missed just one of his attempts.

At the end of the third quarter, Redd had 32 points, with 17 in the third quarter, but his scoring outburst had little effect on the scoreboard. Milwaukee still trailed 86–69.

Even with just 3:20 left in the game, it looked like garbage time was just a few possessions away as Jazz forward Matt Harpring made a free throw to put the Jazz up 104–92. Redd had already tied his career-high with 43 points, but he still had some more left in the tank. As they had done throughout the game, the Bucks sent Redd all over the floor, weaving from screen to screen with Jazz players unsuccessfully chasing him and attempting to keep the ball out of his hands.

With 3:08 left, Brian Skinner screened Harpring just enough on the right wing to free Redd for a curl cut and a bucket through contact from backside helper Mehmet Okur. With the free throw, Redd had a new career high with 46 points. On the next possession, Redd set up a similar curl cut, but with rookie center Andrew Bogut screening this time. Harpring saw it coming and jumped the route. Redd countered with a flare to the corner and hit a three for 49 points, but the Bucks still faced a 107–98 deficit with 2:30 left.

After Bogut took a charge and forced a Carlos Boozer turnover, Redd established position on the left side of the floor inside the three-point line with his back to the basket. Charlie Bell fed him the ball and Redd quickly turned over his right shoulder for a baseline take. Lefty floater with a little contact and Redd had 51 points with 1:59 left.

The Jazz answered immediately and pushed the lead back up to nine, but Redd drew a foul on the next possession, hitting both free throws to cut the Jazz lead to seven with 1:34 left. On the next possession, Redd grabbed a steal and Ruben Patterson hit two free throws to cut the deficit to five. The Bucks forced a miss from rookie point guard Deron Williams and then a Bogut bucket, plus a free throw for a foul, cut the Jazz lead to just 109–107 with 39.7 seconds left.

At the end of the shot clock, the Bucks forced a missed three from Williams and quickly got down to the other end of the floor where Redd was fouled by Boozer. Despite being in the midst of the highest scoring night of his career, he somehow missed the first of two free throws before hitting the second.

Redd immediately fouled Boozer, who went to the line and hit both free throws to give the Jazz a 111–108 lead with 11.7 seconds left and set the stage for Redd's most difficult shot of the night. Milwaukee needed a three and everyone in the building knew only one guy would be shooting it. The Bucks called a timeout to advance the ball and then positioned Redd off the ball.

Like he had so often that night, Redd started on the right side of the floor and took a bump from Williams before shaking loose and sprinting off Bogut's right hip. He ran tight enough to Bogut to help the center make contact with Williams and get a foot or so of space. Bell delivered a pass from the top of the floor and the lethal lefty let one fly with Williams and Bell's defender Dee Brown each trying desperately to contest it.

Bang. Redd had 57 and tied the game.

The night ended on a sour note, however, because Milwaukee's defense failed to send the game to overtime as it took just five seconds for the Jazz to get down the floor and score to retake a 109–107 lead. Redd would have one last chance, but the Jazz defended him better the second time around and he missed a three as time expired.

It was a fitting ending to Redd's historic night. In the 2005–06 season, he had two more huge scoring nights with 45 points in a four-point victory over the Lakers and 52 points in a five-point loss to the Bulls, but his scoring just couldn't seem to lead to Bucks victories. Ultimately, some fans may choose to remember Redd as just a scorer, but few could score quite as well as Redd as evidenced by no one topping his performance against Utah to this day.

# 20 Jennings' Double Nickel

"It's another night to compare a pair of flashy rookies," Bucks television broadcaster Jim Paschke said to open the broadcast of the Milwaukee Bucks and Golden State Warriors matchup on November 14, 2009. "The light on Brandon Jennings is as bright as it gets after scoring 32 against Denver. Stephen Curry, with his own pedigree as son of former Bucks star Dell Curry, was taken three spots ahead of Jennings. They will compare notes tonight."

Jennings, the 10th pick of the 2009 NBA Draft, had just dropped 32 points and nine assists on the Denver Nuggets in his sixth NBA game. Curry, the seventh pick, had played just two minutes and 35 seconds against the New York Knicks in the eighth game of his NBA career.

Eight years later, one of them would be celebrated as a revolutionary basketball talent who changed the game of basketball in the modern era and the other would be playing basketball in China. On this night, it appeared clear which one would be which.

Jennings was scoreless in the first quarter, missing his first three shots. In the second quarter, Jennings got comfortable as he started to figure out how the Warriors would be covering pick and rolls, but it was a quarter largely typical of the concerns scouts had for him before he joined the NBA.

A lightning-quick lefty but rail-thin, Jennings was an interesting draft prospect. He possessed the quickness necessary to get to the rim, but couldn't always finish there. He had the instincts and floor vision necessary to be a passing maestro, but failed to make the best decisions consistently. He carried himself with the confidence and swagger of a sharpshooter from deep, but wasn't much of a long-distance threat.

Ultimately, with some misses from the midrange and a few shots blocked, Jennings went 3-of-9 from inside the arc and hit his only attempt from deep in the second quarter. With the addition of one made free throw, Jennings put up 10 points in the quarter and there wasn't even a hint of what was going to come next.

Jennings came out for the second half and couldn't miss. Literally. His first miss in the half came with 5.9 seconds left in the third quarter. Before that, a pristine 12-of-12:

Andrew Bogut high ball-screen. Hesitation dribble with the left hand. Pull-up free throw line jumper. Good.

Bogut high ball-screen to left. Bogut screen around the elbow right. Pull-up 19-footer. Good.

Bogut post-up. Kick-out to Luke Ridnour. Extra pass to Jennings for three. Good.

Bogut high ball-screen. Dribble to the left, take to the rack. One-handed lefty finish at the rim. Good.

Dribble up the left side in transition. In-between-the-legs step-back dribble at the three-point line. Good.

Bogut high ball-screen. Dribble to the right. Hesitation into a right-hand finish at the rim. And-One. Good.

Free throw. Good.

Bogut high ball-screen. Inside-out dribble. Pull-up to the left just inside the three-point line. Good.

Bogut high ball-screen in transition. Dribble left, pull-up three behind the screen to the right. Good.

Toss forward to Luc Richard Mbah a Moute on the left side to start possession. Dribble handoff. Fly-by finish at the rim. Good.

Bogut high ball-screen. Warriors big high hedge. Reject the screen, dribble left, floater from 10 feet out. Good.

Bogut high ball-screen. Dribble left. Top of the key pull-up three. Good.

Bogut high ball-screen. Warriors big high hedge. Dribble left, then right. Pull-up from the right elbow. Good.

Jennings was 12-of-13 in the quarter, 8-of-8 on two-point field goals and 4-of-5 on threes, for 29 points.

"The Warriors kept going under the screens, and in the first half, I wasn't taking advantage of it," Jennings told the *Milwaukee Journal Sentinel* after the game.

"In the second half, I was like, 'If they're going to keep going under screens, I'm going to shoot it until it goes into the basket.'

*Brandon Jennings reacts near the end of his 55-point scoring effort against the Golden State Warriors in 2009.*

Luckily, I hit the first two, and it seemed like the rim kept getting bigger and bigger and I couldn't miss."

Despite 39 points from Jennings, the Bucks still had some work to do in the final quarter as they led just 92–83. Jennings went cold to start the final period and had a few turnovers, which allowed the Warriors to sneak back into the game and take a 108–107 lead with 4:24 left.

The teams battled back and forth throughout the remaining time, but Jennings' magic hadn't run out quite yet, as he added 12 points in the final four minutes, including a three off, what else, a high ball-screen from Bogut to put the Bucks up 124–118 with 34.3 seconds left. Two more free throws helped seal the 129–125 victory.

On the night, Jennings went for 55 points, tying the franchise's rookie record for points in a game with Kareem Abdul-Jabbar and finishing just two points short of Michael Redd's franchise-record 57 points in a game. It's a night Bucks fans will remember forever because it was a truly incredible performance, but also because Jennings never recaptured that same magic.

Everyone knew he'd stop hitting half of his threes like he did in that first month of his career, but surely someone that confident would be able to develop other parts of his game to make up for it. He'd be able to find ways to use his turbo speed and instant change-of-direction dribbles to become an impactful NBA player. He'd become a great decision-maker or respectable shooter from the outside. But none of that ever happened for Jennings.

And, because of that, his 55-point outburst in his seventh NBA game will live forever in Milwaukee Bucks lore.

# 21 The Big Dog

$3+6+8+14=1.$

It's not an equation taught in any schools, but it was correct for the Milwaukee Bucks on March 22, 1994. The combination of those four numbers at the 1994 NBA Draft Lottery meant the Bucks would select first overall in the 1994 NBA Draft, despite holding only the fourth-highest odds.

Waiting for them at No. 1: Glenn Robinson. The junior from Purdue University was the Naismith Player of the Year, John R. Wooden Award winner, Big Ten Player of the Year, and the nation's leading scorer. At 6-foot-7, Robinson averaged 27.5 points per game, dominating college competition with size, athleticism, and incredible scoring ability. He even earned the nickname "Big Dog" for his tenaciousness and desire to dominate his competition.

On draft night, June 29, 1994, the Bucks made the simple decision and selected Robinson first overall. Unfortunately, things would get complicated from there.

For the next three months, Robinson and the Bucks failed to come together on a contract. Rumors and opinions flew around, with many believing Robinson and his camp were demanding at least $100 million. Rumors of Robinson's demands became such a big story they actually became a part of Bucks owner and Wisconsin senator Herb Kohl's re-election campaign.

Looking to appeal to the common man in his 1994 campaign against Republican challenger Bob Welch, Kohl and the team held a news conference on October 17. During the press conference, the team broke their typical negotiation policies and claimed Robinson had turned down a nine-year, $60 million contract and actually wanted a 13-year deal worth $100 million.

*Glenn Robinson was the consensus top pick in the 1994 NBA Draft and spent eight seasons in Milwaukee.*

Bucks head coach and general manager Mike Dunleavy emphasized the need to make the negotiation details public to make sure people understood they would be able to sign their draft pick, despite being a small-market team. He also wanted to correct some of the figures that had been reported.

Robinson and his agent Charles Tucker were not particularly happy with the way they were represented in the press conference, despite the organization's attempts to affirm their belief in the young star and its desire to sign him as quickly as possible.

"If they want to portray Glenn as a greedy, little black athlete, well, I look at it as a business and it was something that was not a very productive way of doing things, but you just try to remain positive," Tucker told the *Milwaukee Journal*.

The contract dispute continued until November 3, the day before the Bucks were scheduled to open the season in Philadelphia against the 76ers. With Kohl himself getting involved in the negotiations on November 2, the deal got done at 2:00 AM on November 3.

In the end, Robinson signed a 10-year, fully guaranteed deal worth $68 million with no incentive clauses, performance goals, or opt-outs. It was the largest guaranteed deal ever signed by an NBA rookie and actually led to massive changes in rookie contracts the very next season. The league was terrified of deals of that size for rookies becoming a trend and commissioner David Stern implemented a rookie scale to make sure future rookies would be unable to do the same thing Robinson did.

Despite missing the season opener because of the contract dispute, Robinson went on to have a huge rookie season. The 22-year-old showed off the innate scoring prowess that garnered him all the accolades at Purdue during his college career and led all rookies with 21.9 points per game. His scoring, though, was not enough for him to take home Rookie of the Year as he finished third in voting behind Grant Hill and Jason Kidd, who split the award in the 1994–95 season.

Robinson's performance in his rookie year helped the Bucks add 14 wins to their 20-win total from the 1993–1994 season. It wouldn't end up being the first year of a magical run or the dawning of a new era, as the Bucks failed to compile a .500 record in each of the next four seasons, but Robinson would end up being one of the, let's say, three most important players on Milwaukee's next great team.

# 22 Allen Hits 10 Threes in One Game

All Milwaukee Bucks guard Ray Allen could do was shake his head and shrug his shoulders. His Jordan footwear might not ever have been more appropriate than it was in that moment, as Allen did a near-perfect impression of the famous shrug the man whose likeness adorned Allen's sneakers had done in the 1992 NBA Finals against the Portland Trail Blazers.

Allen had just hit his ninth three-pointer of the game and it might have been his most ridiculous of the night. Teammate Tim Thomas had missed a midrange jumper on the left wing and the ball ricocheted off the rim and out toward the left corner. Allen sprinted out from the lane and beat Hornets forward Robert "Tractor" Traylor to the long rebound. In one motion, Allen grabbed the ball, planted both feet behind the three-point line, and rose up for a jumper from deep in the corner.

Splash.

Allen was in the zone and doing everything he could to drag his Bucks team to a victory in their third-to-last game of the season against the team they had eliminated in the Eastern Conference semifinals the previous season. The team had yet to be eliminated from playoff contention, but focusing on whether the Bucks would be in the playoffs rather than their playoff seed on that Sunday afternoon was an outcome unimaginable at the beginning of the season and even as recently as a month previous.

On March 6, 2002, the Bucks beat the Clippers 92–86 and sat tied for second place in the Eastern Conference with the Detroit Pistons. Over the next 39 days, the Bucks would win just four games and drop 15 of 19 to find themselves one game under .500 at 39–40. The team's strong early start meant they were still in the thick of the playoff conversation, but hanging on for dear life heading into their game against the Hornets on April 14, 2002, tied for the Eastern Conference's final spot with the Indiana Pacers.

Milwaukee needed every win it could get and Allen was dead-set on getting the one they needed that Sunday afternoon. He got off to a solid start with 17 points on 6-of-11 shooting, including 2-of-4 from deep and hitting all three free throws he attempted, but the second half would be where he found his groove.

Allen put up 30 points in the second half, while only missing three shots and only shooting four free throws. It was a shooting performance only one of the greatest shooters in the history of basketball could have pulled off.

Allen never stood still. He was always moving and impossible for the Hornets to track. His first three of the period came just 12 seconds into the second half as he whipped around teammate Anthony Mason and pulled the forward into the path of defenders like a bad guy throwing a garbage can in the path of a pursuing cop in a bad action movie.

Later, Allen whipped around a double-screen on the right side of the floor to the top of the key, pump faked, drove down the left lane line, kicked it out to Bucks point guard Greg Anthony on the right wing, ran under the basket on the baseline, and received a no-look pass dropped from Mason, who had just received a pass from Anthony and then screened for Allen as he finished his route to the corner. All of that just for one open look from deep.

Allen ran around the floor, expertly navigating the halfcourt obstacle course created by his Bucks teammates, for the rest of the half. If a Hornets defender managed to get through all of that to contest a shot at the three-point line, the sharpshooter simply drove to the basket. If a teammate missed a shot, Allen was improbably there to keep the ball alive or hit a shot immediately after corralling it. In the end, he had hit 9-of-12 in the second half, including 8-of-9 from behind the line for 30 points in the final two periods and a career-high 47 points on the night.

Allen carried the Bucks to victory and kept their playoff hopes alive for another day, but they would ultimately fall short of the playoffs, which started a playoff-series-victory drought that still exists to this day. The team's second-half collapse in 2002 would ultimately lead to the disbandment of the Big Three (Allen, Sam Cassell, and Glenn Robinson would all be traded in the next 16 months), the firing of George Karl, and a decade of mediocrity in Milwaukee. There was no way of knowing it at the time, but Allen's 47-point game would be the last great moment for one of the most beloved eras of Bucks basketball.

# 23 Abdul-Jabbar's Punch

It was going to be a difficult professional debut no matter what for Bucks center Kent Benson. He was the first pick of the 1977 NBA Draft and he was going up against four-time NBA MVP Kareem Abdul-Jabbar, who just so happened to lead the Bucks to the franchise's only championship in 1971.

Between the weight of the expectations that come along with being the first pick and playing a franchise legend now in another uniform, it would likely be a long day for Benson and he had no illusions of anything different.

"He's got a great hook shot and is almost unstoppable on offense," Benson told the *Milwaukee Sentinel* the day before the 1977–78 season opener. "All I can do is use my body to the best of my ability. I'm going to try and push and shove. But how much I can get away with, I don't know. I don't mean I'll be dirty, but I can't be hesitant or scared. I've learned how to use my body, my strength, and my hands to guard the other centers."

Little did he know what he could get away with was different for officials and Abdul-Jabbar.

Benson actually got off to a strong start against the league's best player. On the opening tip, he beat Abdul-Jabbar to the basketball and got it to a teammate. Bucks guard Brian Winters missed a shot early on and Benson grabbed the rebound before ultimately finishing it against Abdul-Jabbar. Then came a defensive possession just short of two minutes into the game, the outcome of which is subject to interpretation.

As Benson tells it, he followed his defensive assignment and got to the middle of the floor where Abdul-Jabbar liked to set up for his hook shot. As the four-time MVP came down the floor, he drove his elbow into Benson's chest and began jostling for position. Benson jostled right back and hit Abdul-Jabbar with an elbow to the chest.

Abdul-Jabbar doubled over in pain and staggered away toward the baseline. After composing himself, he ran up from behind Benson, tapped him on the left shoulder with his left hand, and "sucker punched" Benson with his right hand, knocking Benson to the floor.

If you were to ask Abdul-Jabbar about the series of events, he would surely mention the elbow and the regular abuse he believed he suffered throughout his career as one of the league's largest and most dominant players.

"Everyone's attitude was that it was totally my fault," Abdul-Jabbar said to *Sports Illustrated*. "So again it was me against the world. I can understand how the punch happened. He was a rookie, he made a mistake. When he did that I thought of all the times I was provoked, abused, bullied, scorned, and I was not going to take one more thing."

The incident was an interesting juxtaposition of two very different viewpoints. Benson, a highly rated rookie center, needed to show to his teammates and the entire league he was strong and tough enough to play with the league's best. Abdul-Jabbar, on the other hand, had grown tired over the years of being treated as a player to prove something against and general mistreatment from officials who rarely gave him the calls he felt he deserved because he was the league's most dominant player.

"My reaction was extreme, no two ways about it, but the league's reaction was wrong," Abdul-Jabbar said. "It was neither my fault nor Benson's, totally. It was the system's."

Abdul-Jabbar broke his hand on the punch and would miss 20 games of the regular season. Benson would only miss one game from the punch to the temple, but complained a week later of a steady pain across his forehead. Critics said the incident changed Benson's career forever and kept him from reaching his potential, but Benson doesn't buy that and points to putting together a successful 11-year career as all the evidence he needs.

Ultimately, Benson would not enjoy those 11 years in Milwaukee. After just two and a half years, Benson and the Bucks' 1980 first-round pick were traded to the Detroit Pistons for Bob Lanier. The trade helped the Bucks start a 12-year streak of playoff appearances, but most fans can think of little else than Abdul-Jabbar's infamous punch when reflecting on Benson's time in Milwaukee.

# 24 Bucks Win 2005 NBA Draft Lottery

So, get this, Bucks general manager Larry Harris walked into a room with a fishing lure, a bracelet, and a rooster.

This isn't the setup to a joke, but rather exactly what happened at the 2005 NBA Draft Lottery, where Harris and the Bucks left Secaucus, New Jersey, with the first pick in the draft. Actually, maybe there was something there with the fishing lure and the biggest catch, but never mind.

Heading into that night, Milwaukee had the sixth-best chance of getting the first overall pick at just 6.3 percent. After first-year head coach Terry Porter led the team to the playoffs in the 2003-04 season, the Bucks couldn't capture the same success in his second season. Both the offense and defense declined slightly as a few rotation players changed roles, which kept Milwaukee from winning games and dropped them into the league's bottom 10 in the 2004–05 season.

To get some extra luck, the Bucks held a contest to find the perfect lucky charms and eventually landed on two winners for Harris to take with him to Secaucus. Sixteen-year-old Michael Millies of Milwaukee sent along a fishing lure, which had aided him in catching his biggest fish, and 20-year-old Emily Dunne sent a bracelet that led her to her boyfriend and always seemed to bring her good luck.

Harris happily took each of the lucky charms with him, along with his own—a small, wooden rooster—and ended up with a big smile on his face when he heard the Portland Trail Blazers announced when the sixth pick came up. And then again, when the Utah Jazz came up with the third pick. And once more, when the Atlanta Hawks were announced as the team selecting second, which meant the Bucks would have the first overall pick.

With that, it became much simpler. Picking sixth, there could have been any number of players potentially on the board: high schooler Martell Webster, Connecticut's Charlie Villanueva, Arizona's Channing Frye, North Carolina's Raymond Felton, or Arizona State's Ike Diogu, among others.

*A decade after winning the NBA draft lottery and selecting Glenn Robinson, the Bucks defied the odds again in 2005 and picked Andrew Bogut, a center from the University of Utah.*

At No. 1, there were really only two consensus options: Utah's Andrew Bogut or North Carolina's Marvin Williams.

Bogut was the consensus National Player of the Year as a sophomore at the University of Utah. A true 7-footer with incredible touch around the basket, excellent court vision, and the ability to hit jumpers from the midrange, Bogut was a terrific offensive player who seemed destined to anchor an NBA offense for the next decade.

Williams was the sixth man on the national champion North Carolina Tar Heels. As a freshman, the 6-foot-8 forward averaged 11 points and six rebounds in just 22 minutes per game off the bench with a mixture of size, length, athleticism, and upside that dazzled scouts. With a great jump shot as well, organizations were enamored with what Williams could do once he got to the NBA.

(In hindsight, it would ultimately prove ridiculous for Bogut and Williams to be viewed as the only choices. Deron Williams and Chris Paul were drafted with the third and fourth picks of the 2005 NBA Draft and both turned into generational talents at point guard, a position that took over the league around the same time.)

Ultimately, the Bucks made the conventional pick and opted for the 20-year-old big man to anchor the middle for years to come. Bogut put together a decent rookie season and helped the Bucks win 10 more games to sneak into the playoffs at 40–42, while Paul ran away with Rookie of the Year. Bogut would never find the individual success of Williams or Paul, but his career will always have one big question mark.

After four years of solid, if unspectacular, work in Milwaukee, Bogut put together a fantastic fifth season. The center vaulted up the leaderboard with 2.5 blocks per game after averaging just one per game the previous season. He became a force defensively, all while managing to improve offensively on his way to a career-high 15.9 points per game.

His two-way performance garnered Third Team All-NBA recognition, but the best season of his career came to an abrupt end in the 69th game of the season. Bogut went up for a running dunk against the Phoenix Suns. Forward Amar'e Stoudemire tapped him while he was hanging on the rim and he tumbled to the floor, brutally shattering his right arm. Bogut was never the same after the fall and Bucks fans were robbed of getting to see what his career in Milwaukee would become. Instead, they were forced to wonder what could have been if that moment never happened.

# 25 Bayless' Buzzer-Beater

It felt inevitable. There was just no way the Bucks were going to escape on that Saturday afternoon in 2015 with a win.

Trailing 3–0 in their best-of-seven series with the Chicago Bulls in the first round of the Eastern Conference playoffs, it was over. The sixth-seeded Bucks had struggled in the second half of the season and simply wouldn't be able to manufacture a win against the third-seeded Bulls. Even with a fourth-quarter lead, it would all fall apart and the Bulls fans who occupied a not insignificant portion of the BMO Harris Bradley Center would go home happy.

Khris Middleton and the Bucks' bench mob of veterans Jerryd Bayless, Jared Dudley, and O.J. Mayo, plus John Henson, started the fourth quarter with a two-point lead at 73–71. They proceeded to push that lead out to 80–73 on back-to-back buckets from Mayo, forcing Bulls coach Tom Thibodeau to call a timeout with 9:03 on the clock. They led 85–79 following a Bayless bucket, when an official timeout came up with 5:51 left in the game. They even pushed the lead out to eight points again at 87–79, following a turnover from Bulls star Derrick Rose and a layup by Dudley, which forced another Thibodeau timeout with 4:33 left. All the while, Bucks coach Jason Kidd stuck with Middleton and his veterans.

"You can only have so many moral victories," Dudley told the *Milwaukee Journal Sentinel* after the game. "This was more of a veteran game today. All the vets were in [to close the game]. It's something you have to show the young guys."

Kidd kept them on the floor for the entire fourth quarter, even as the seemingly inevitable was set in motion. Henson missed two free throws and Middleton missed one from in close before Rose slithered through the lane for a layup. Mayo had the answer on the next possession and pushed the Bucks' lead back out to nine at 90–81. Jimmy Butler hit a tough three to bring the Bulls within six, but a review following a foul by Nikola Mirotic revealed Mayo's three didn't count. And just like that the Bulls were within three at 87–84.

Mayo made sure he got credit for his next attempt from deep, but still the Bulls would not go away and ended up tying the game at 90–90 with a Rose three and then a Pau Gasol and-one bucket and free throw with 38 seconds left. The Bucks would have a chance to take the lead, but Bayless missed a shot at the rim. The Bulls secured a rebound with 23 seconds left and it felt like the ending every Bucks fan feared was upon them.

Derrick Rose. Last shot. Bulls fans celebrating in Milwaukee. Sweep.

But that wasn't how it went down. Rose did try to get the last shot, but the savvy veterans were ready for him. Isolating Bayless on the right wing, Rose tried to drive to his left, but he saw Middleton waiting for him, so he crossed over to his right. Bayless stayed in front of him and forced him to turn again. This time, Rose put his dribble behind his back and went back to his left and there Bayless, Middleton, and Dudley converged on the ball; Middleton, from the top of the floor, and Dudley, helping all the way off Joakim

Noah and Taj Gibson from the left baseline. Together, they knocked the ball away and Middleton secured the turnover. He quickly turned to chuck it from the opposite three-point line in an attempt at a buzzer-beater, but Kidd called a timeout and gave the Bucks a chance to draw up a play.

Sideline out of bounds with 1.3 seconds left. Dudley would serve as the trigger man on the left side. Middleton on the left block. Bayless on the right. Henson and Mayo just above each elbow. Middleton came up the left lane line and around a double-screen from Henson and Mayo, which would take him away from Dudley and set him up for an over-the-shoulder catch and shot from the right wing, reminiscent of a shot Rex Chapman hit for the Suns in the 1997 playoffs that was assisted by Suns guard (and future Bucks coach) Jason Kidd.

But it was all for show. Despite appearing to be just a decoy, Bayless was Dudley's target the entire way. The Bucks guard came across the lane beneath the basket as though he was running to the corner to provide an extra outlet to Dudley and clearing out the backside of the defense. He was trailed by Rose. Just outside of the lane, Bayless stopped and quickly cut underneath the basket. Rose was overextended. With the 7-foot Noah on the ball, Dudley lobbed a pass from the wing to directly underneath the basket. Bayless caught it and laid it in.

Bucks win. With the opportunity to fight another day.

Unfortunately, the Game 4 victory would be the bright spot in the 2015 NBA postseason for the Bucks. They were ultimately able to steal Game 5 on the road and force Game 6 in Milwaukee, but it went poorly as they were blown out 120–66. Giannis Antetokounmpo was ejected from that game when he tackled Mike Dunleavy Jr. after the Bulls forward attempted a three. He was upset over what he believed to be dirty play from Dunleavy Jr., but it would nonetheless be one of the two plays that stuck out from the series and a scene perfectly juxtaposed to Bayless' buzzer-beater.

On one hand, a youngster not quite yet ready for the biggest stage. On the other, a group of experienced players pulling together for a surprise victory through timely play and veteran savvy.

# 26 Kohl Doesn't Sell to Jordan

Michael Jordan, owner of the Milwaukee Bucks.

For a week in June of 2003, the statement above was almost a reality. Bucks owner Herb Kohl was reportedly openly trying to sell the franchise in the off-season of 2003 and the greatest basketball player of all time was interested.

Jordan was coming off a two-year stint with the Washington Wizards, in which he served as an owner and then a player. He started with Washington as an executive and part owner, even serving as president of basketball operations from January 2000 to September 2001, before needing to relinquish his ownership stake to return to the floor in 2001.

After retiring for a third time two seasons later, Jordan hoped to return to his role in the front office, but Washington's ownership group was no longer interested in bringing Jordan back in such a role. With frustrations during his time with the Wizards lingering, Jordan was adamant that his next ownership move would need to afford him organizational control.

At the time, just two teams were up for sale: the Bucks and the Charlotte Bobcats, an expansion franchise. NBA commissioner David Stern helped broker the negotiations between Kohl and Jordan because, as sources told the *Chicago Tribune*, Stern believed it was important to keep Jordan and other legendary players, such as Larry Bird, in the NBA in ownership roles.

In Charlotte, Jordan had been rebuffed in his desire to be in control of the operation because he would never be put higher on the organizational chart than owner Robert Johnson. That was not the case in Milwaukee. Jordan's ownership group would have bought the team and Jordan would have been in full control.

Jordan owned a home in northern Illinois, which placed him just an hour away from Milwaukee. Although that could be construed as some level of knowledge of the area, many Milwaukeeans were concerned about Jordan's lack of connection to the area. Some feared Jordan would move the team or use the threat of moving the team to leverage the city and state of Wisconsin to pay for a new arena or change the lease of the Bradley Center.

Those fears did not dissuade Kohl as the two sides continued to discuss a potential sale of the team. In fact, discussions got so far along ESPN's Chad Ford reported Jordan's group would be purchasing the Bucks on the night of the 2003 NBA Draft. Ultimately, Senator Kohl decided against selling the team and released the following statement:

"I have decided not to sell the Milwaukee Bucks at this time, and will continue to own them, improve them, and commit them to remaining in Wisconsin...I must say that I enjoyed those conversations and was pleased with Michael's commitment of substantial personal time and personal financial resources to the proposed transaction...I was also impressed with the quality of the professionals that he was prepared to engage had we gone forward, as well as his willingness to make every effort to keep the team in Wisconsin.

"I think Michael will be an excellent owner of an NBA franchise and have encouraged him, for the benefit of the NBA, to continue his consideration of such an investment. On balance, I simply decided that I am not yet prepared to sell the team at this time and have instructed my representatives, accordingly."

Kohl ended up keeping the team for another 11 years before selling the team to an ownership group led by Wes Edens and Marc

Lasry. It appeared Jordan would have willingly kept the team in Milwaukee, but anyone doubting Kohl's conviction on the issue would be shown just how much that meant to Kohl.

"Somebody could have offered me $5 billion and I couldn't do that," Kohl told the *Journal Sentinel* in 2016. "I couldn't do it. How could I still live here? How could I live with myself? I never thought in any way that anybody could offer me the price that would be sufficient to say to Milwaukee and Wisconsin, 'I'm taking a lot of money, and good-bye.'"

And it wasn't just lip service with Kohl either. He eventually sold the team to an ownership group committed to keeping the team in Milwaukee, but also pledged $100 million toward the construction of a new downtown arena to ensure it happened. In the end, Kohl's decision in 2003 meant Jordan's impact on Bucks history is limited to his performaces on the court.

# 27 Bucks in Six

Bucks in Six.

It was a prediction by Bucks guard Brandon Jennings no one thought could come true and Jennings' smile after relaying the prediction to the assembled media at the 2013 Wisconsin Sports Awards seemed to suggest he knew the same. Regardless, it became one of the prevailing storylines in the Bucks' bid to upset the No. 1 seed Miami Heat, led by their big three of LeBron James, Dwyane Wade, and Chris Bosh.

"There's no pressure on us," Jennings exclaimed, in response to the media onlookers who found the claim preposterous.

He was right about that, though. The Bucks had no pressure heading into their first-round matchup against the Heat in the 2013 NBA playoffs. No one thought they had a chance against Miami, who finished out the season winning 37 of their final 39 games, including a 27-game win streak. In short, the Heat were at the peak of their powers and compiled a 66–16 record on their way to the East's top seed. They were regularly brought up in discussions of the greatest teams of all time.

Despite discussion of his comments creating the oft-mentioned fear of providing bulletin board material for his opponents, the Heat largely appeared unbothered by the comments.

"It doesn't matter," Wade told *Sports Illustrated*. "He's supposed to [say that]. If he comes out and says they're going to lose in six, everyone's going to say there's something wrong with him... He's supposed to have confidence in his team."

In the end, it didn't much matter, which was quite disappointing for the Bucks, who had made a series of moves during the season to increase their playoff chances. After 32 games, the team fired head coach Scott Skiles and asked Jim Boylan, one of Skiles' assistants, to step in as interim head coach for the rest of the season. With Boylan at the helm and pretty much the same roster, the Bucks went just 10–10 leading up the All-Star Break. So, just minutes before the trade deadline, the team dealt promising young forward Tobias Harris, Doron Lamb, and Beno Udrih for veteran guard J.J. Redick, Gustavo Ayon, and Ish Smith in an effort to strengthen the roster for the playoff run.

After adding Redick at the All-Star Break, there wasn't any improvement either, as the Bucks went just 12–18 to close out the season. The Bucks had fired a coach and traded away a potential future asset for a veteran to help boost their playoff odds, but there was little chemistry between the Bucks' three lead guards in Jennings, Monta Ellis, and Redick, and the team limped into the playoffs.

In their playoff series, the Heat swept the Bucks and Milwaukee lost each of the four games by double-digits. The series was not particularly close and the 2013 team was quickly broken up. Redick was moved to the Clippers in exchange for Jared Dudley and a first-round pick. The Bucks traded Jennings to Detroit for Brandon Knight and Khris Middleton. Ellis signed with the Dallas Mavericks.

The team was gone, but somehow "Bucks in Six" has lived on.

Maybe it was the carefree nature of the comment, the swagger necessary to make such a confident statement against such impossible odds, or the hope inherent in any such statement, but something about the phrase resonated. It has remained a part of the vernacular of Bucks fans from the moment it came out of Jennings' mouth.

Now, as the Bucks go into a playoff series, it's nearly impossible to ask for predictions without at least one news outlet or analyst making a "Bucks in six" prediction. At times, it has even become a rallying cry for fans.

In their 2017 first-round playoff matchup against the Toronto Raptors, the Bucks stole a game on the road in Toronto and went into Game 4 with a 2–1 series lead. That game did not go particularly well for the Bucks. They ended up losing 87–76, but that didn't stop fans from ringing out from all parts of the BMO Harris Bradley Center with the familiar chant.

"Bucks in six! Bucks in six! Bucks in six!"

Did the Bucks end up winning the series because of the inspiration of the chant by their home crowd? No. They lost in six games, but the chant cemented it. Just four years after his initial comment, Jennings words had transformed into a symbol of hope and a carefree attitude for an entire franchise trying to win its first NBA title since 1971.

# 28 Monroe Chooses Milwaukee

Milwaukee versus Los Angeles?

Milwaukee versus New York City?

Milwaukee versus Los Angeles *and* New York City?

In most circumstances, the money in Vegas would lean heavily in the favor of the large metropolitan areas on each coast, but in the summer of 2015, Milwaukee came out on top.

With both the Knicks and the Lakers vying for his services, free agent center Greg Monroe opted to sign with the Milwaukee Bucks.

"Many in the league were stunned," ESPN reporter Brian Windhorst wrote three months after the deal was made. "No one could remember the Lakers or Knicks losing out on such a high-profile unrestricted free agent to a low-profile team like the Bucks."

On the floor, the Bucks have bested both the Knicks and Lakers plenty, but that is all about the talent on the floor. If you have the best roster and coaching on a given night, you can beat the other team. Off the floor, however, how does Milwaukee try to compete?

Los Angeles' population is nearly seven times that of Milwaukee's. New York has 14 times more people than Milwaukee. Each city contains a level of diversity and culture a smaller city like Milwaukee simply couldn't offer. Los Angeles has the warm weather and sunshine. New York has the appeal of the country's largest city. Each serves as the hub for multiple national media outlets. For a younger player looking to improve his popularity among casual NBA fans across the country, L.A. and N.Y.C. simply offer an access to media outlets that Milwaukee could never even attempt to match.

Yet, in the summer of 2015, Monroe chose Milwaukee. Why?

"I knew what they had going on [in Milwaukee]," Monroe told ESPN. "I enjoyed all my free agent meetings, but after hearing what [the Bucks] told me, I knew [Milwaukee] was my best option."

What Milwaukee had going on was an up-and-coming team with some buzz around the league. In head coach Jason Kidd's first year in Milwaukee, the Bucks improved from the league's worst record to a spot in the playoffs and a competitive series against the Chicago Bulls. Much of the team's success stemmed from an aggressive defensive scheme that, for a year, stumped the entire league.

They had Jabari Parker, the No. 2 overall pick in the 2014 NBA Draft returning from a left ACL tear he had suffered just 25 games into his rookie season. They had Giannis Antetokounmpo, a long-limbed mystery man from Greece, who had just put up a strong second season. And maybe most importantly, they had Khris Middleton, a friend of Monroe's from his days in Detroit and a deadeye shooter on the wing.

On top of that, they also had the money. Milwaukee's new ownership group of New York hedge fund–managing billionaires were prepared to step up and give Monroe the contract he believed he deserved. They would match whatever numbers the owners from Los Angeles, New York, and Portland would be willing to give Monroe.

Maybe the Bucks had a slight advantage with the potential and perception of their roster, but ultimately the money would be equal anywhere Monroe wanted to sign, so the Bucks would need something to take their offer over the top. That thing ended up being co-owner Marc Lasry.

Lasry attended the meeting with Kidd and general manager John Hammond and helped blow Monroe away. The Bucks showcased renderings of the new arena they had secured funding for earlier in the year, pictures of their new uniforms, and even a video featuring comedian Marlon Wayans, but it was Lasry who sealed the deal as he sold Monroe on each detail of the Bucks' future.

In the end, Monroe signed a three-year max contract with the Bucks worth $52 million, with a player option in his third year. Reports at the time would differ as to what player options and contract lengths each team had offered, but Milwaukee went to the same meetings Los Angeles and New York went to and came out on top.

After Kareem Abdul-Jabbar made it clear he would prefer New York or Los Angeles to Milwaukee 40 years earlier, the city and organization struggled to even get meetings with the league's top free agents. Largely, the franchise relied on developing homegrown talent and fighting hard to retain them when other teams came calling. Often, the strategy led to overpaying their own players undeserving of such large contracts just to keep them in the city.

Monroe's time in Milwaukee would end in similar fashion, as he never found a solid footing with the Bucks and failed to live all the way up to his max contract, but the value obtained from Monroe's play is almost secondary to actually signing a big-time, big-money free agent.

The Bucks paid too much for a free agent, which was not unusual for Milwaukee or any other franchise, but for the first time in a long time, they signed one of the most coveted free agents on the market, even with teams from the biggest markets competing for his services.

# 29 Jabari Parker's Journey

The Bucks compiled the league's worst record during the 2013–14 season, which earned them the best chance at selecting first in the 2014 NBA Draft, but things didn't end up going that way.

Really, it was a fitting start to Jabari Parker's journey in Milwaukee.

The Cleveland Cavaliers ended up jumping from the ninth pick in the lottery to grab the first pick and move the Bucks down to the second spot. The drop was certainly disappointing for the franchise, but there were three players at the top of the 2014 draft seen as franchise-changing talents: Andrew Wiggins, Jabari Parker, and Joel Embiid.

No matter what happened with the first pick, the Bucks would come away with a great player to help rebuild their roster. In the lead-up to the draft though, Parker made headlines by talking about his desire to play in Milwaukee.

"I've got some comfort level with [the Bucks], especially with them just telling me 'We want you,'" Parker told the *Washington Post*. "I didn't get really any answers from the Cavs, so I'm just going with what I'm certain with. I got just that answer, that fair assessment. They sat with me and said, 'We're going to go with you.'"

That is exactly what ended up happening. Wiggins went first overall, before ultimately getting traded to Minnesota, while Parker went second to the Bucks. During the team's introductory press conference for Parker, the organization made its desire to get him in Milwaukee very clearly known and believed it had gotten the right guy when the Cavaliers decided on Wiggins.

The Bucks hoped the rookie would run alongside Giannis Antetokounmpo in his second year, and the two would develop together on their way to turning the team into a playoff contender. But things didn't end up going quite that smoothly.

Parker started the first 25 games of the season and averaged 12 points and five rebounds per game to put himself squarely into contention for the Rookie of the Year award, but then Parker collapsed while trying to complete a Euro step against the Phoenix Suns on December 15, 2014. In a single move, Parker had torn his left anterior cruciate ligament (ACL) and significantly altered his career path and the future of the Bucks.

The next year of Parker's life would be consumed by rehab. The Bucks tried to make the process as effective as possible by hiring rehab specialist and sport scientist Suki Hobson. Hobson and Parker would be inseparable for the entire year, even venturing to the Andes Mountains to hike in the mountain's altitude to improve his stamina.

On November 4, 2015, Parker returned to the floor against the Philadelphia 76ers. In just 11 months, he had recovered from his torn ACL and a number of people in the organization, including head coach Jason Kidd, thought he looked "bigger and stronger" after the injury. Parker's play clearly improved as he went on to average 14 points per game in 76 games in the 2015–16 season.

The 2016–17 season would be Parker's first full season, as well as the first off-season without rehab as a professional. He would not be playing catch up with the health of his body and could instead focus on the things he needed to improve upon as a player. It showed as Parker averaged more than 20 points per game. He looked like a potential winner of the NBA's Most Improved Player award, but again, things didn't end up going that way.

Against the Miami Heat on February 8, 2017, Parker collapsed to the floor as he drove to the basket, which resulted in a torn left ACL. Same injury, same knee, same difficult rehab. Parker would be forced to work his way back into game shape for the second time in his career. Hobson and the team's training staff helped Parker through the difficult rehab for a second time

Before Parker returned to action on February 2, 2018, against the New York Knicks, Bucks director of performance Troy Flanagan told the *Milwaukee Journal Sentinel*, "He's faster than he's ever been, he's stronger than he's ever been, and he's leaner than he's ever been." In his first game back, Parker scored 12 points in 15 minutes, showing off the same scoring ability he displayed before his second left ACL tear.

Parker went on to average 12.6 points and 24 minutes per game in 31 appearances to end the season. Joining a team in the middle of a playoff push, Parker was responsible for figuring out how he fit in and play a supporting role, something he really never had been forced to do in his entire life as a basketball player.

The smaller role and spot minutes frustrated Parker during the Bucks' first-round playoff series against the Boston Celtics. After Milwaukee dropped the first two games of the series, Parker told reporters he wanted more minutes in Game 3. He had struggled greatly during the first two contests in Boston, so his public request for more minutes drew criticism from some. Ultimately, though, the request may have motivated Parker to play some of the best basketball of his NBA career, including a sterling, 12-point first-half performance in Game 4.

In the end, though, Parker's up-and-down playoff performance just ended up contributing another variable to an already difficult off-season decision. Could a potential attitude problem pop up again in the future? Will Parker become a passable defender? How serious of an injury risk is his left knee?

With Parker's restricted free agency looming in the summer of 2018, the Bucks were forced to weigh each of these questions and decide how much they valued him going forward. It turns out they didn't value him as much as the Chicago Bulls did, who signed

Parker to a two-year, $40 million deal with a team option for the second year, ending his time in Milwaukee.

Four years after selecting Parker with the second pick in the 2014 NBA Draft, he was joining a different team. He had yet to make an All-Star team or even play a full NBA season, and now he was leaving the Bucks before having a chance to fulfill any of the hopes the team had when he was drafted.

# 30 24–1

It may be the first time a team has ever called its shot on a T-shirt, but that's exactly what the Bucks did before their game with the Golden State Warriors on December 12, 2015.

The Warriors entered the BMO Harris Bradley Center with a perfect record. They had won each of their first 24 games in the 2015–16 season on their way to a record-breaking 73-win regular season, but that didn't stop Bucks owner Wes Edens from deciding to try his hand at predicting the future.

"I got the idea when I was at a game a week ago against the Trail Blazers," Edens told the *Washington Post* a few days after the game. "I was talking to Jason [Kidd] and I said, 'If Golden State wins, we should print up shirts.' I was thinking of that story about Babe Ruth and the called home run and the only reason people remember that is that he pointed at the wall."

With clearance from the head coach, Edens went ahead and created the shirts. As the Bucks and Warriors stepped on the floor, the Bucks' cheering section was a sea of green shirts adorned with 24–1 printed in cream.

*The brainchild of owner Wes Edens, T-shirts emblazoned with 24–1 were distributed to fans prior to the Bucks–Warriors game in 2015, a reference to Golden State's 24–0 record at the time. The Bucks made good on the promotion's promise, winning 108–95.* (AP Photos)

With the challenge clearly laid out in front of them, the Bucks would have to play the best basketball of their young season. At just 9–15, they were struggling with the weight of elevated expectations after a surprise playoff run in Kidd's second season and the integration of new center Greg Monroe, the biggest free agent signing in franchise history.

Both teams were coming off a game on the road the previous night, but the Warriors would probably claim a slight edge in difficulty as the Celtics forced two overtimes before Golden State escaped Boston with a win. Their fatigue showed in the first half against the Bucks as they hit just two of the 13 threes they attempted, while the Bucks were 6-of-9 from beyond the arc and roared out to a 59–48 lead at the half. Giannis Antetokounmpo took over in the second quarter as he attacked the Warriors' defense relentlessly, tallying nine points and five assists as the Bucks opened their lead up from just two after one quarter.

The Bucks knew the Warriors would come back with a vengeance in the second half because the defending NBA champions truly cared about their win streak. And at some point, Milwaukee would be forced to see the "Death Lineup." The Warriors regularly deployed a small-ball lineup of Stephen Curry, Klay Thompson, Andre Iguodala, Harrison Barnes, and Draymond Green, which ran most teams off the floor with its combination of versatile defenders, three-point shooting, and athleticism.

The Warriors chipped away at the Bucks' lead in the third quarter and pulled to within three entering the final period. It seemed like a perfect time to deploy the Death Lineup, but Warriors interim coach Luke Walton waited and point guard Michael Carter-Williams and Monroe went to work. By the time the Death Lineup hit the floor with 6:57 left, the Bucks had pushed the score to 91–79.

The Death Lineup didn't matter this night. Many teams tried to deploy their most athletic lineups to counter it, but the Bucks went in the opposite direction. They turned to their big free agent acquisition. Possession after possession, the Bucks fed the ball to Monroe as Green attempted to cover him in the post, but he was no match for the player affectionately nicknamed "Moose."

Monroe used his strength and nimble feet to back down Green for a couple buckets from the blocks. He deftly ran the offense on a number of touches at the elbow. He found Carter-Williams and Antetokounmpo for great looks at the rim and the Bucks kept Golden State quiet on the other end. Despite their best efforts, the Warriors could not claw their way back into the game and Carter-Williams closed it out with a one-handed slam with 43 seconds left as the capacity crowd went crazy.

"What was the worst that could happen?" Edens asked a few days later. "If it didn't work out, we'd have donated the shirts to charity and some kids in Ethiopia would be wearing 24–1 shirts."

Instead, the Bucks beat the Warriors 108–95, allowing Edens and fellow Bucks owner Marc Lasry to pose with 24–1 shirts courtside immediately following the game. The Bucks had cashed the check their owner had written and beaten the Warriors, ending the second-longest winning streak the NBA has ever seen.

# 31 Antetokounmpo's First All-Star Game

Anthony Davis of the New Orleans Pelicans was the MVP of the 2017 NBA All-Star Game, but the most memorable moments came courtesy of Giannis Antetokounmpo in his first All-Star Game appearance.

In a bit of a surprise, the Bucks forward picked up a ton of votes from fans, media, and players alike. Among fans, Antetokounmpo picked up the third-highest number of votes, trailing only LeBron James and Kevin Durant, with 1,604,463. In just one year, Antetokounmpo increased his total votes by more than 1.5 million, as he only garnered 84,617 votes for the 2016 All-Star Game.

He also did incredibly well in the first year the NBA instituted player and media voting. Again, only James (198) and Durant (170) bested him in player voting, as Antetokounmpo collected 162 votes from the 324 players who voted. The same was true of media voting, as 93 out of 100 possible votes put him behind just those two superstars.

Despite the impressive vote tallies, Antetokounmpo still wasn't quite sure he belonged when he arrived in New Orleans for the game. After wrapping up shootaround, he admitted to having some nerves as he prepared to hit an All-Star court for the first time, but relayed he received some helpful reassurance from New York Knicks forward Carmelo Anthony.

"I saw him out there, he was antsy," Anthony told reporters. "So, I just told him, 'Relax, man. Just play your game. You're too tall to be nervous. With a name like the 'Greek Freak,' you can't be nervous out here."

Any nerves Antetokounmpo had seemingly disappeared by tipoff on Sunday night, because it didn't take long for him to put his stamp on the game. On his first touch of the night, the lanky forward drove baseline against Davis, collected himself under the rim with a jump stop, and eventually threw down a two-handed flush.

Two minutes later, he swatted a Davis midrange jumper from behind. When he got down to the offensive end, he received a short pitch from Cavaliers guard Kyrie Irving at the free throw line on his way to a tomahawk slam.

*Giannis Antetokounmpo made quite an impression during his first All-Star Game appearance in 2017.*

A minute after that, the 22-year-old applied some pressure to Houston Rockets guard James Harden as he brought the ball up the floor with the malaise typical of a modern All-Star Game; Antetokounmpo simply stole it and the hammered home a windmill slam. The first half would feature three more of his dunks, as well as some tricky ballhandling to set one of them up, another steal, and a no-look left-handed assist to a slashing James.

None of that would compare to the fireworks the first-time All-Star saved for the second half.

Just two minutes into the third quarter, James threw the ball ahead to Irving, who saw Antetokounmpo trailing behind him. They attacked the only defender back for the Western Conference, Warriors guard Stephen Curry, and Irving threw Antetokounmpo a lob, which he pounded through the rim with two hands for a loud and powerful finish.

Harden brought the ball back up the floor, but got a little loose with his dribble and Antetokounmpo stripped it away again. He collected the ball around midcourt with Curry serving as the only defender back to defend a 4-on-1 break once again. Instead of attempting to defend it, Curry laid down on his stomach and covered his ears to protect himself from the carnage coming his way and save himself from the potential embarrassment of challenging the Greek forward at the rim.

The potential embarrassment might have been his destiny though, because Antetokounmpo got Curry four minutes later. Pacers forward Paul George isolated Clippers center DeAndre Jordan off the dribble on the left wing before trying a pull-up jumper from 19 feet out. It bounced off the front of the rim, where Curry stood nearly underneath the basket waiting to grab the ball, either make or miss. Antetokounmpo came streaking in from the right wing, jumped from behind Curry, reached over the top of the former MVP, and threw it down with two hands.

Warriors center Draymond Green's hands went to his head in the middle of the lane. Jordan's head quickly whipped around with his mouth agape. Curry's coach Steve Kerr smiled, but quickly put his hand to his mouth to try to hide it. Durant looked on with concern for his teammate. James smiled with eyes wide on the Eastern Conference bench, while Anthony and Toronto Raptors guard Kyle Lowry hopped up off the bench smiling and clapping.

In short, Antetokounmpo's thunderous dunk would be the moment everyone remembered from the game and a perfect symbol of the impression he left on the league's best players in his first All-Star Game.

"He did well," George said. "I think he was the only one that had the intensity level as high as he had it. And that's what you love to see. Guys that come out and play both ends like Giannis did. Have fun. Still put on a show. I thought he just enjoyed the moment."

With three steals and a block in just over 23 minutes of action, Antetokounmpo might have been exerting a little bit more effort than some of his contemporaries, but his 30 points and plethora of highlight dunks more than adequately showed he understood what the All-Star Game is all about. He put on an entertaining show for fans across the world and more than justified his standing next to James and Durant. He might have even earned the right to get invited to a few more by the time his career is through.

# 32 Dr. J in Milwaukee?

Can you imagine Dr. J playing next to Kareem?

It's one of the great "what-ifs" in the history of the Milwaukee Bucks and maybe even the entire league. Julius Erving with Kareem Abdul-Jabbar in Milwaukee. It almost happened, and if you listen to anyone with the Milwaukee Bucks in the 1970s, they'll tell you that it should have happened.

The Bucks had two first-round picks in the 1972 NBA Draft, sixth and 12th overall. At the time, the draft was much longer than the two-round draft we've come to know, with 18 rounds and about 200 players selected as the NBA's 13 teams tried to fill their rosters. With their first pick, Bucks general manager Wayne Embry selected Russ Lee, a quick guard from Marshall University. Embry had a special plan with the team's second pick, but Bucks owners Wes Pavalon and Marvin Fishman were not quite sure of it.

"I said I would like to draft Julius Erving," Embry later recounted to the *Racine Journal-Times*. "I told them he's playing in the ABA and he's going to be a great player. They didn't know who he was. They had never heard of him. They said, 'Are you sure you want to waste a draft pick on him?' And, again, I told them he is playing in the ABA—that's when the ABA just started out—and that I think we just ought to take a chance and draft him because we don't know if the ABA is going to last."

Embry put together an 11-year NBA playing career before transitioning to the front office in Milwaukee in 1970, so he actually got introduced to Erving as a player. Like many players, Embry would work at basketball camps in the summer as a way to make extra money because professional basketball didn't pay all that well in the early days of the league.

While with the Boston Celtics, Embry was asked to help out at a camp for some of the area's best college players in upstate New York. The 30-year-old center made his way up to the camp for the weekend and hit the court after dinner on Saturday. He started shooting around before one of the coaches at the camp told him he wanted to grab one of the kids at the camp for a game of one-on-one against the NBA veteran.

"I don't want to play against a kid because I'm pretty physical," Embry remembered telling the coach.

At 6-foot-8 and 240 pounds, Embry was known as a very physical player, so his concern for a young player was justified, but ultimately not necessary. Embry started out shooting jumpers instead of using his normal physical play and quickly went down 3–0 to the kid in a game up to seven. He relayed that he was going to start playing harder and the kid said that would be fine. It didn't end up mattering. The kid beat him 7–5.

After the game, Embry told the kid that he was pretty good. The coach who set up the game jumped in the conversation and told Embry the kid was actually one of the best players in New York City. Embry was impressed and asked the kid for his name. He said, "Julius."

His one-on-one game versus a skinny kid from New York City stuck out in his mind as he decided to use the 12th pick in the 1972 NBA Draft on Julius Erving on April 10, 1972. Little did he know his pick would turn into a massive controversy.

By the time Embry drafted Erving, the forward had already completed a season as a professional basketball player. Erving had left the University of Massachusetts after his junior year to join the Virginia Squires in the ABA. He had signed a four-year, $125,000 contract with the team and earned ABA All-Rookie and All-ABA Second Team honors in the 1971–72 season.

The 1972–73 season would be the first year Erving could play in the NBA because of a rule prohibiting teams from signing players before their college class graduated. It's unclear whether Embry actually believed Erving would join the Bucks for the upcoming season, but he did believe it was important to have his rights. So, he drafted Erving, only to have the Atlanta Hawks announce they had signed Erving to a five-year, $1 million deal the day after the draft. Apparently, they had signed a deal in secret before the draft and were desperately trying to trade up in the draft to take Erving and bring their deal above the table, but the Bucks beat them to it.

In turn, everybody sued everybody. Erving sued his agent because he believed he was working for the ABA. The Squires sued the Hawks for stealing Erving because he still had signed a deal with them. The Bucks sued the Hawks for signing a player they believed they had the rights to. All of which led to a long, drawn-out court battle.

While all of that got sorted out, Erving started suiting up for the Hawks and playing with their phenom Pete Maravich. The NBA soon put a stop to that by fining the Hawks $25,000 for every game Erving played with them, even exhibitions, before a vote among the league's owners ultimately ruled the Bucks should have the rights to Erving.

"The vote could not have gone any other way," one of the league owners told *The New York Times*. "The entire credibility and structure of the college draft was at stake if Milwaukee had not been able to retain the rights to Erving. Milwaukee drafted him and Atlanta signed him even before the college draft was held. They had no rights to him."

In the end though, the victory meant nothing—the courts ruled the NBA didn't have any rights to Erving to begin with, because he needed to honor his contract with the ABA's Squires. Erving played the next year with the Squires and became one of the league's best players before getting sold to the New York Nets. Erving would honor the remainder of his contract in New York and win three ABA Most Valuable Player awards before coming to the NBA in 1976. The Philadelphia 76ers signed him before the Bucks got a chance to meet with Erving the second time around. Today, fans can only dream about what could have been if Dr. J would have got the chance to play next to Abdul-Jabbar and Oscar Robertson.

# 33 Trading for Oscar Robertson

"It was a phone call for me. Wayne Embry was telling me, 'We got the 'Big O,' and things are looking up.' There wasn't any hype, but all I needed to know was that we got Oscar Robertson. I thought, 'We're a legitimate team now.'"

"When I heard that Oscar was coming to play with the Bucks, I was very happy. I thought that really made it easy for us to win because of his abilities on both ends of the court."

"After we got Oscar, we knew that we had a championship-caliber team. We had all of the other pieces in place."

The quotes above come from Bobby Dandridge, Kareem Abdul-Jabbar, and Jon McGlocklin, respectively. They each speak to the level of excitement among Bucks players when they heard the Bucks would be trading for Oscar Robertson immediately following the 1969–70 season.

Just one day after the Bucks were eliminated from the Eastern Division Finals by the New York Knicks, they traded Flynn Robinson and Charlie Paulk for the 10-time All-Star. Such an immediate move after elimination might suggest something that came together quickly, but the move for Robertson actually took quite some time.

Robertson was a star during his four years at the University of Cincinnati, vaulting the Bearcats into the national spotlight by leading the nation in scoring three straight years and leading them to Final Four appearances in 1959 and 1960. He then went on to play 10 years for the Cincinnati Royals, becoming the first player to average a triple-double for an entire season in his second NBA season.

Despite Robertson's brilliance, the Royals were never able to beat the Boston Celtics in the Eastern Division and advance to the NBA Finals. With the team struggling to find more success, the Royals decided to go in a different direction and hired former Celtics great Bob Cousy as their new head coach before the 1969–70 season. Cincinnati gave him the right to make the personnel moves he saw fit and rebuild the team in his own unique vision.

Playing under all-time great coach Red Auerbach for the Celtics instilled in Cousy an emphasis on fast-paced play and defense. He intended to replicate the same model in Cincinnati and started trading away players he felt didn't fit those principles. He was even willing to trade Robertson.

"The team was going to move to Kansas City," Robertson later told Bucks.com. "Bob Cousy was going to trade me to Baltimore, but I vetoed that trade because I had a clause in my contract that I could do that. Cousy had no idea I had that clause. The way they handled that situation, they acted as if I hadn't done anything there. It was emotional. I didn't want to go anywhere. But they were destroying the team, and I didn't want to go to Kansas City, anyway."

With a trade to Baltimore vetoed, discussions continued throughout the rest of Cousy's first season. Robertson didn't prioritize the teams where he could win a championship or cities that featured warm weather, but rather teams that would allow him to keep his family in the Midwest. He wanted to make sure that his three daughters were in a good school system and he had a place where he could raise his family.

Robertson was eventually convinced to accept a trade to Milwaukee by a former teammate. Bucks owner Wes Pavalon hired Wayne Embry as a front office assistant after he had retired from the NBA in 1969. Before spending his final season with the Bucks, Embry had backed up Bill Russell in Boston for two years and starred with Robertson in Cincinnati.

"I think Oscar had a no-trade contract or approval, and [Pavalon] asked me if I'd pick up the phone and give him a call, and kind of push him our way," Embry told NBA.com. "I told Oscar I was going back and it'd be great for him to win a championship after all these years. And of course I was interested in pushing it along, if I was going to go back there too."

With his former teammate's recommendation and comfort with a Midwestern city, Robertson approved a trade to Milwaukee and he prepared to join the Bucks for the 1970–71 season. He was nearing the end of his career, but Robertson and Lew Alcindor (later Kareem Abdul-Jabbar) would be one of the league's most formidable duos.

"After I got there, and started practicing with the guys, I started thinking that maybe we could win a championship," Robertson later told Bucks.com. "We didn't talk about it right away, though. We didn't know each other. We really had to get together, get to know each other, and start playing together as a team."

Robertson's unspoken premonition upon first playing with the team was right as the Bucks went on to win their first NBA championship the very next season.

# 34 The 1974 NBA Finals Disappointment

After falling 95–83 in Game 3 of the 1974 NBA Finals, the questions grew louder during Kareem Abdul-Jabbar's postgame media availability. From the May 13, 1974 issue of *Sports Illustrated*:

"During his early years with the Warriors," asked a reporter, "when Wilt Chamberlain was criticized for never winning championships, he used to defend himself by saying he wasn't getting much help from his teammates. Do you sometimes feel the same way?"

"You're trying to get me to say that my teammates aren't any good," answered Abdul-Jabbar.

"I guess so," the reporter admitted.

"I have no comment on that," said Abdul-Jabbar.

During the 1971 NBA Finals, Abdul-Jabbar could have told the reporter about Oscar Robertson's sterling play at point guard and Jon McGlocklin's shooting and the strong forward play of Bobby Dandridge and Greg Smith and the boost from Lucius Allen's play off the bench and the steady play of Bob Boozer and McCoy McLemore and Dick Cunningham.

But things had changed by 1974.

Robertson wasn't the player he used to be. The legendary NBA point guard still understood the delicate ballet of NBA basketball better than anyone else in the world, but he simply couldn't move quick enough or handle the pressure of ballhandlers like he did at the beginning of his time in Milwaukee. Father Time had caught up with Robertson and no amount of knowhow and understanding of the game could make up for his diminished skills. Still a fine player, but no longer the star who originally joined the Bucks, he was also hampered with a torn groin muscle heading into the Finals.

In just three years, Dandridge had developed into an even greater threat in the frontcourt and Abdul-Jabbar's strongest teammate, scoring 18.9 points per game. Allen had done the same by bumping his scoring average up to 17.6 points per game, but he was lost to a knee injury before the postseason began. Despite their improvement and continued growth, neither player made the 1974 All-Star Game or received All-NBA honors in the 1973–74 season.

Milwaukee also didn't have the depth it had in 1971 and it showed late in 1974 as the Bucks piled up injuries. Despite those struggles, Abdul-Jabbar led the Bucks to the league's best record at 59–23 and the NBA Finals, needing just one more game than the minimum to get through the first two rounds of the playoffs. The UCLA product was brilliant throughout the season, averaging 27 points, 14.5 rebounds, and 4.8 assists per game on the way to his third Most Valuable Player award.

The Bucks' injuries helped set the stage for an epic seven-game NBA Finals. With no Allen and a hobbled McGlocklin (torn calf) and Robertson, the Celtics entered the matchup with a little extra confidence, despite splitting four regular season games with the Bucks. Celtics center Dave Cowens was five inches shorter than the 7-foot-2 Abdul-Jabbar, but he was no David to Abdul-Jabbar's Goliath. He took home the NBA MVP award the previous season and perfectly fit the Celtics' fast-breaking, full-court-pressing style.

With Cowens making Abdul-Jabbar work for every touch on the inside, the series was largely decided by the other players on the floor. The Celtics guards—John Havlicek, Jo Jo White, and Don Chaney—tormented Robertson and other Bucks guards as they attempted to bring the ball up the floor, forcing the league's best offense into more than 20 turnovers per game.

The two teams traded victories on their way to one of just 19 NBA Finals to reach a seventh game. The Bucks dropped Game 1 by 15 on their home court before saving face with a nine-point win in Game 2. The Celtics looked to have the Bucks on the ropes, forcing 27 turnovers in a Game 3 loss, 95–83, before Abdul-Jabbar responded with a 48-minute, 34-point performance to lead the Bucks to a 97–89 win to even the series at 2–2. Game 5 featured the typical strong performance from Abdul-Jabbar, as well as a vintage 23-point, six-assist game from Robertson, but the Bucks couldn't pull it out, falling 96–87.

The Bucks would need to win Game 6 in the Boston Garden. Backs against the wall in the league's loudest arena and somehow Milwaukee would have to find a way to win. It took two overtimes and 58 minutes from both Robertson and Abdul-Jabbar, but the Bucks pulled out a 102–101 victory with the MVP nailing a double-teamed skyhook with three seconds left in the second overtime to seal the victory and force a Game 7.

After Game 6, former Celtics great Bob Cousy found his way into the office of Celtics coach Tommy Heinsohn and asked one question: "Why don't you double?" Heinsohn disagreed with the strategy and believed it was best to make it difficult on an opposing star without conceding open shots to his teammates. After an extended discussion with Cousy, Heinsohn decided to give it a try in Game 7 and it worked. While the Bucks struggled to adjust, the Celtics took a 53–40 lead into the half and ultimately defeated Milwaukee 102–87.

No one really knew it at the time, but it would herald the end of an era. Robertson would retire before the next season. Abdul-Jabbar would request a trade out of Milwaukee in October and be out of town the following season. The 1974 NBA Finals would be the last time Bucks fans would see Abdul-Jabbar and Robertson share the floor in Milwaukee.

# Retired Jerseys: Bob Dandridge's No. 10

On March 7, 2015, Bob Dandridge got to see something he thought he might not ever see: his No. 10 jersey up in the rafters of the Bradley Center.

"I've thought about it for quite a few years and then it sort of crumbled on the back burner," Dandridge told OnMilwaukee.com. "Then when new ownership came in and felt that this was something they wanted to do…I guess, patience pays off."

The Bucks have retired eight jerseys in their 50 years as a franchise. Six of the men who wore those jerseys—Oscar Robertson, Junior Bridgeman, Sidney Moncrief, Jon McGlocklin, Bob Lanier, and Brian Winters—were honored almost immediately after the respective players retired. Kareem Abdul-Jabbar's No. 33 jersey was retired four years after he retired from the NBA.

Dandridge's No. 10 was raised *33 years* after he retired from the NBA.

Ask any of his teammates honored by the Bucks and they will wonder why the franchise didn't figure it out sooner.

"Bob made it very difficult for our opponents to guard us because of his quickness," Abdul-Jabbar told ESPN. "He could hit the open midrange jump shot and he was a very good defensive player."

Drafted in the fourth round the same year the Bucks selected Abdul-Jabbar, Dandridge always had something to prove and played that way. In his rookie season with the Bucks, Dandridge earned more than 30 minutes of playing time a night and averaged 13.2 points, 7.7 rebounds, and 3.6 assists per game. Milwaukee traded for Robertson immediately after the season, but their 6-foot-6 small forward didn't plan on taking a back seat.

"I wanted to remain the team's No. 2 scorer and rebounder and I did even with Oscar," Dandridge later told the *Washington Post*. "You set goals and you want to be recognized when you travel around."

In the next season, Dandridge improved his scoring average by nearly five points and helped Milwaukee win its first and only NBA championship. Abdul-Jabbar and Robertson got the attention, but Dandridge was just as steady and vital to the team's success. He even turned it up come playoff time. In the Finals against the Baltimore Bullets, he was one of three Bucks to average more than 20 points per game.

"Bob Dandridge was a great player, a great forward," Robertson later told Bucks.com. "I enjoyed playing with him. His contributions were often overlooked, but his value to the team was shown as he played a critical role in helping us win our only NBA championship in 1971."

Dandridge's improvement didn't stop there either. By the time the 1974 NBA Finals came around, he was clearly the team's second-best offensive option. As Robertson aged and injuries plagued his final season, Dandridge stepped up, but it wasn't quite enough and the Bucks fell to the Celtics. After the "Big O" retired, Dandridge, affectionately named "The Greyhound" by Bucks radio announcer Eddie Doucette for his fast-break abilities, took an even bigger step forward, making his second All-Star Game and even serving as the Bucks' lead option while Abdul-Jabbar missed a number of games with an injury at the start of the season.

His experience as the team's No. 1 option would prove helpful the next season after the Bucks were forced to trade Abdul-Jabbar and put the team in Dandridge's hands. The Norfolk State product took full advantage of the opportunity, compiling the highest scoring total of his career with 21.5 points per game. He averaged 20-plus points again in the next season, but it would be his final season in Milwaukee because of an ugly contract dispute throughout the season.

Dandridge felt the Bucks were not willing to pay him what he was worth considering he was, in his words, "the big scorer on the team ever since they broke up the championship team we had." During his time in Milwaukee, Dandridge was unafraid to speak his mind and believed he suffered for it.

"They weren't used to the semi-intelligent black athlete who spoke what was on his mind instead of being totally humble," Dandridge told the *Washington Post* a year after leaving Milwaukee. "They still don't really know me. The last thing [Bucks coach] Don Nelson said about me was he regretted that I said what was on my mind. How about that? A man can't say what is on his mind."

The breakup was ugly. Dandridge left for Washington and Bucks owner Jim Fitzgerald told him he "wasn't as valuable to the Bucks as he thought he was." With the Bullets, he played alongside two Hall of Fame players again in Wes Unseld and Elvin Hayes. He would win his second championship in 1979 after a number of clutch performances in the playoffs, including a 37-point game in Game 7 to close out the San Antonio Spurs.

"If I say a guy is an 'excellent professional player,' that's the highest compliment that I can say about a player," former Bucks assistant coach and legendary NBA analyst Hubie Brown told ESPN. "That's Bobby Dandridge, because he was complete. Athletically, offensively, and defensively. In the pressure moments he could deliver at both ends of the court and then he was an excellent teammate. That, to me, completes the pro."

Dandridge returned to Milwaukee for the 1981–82 season, but would only appear in the first 11 games before retiring. After retiring, Dandridge worked with the NBA to develop the NBA Rookie Transition Program, a way for the league to help give rookies guidance as they entered the professional ranks. Despite staying close to the league, Dandridge never received a call from the Basketball Hall of Fame or the Bucks about a possible honor, even with numbers that might deserve it. Dandridge is still first in Bucks franchise history in minutes played, second in rebounds and field goals made, third in games played, and fifth in points.

"As a player, Bob Dandridge embodied everything we want this franchise to stand for: hard work, passion, toughness, and, above all else, excellence," Bucks co-owner Wes Edens said when announcing Dandridge's jersey retirement. "This honor is long overdue, and the entire organization is thrilled to finally put his number in the rafters along with the other legends who have helped shape this franchise."

Nobody understood the honor, or the wait for that honor, better than Dandridge.

# 36 The 20-Game Win Streak

If the 1970–71 season went anything like their first meeting, Oscar Robertson and Lew Alcindor might have ended up at each other's throats instead of passing around the Walter A. Brown Trophy, soaked in champagne in the visiting locker room of the Baltimore Bullets.

"First time I ever met Oscar was a couple of years ago in an exhibition game in the Catskills, and Oscar and I got put on the same team," Alcindor told *Sports Illustrated* in April of 1971. "He got the ball and he drove, and I cut the wrong way. Man, he yelled at me! He said, 'Listen, you got to do it this way!'

"When Oscar Robertson talks, you listen! And it helped me. The next time he drove, I cut the right way, and he got the ball to me and I scored. And I said to myself, 'Well, well! You've just met Oscar Robertson, and already he's taught you something!'"

Robertson's demanding ways pushed away many teammates throughout his career, but Alcindor accepted his demeanor and the two formed a dynamic pairing early on in their first season. After splitting their first two games, the Bucks won 16 straight contests. To kick off the new year, they won their first 10 games of 1971. Those two streaks, though, would not compare to their 20-game win streak in February and March, an NBA record at the time.

During the win streak, which ran from February 6 to March 8, the Bucks' average margin of victory was 17.95, with just six of the games remaining within single digits. They won four games by 30 or more points and nine games by 20 or more points. Their point differential is one of the highest in the history of basketball. They weren't just beating teams, they were destroying them.

Much of their dominance was due to Alcindor's brilliance on the way to his first NBA Most Valuable Player award, but their depth often gets overlooked.

"I really think the key to us winning the championship was our subs," Robertson later told Bucks.com. "We had McCoy McLemore and Bob Boozer and big Dick Cunningham, who was my roommate. Then Lucius Allen came along. Once we all got together and started playing a few exhibition games, we just blew everybody out of the water. At that point, I thought, 'We've got something special.'"

Adding Robertson gave Alcindor a true running mate, but a preseason trade with the Seattle Supersonics gave the Bucks depth they simply didn't have before. On September 17, 1970, Milwaukee traded Zaid Abdul-Aziz to Seattle for Allen and Boozer. On February 1, 1971, the Bucks also sent Gary Freeman and a second-round pick to the Cleveland Cavaliers for McLemore.

With Jon McGlocklin in the backcourt next to Robertson and Greg Smith and Bobby Dandridge next to Alcindor in the frontcourt, the starting lineup was as strong as it would ever be. Dandridge, McGlocklin, and Smith could all go off on any given night. McGlocklin had seven games with 20 or more points during the streak. Smith had three and Dandridge had six such games, including a 33-point game in a win over the San Diego Rockets on February 24, 1971.

From top to bottom, the Bucks didn't have any holes and proved it during their 20-game win streak. They proved worthy defensively as they pulled out a 107–106 victory in the third game of the streak against the Pistons, who were led by Dave Bing, the man Alcindor believed to be the MVP. They beat up on Wilt Chamberlain and the Lakers twice, including a 34-point drubbing in the streak's fourth game. They survived a three-game West Coast road trip.

Their record would be broken the very next season by the Los Angeles Lakers, but their standing as one of the greatest teams in the history of basketball would stand forever and their win streak would be a nice memento of their dominance.

# 37 Retired Jerseys: Jon McGlocklin's No. 14

Jon McGlocklin's relationship with the Bucks is simple.

He is "Mr. Buck."

McGlocklin has been in Milwaukee for all of it, so maybe it comes as no surprise the Bucks decided to hang his jersey up in the rafters on December 10, 1976.

"Do I remember making the first Bucks basket?" McGlocklin asked, during the announcement ceremony for the team's return to the MECCA in 2017. "I didn't, but one of our long-time scorers who has been with us all 50 years brought the official stat sheet one time, and I got to see the fact that I had the privilege of scoring the first Bucks basket."

McGlocklin did a bunch of scoring for the Bucks in their inaugural season. McGlocklin (19.6 points per game) and Flynn Robinson (20.3 points per game) led the way in their first season and McGlocklin was invited to the 1969 NBA All-Star Game. It was quite an accomplishment for a player who had been made eligible for an expansion draft by two different franchises.

The shooting guard from Indiana University got his career started in Cincinnati when he was drafted by the Royals in the third round (27th pick) of the 1965 NBA Draft. He played two years for the Royals before they decided not to protect him from the 1967 NBA Expansion Draft for the Seattle Supersonics and San Diego Rockets.

*Jon McGlocklin, known to many as "Mr. Buck," scored the franchise's first basket during its inaugural season in 1968.*

The Rockets drafted McGlocklin and he quickly started to play a much larger role than he did in Cincinnati, averaging 12.1 points per game and playing nearly 30 minutes a night. Despite that larger role, the Rockets decided against protecting McGlocklin the next season, which allowed the Bucks to snag him in the 1968 NBA Expansion Draft.

"And I got to shoot a lot that year, but then we got Kareem [Abdul-Jabbar], and I didn't get to shoot anymore," McGlocklin continued at the 2017 ceremony. "And then we got Oscar [Robertson], and I never got to shoot! But, we won a championship."

McGlocklin would not end up having a better individual season than his fourth NBA season, his first in Milwaukee, but he would end up enjoying much more successful basketball as his time in Milwaukee progressed. After winning just 15 games in his lone season in San Diego, McGlocklin won 56 games the next season with the Bucks.

As he mentioned, Abdul-Jabbar did take over as the Bucks' leading scorer in his rookie season, averaging 28.8 point per game, which cast McGlocklin in a smaller, supporting role, but the sharp-shooting guard wasn't irrelevant. He still averaged 17.6 points per game in his second Milwaukee season. His scoring role lessened again the next season with the addition of Robertson, but McGlocklin held his own, averaging 15.8 points and 3.7 assists per game.

McGlocklin's averages continued to decrease over the years as he aged and younger players came along, but he still found ways to contribute to the team that went on to play in the 1974 NBA Finals against the Boston Celtics. The man affectionately known now by Bucks fans as "Jonny Mac" played two more seasons after that series loss.

To this day, McGlocklin remains 12th all time in career points at 7,505, 10th in minutes with 17,008, and sixth in free throw percentage at 86.0 percent, but those aren't really the things that got his jersey retired. More than anything, it was the firsts that

McGlocklin was a part of in Milwaukee. He made the franchise's first basket on October 16, 1968. He was the team's first All-Star honoree in 1969. He was a leader on the team's first championship team. And he did all of those things proudly as a Milwaukee Buck.

"Every owner, every coach, every general manager, every player, every trainer," McGlocklin told the *Milwaukee Journal Sentinel.* "I've seen all of them. The Bucks, to me, they're our family. I realize it's changed but it's still the franchise, the organization, the logo. That's family to us. We've been here since June of '68. We raised our family here."

As his playing career came to an end, McGlocklin made a commitment to stay in Milwaukee and remain a Buck. He decided to start the MACC Fund and truly become a part of the city. The accomplishments were nice and what he did on the floor was great, but really, McGlocklin was the first person to proudly proclaim, "I am a Milwaukee Buck," and for that, his jersey will hang in the rafters for the rest of time.

# 38 Squad 6/Clutch Crew

"Novak's better! Novak's better!"

The statement was clearly untrue. Skinny 6-foot-10 sharpshooter Steve Novak was not, in fact, better than Dwyane Wade, but the chant rained down on the former Marquette star anyway as his Miami Heat played the Bucks on February 1, 2010, in the Bradley Center.

The playful chant originated from a group of fans in the top 10 or so rows of the first level behind the Heat bench. It wasn't just a random group of fans emboldened by a few too many hops-based beverages and organized through some makeshift discussions. It was a well-organized group of 100 fans in lockstep, making noise on every possession and executing a number of chants and cheers. And it was all the brainchild of Bucks center Andrew Bogut, with an assist from the Houston Rockets.

The idea for a fan section, resembling what you commonly find in European soccer stadiums, had been bouncing around in the Australian center's mind for a couple of years, but he had never seen it actually executed. But during a preseason game in Houston, Bogut realized the Rockets had a small group of fans—the Red Rowdies—going crazy during the game, which meant his idea might actually work.

"I wanted to do something even before that, but when I saw it there, I thought it can be done," Bogut told the *Milwaukee Journal Sentinel*. "On that flight home, I went and sat next to [media relations director] Dan [Smyczek] and I said, 'Look, I want to put a fan section together. I'm buying tickets for kids, but I want to buy some more, buy another 100 for every game and make sure they're in the lower bowl.'"

With that conversation, Squad 6 was born.

"I wanted to give them to fans who want to be there, fans who want to cheer and might not be able to afford tickets to every game," Bogut said. "It came together pretty quickly."

In a rather short period of time, Bogut had purchased 100 lower-level tickets, priced somewhere between $65 and $95, for every home game in the 2009–10 season and auditions were scheduled. Bogut wanted to put a personal touch on the section, so he would personally judge the fans who believed they deserved to sit in the section.

"We'll give 'em out to fans who are boisterous, outrageous, loud," Bogut told the *Journal Sentinel*. "Bring drums, paint your face, bring flags, signs, whatever you want to do to get rowdy."

Bogut held three auditions: two during the preseason and one more in December once the season had already started. To keep things under control and family-friendly, the Bucks even put an employee in charge of Squad 6—6 was Bogut's jersey number—to make sure the section stayed filled. In the first year, the rowdy fan section had about 100 members with roughly 85 or so showing up each game. Miss three games with unexcused absences? You're out, and the Bucks would go to the next person on the list.

As the first season went on, the group gained more and more notoriety. *The New York Times*, ESPN, and *Maxim* magazine all came to Milwaukee to write features about the squad. After his Dallas Mavericks were in town, owner Mark Cuban tweeted, "Those fans were the most fun fans I have seen on the road EVER. It made the atmosphere 100x better. More PBR for them." Everyone was delighted to see the fan group start to make some noise in one of the league's smallest markets.

Well, not everyone, exactly. The Cleveland Cavaliers made an official complaint to the league because they believed Squad 6 used illegal air horns while the Cavaliers were shooting free throws, but the league actually found they were vuvuzelas, which were legal. (They were later banned.)

Whether or not Squad 6 deserves any credit for it, the team also put together a great 2009–10 season. The Bucks ended up being a surprise playoff team and took the Atlanta Hawks to seven games in their first-round Eastern Conference postseason series.

With the success of the section and the team, Bogut kept Squad 6 around for another season and another after that. When Bogut was traded to the Warriors before the 2012–13 season, Turkish forward Ersan Ilyasova took over and purchased the tickets for the fan section, which he called Sector 7 in honor of his jersey number. When he was traded before the next season, new Bucks head coach Jason Kidd bought the tickets and renamed it the Cream City Clash. Eventually, Harley-Davidson took over and renamed the cheering section the Clutch Crew. No matter the name, the fan section was rowdy and loud at every single Bucks game.

"I think what really has made it a success is just everybody internally was into it," Bucks chief marketing officer Dustin Godsey told the *USA Today*. "It was something that came from the basketball side. Then, as we've changed ownership in the last few years and gone through, they've recognized this as being a part of what it is, so it had that support from the beginning, and then has been allowed to kind of build and create its own culture, which I think is what has to happen."

The fan section went through a multitude of changes, but the passion of the boisterous section remained the same. So, it was no surprise when a familiar chant rained down from the Clutch Crew when the Cavaliers came to town on December 19, 2017.

Eight years had passed. Wade was now in his 15th NBA season and on his third NBA team. Novak, a native of Brown Deer, Wisconsin, was now an analyst for the Bucks, but the Clutch Crew knew the chant their Squad 6 forefathers had started a better part of a decade well and weren't shy about yelling it at the top of their lungs.

"Novak's better! Novak's better!"

# 39 Bucks Trade Abdul-Jabbar to L.A.

Nobody wants to trade the best player in the NBA, a three-time MVP, and a surefire Hall of Famer. Those are not trades you want to make as a general manager, but that was exactly what Bucks general manager Wayne Embry had to do with Kareem Abdul-Jabbar, no matter how much he wanted to avoid it.

"I told Kareem, 'You are the franchise,' and I wasn't anxious to trade the franchise," Embry later told the *Sports Business Journal*. "I told him, 'If it's me, I can go.'"

It all started with a phone call. Sam Gilbert, a UCLA basketball booster and one of Abdul-Jabbar's advisers, called Embry in early October 1974 and requested a meeting.

"When he said he wanted to talk about Kareem's future, I didn't know what the hell to expect," Embry told the *Los Angeles Times*. "I sensed that there was something that wasn't right."

The meeting would take place on the night of October 3, 1974, in a suite of rooms at the Sheraton Hotel in downtown Milwaukee. The assembled Bucks front office members would listen to Abdul-Jabbar and his party tell them he no longer wanted to be in Milwaukee and would not be willing to sign a contract extension when his deal expired after the 1975–76 season.

"I'm not criticizing the people here," Abdul-Jabbar told *The New York Times* in 1975. "But Milwaukee is not what I'm all about. The things I relate to aren't in Milwaukee."

Abdul-Jabbar wanted a larger city that fit him better culturally. He wanted to be traded to New York or Los Angeles to be somewhere with more people and a place where he could "pursue his interests in black culture, the orthodox Muslim faith, jazz, and serious reading." The star center also thought a move to a larger city could help him regain a level of anonymity, which he felt he had lost in Milwaukee and thus left him more cloistered in his life off the court.

Despite wanting to leave Milwaukee, Abdul-Jabbar kept his desire to leave a secret, only sharing his request with the team's ownership. He asked for the trade, but allowed the Bucks to work through each of the scenarios and find the one that fit all parties best.

The Knicks would be given the first opportunity, because New York was Abdul-Jabbar's top choice and his hometown. Unfortunately, they had very little in the way of bargaining chips for a player of Abdul-Jabbar's stature. Thanks to a number of previous moves, the Knicks had few intriguing prospects on the roster and could really only put together some sort of deal if the Bucks would be interested in millions of dollars. Embry made his feelings very clear to New York.

"They thought cash was appealing to everybody, but cash can't play," Embry later told the *New York Post*.

With no deal possible with the Knicks, the Bucks shifted their attention to the Los Angeles Lakers. Unlike the Knicks, the Lakers actually had some young prospects. With some struggles in the 1974–75 season, Los Angeles grabbed the second and eighth pick in the 1975 NBA Draft. They used those picks on Dave Meyers, a big man from UCLA, and Junior Bridgeman, a small forward out of Louisville University.

Those two players would be the foundation of the Lakers' deal for Abdul-Jabbar, but the Bucks needed more. Embry asked for shot blocker Elmore Smith and the Lakers offered aging scorer Gail Goodrich, but Embry insisted that would still not be enough for Abdul-Jabbar. He wanted another young player. He wanted Lakers shooting guard Brian Winters, who was coming off a rookie season in which he averaged 11.7 points per game.

Embry ended up having a motto of sorts as he went back and forth with Lakers attorney Alan Rothenberg and Board of Governors member Jim Locher: "Still no Winters, still no damn deal!"

Winters became a sticking point in negotiations, but the Lakers ultimately relented and included him in the deal. With an agreement in place, Embry had to go in front of the Bucks' board of directors and convince them they needed to trade Abdul-Jabbar. The board was not pleased with the decision, but Embry eventually convinced them just how serious Abdul-Jabbar was about his trade demands and they agreed to let Embry make the deal.

On June 16, 1975, the Milwaukee Bucks traded Kareem Abdul-Jabbar and backup center Walt Wesley to the Los Angeles Lakers for Dave Meyers, Junior Bridgeman, Elmore Smith, and

Brian Winters in one of the most monumental trades in the history of basketball. Abdul-Jabbar would go on to win five NBA titles with the Lakers and captain some of the best teams in the game's history.

Bridgeman and Winters would each find great success in Milwaukee with both players' numbers hanging in the rafters after illustrious careers with the Bucks, but they would not reach the same level of team success as Abdul-Jabbar. The Bucks have not reached an NBA Finals since 1974 with their big man in the middle, a drought that extends to this very day, 44 years later.

# 40 Retired Jerseys: Brian Winters' No. 32

He was one of four players traded for Kareem Abdul-Jabbar. It was an unenviable position. No one wants to be the guy, or even one of the guys, expected to take the place of one of the greatest basketball players of all time. But Brian Winters handled the responsibility with aplomb and ended up putting together eight strong years in Milwaukee, all of which led to his jersey being hung up in the rafters on October 28, 1983.

When he retired, Winters led the franchise in assists (he's since been bumped down to third) and sat at third in career points (now eighth) and games played (now fifth). He functioned as one of the best players on the team after Abdul-Jabbar and then was a valuable member of the next batch of playoff teams the Bucks produced in the 1980s.

"Milwaukee was a hardworking town," Winters said. "Back then it was a blue-collar, Midwestern industrial city. And we had that same mindset. We worked hard. We played hard. And I'm talking about everybody on our team. We had a work ethic about ourselves. We knew it wasn't easy to win games at a high level. We came to do our jobs. And we did them well."

A strong work ethic defines Winters' time in Milwaukee. No matter what was asked of him, he delivered. When he first arrived to the team for the 1975–76 season, the Bucks needed him to be a scorer and playmaker to help fill the void left by Abdul-Jabbar, and that is exactly what the guard from the University of South Carolina did.

In his first season with the Bucks, Winters put up 18.2 points and 4.7 assists per game on his way to being elected a Western Conference All-Star along with teammate Bob Dandridge. Winters and Dandridge ultimately took on a large playmaking role and kept the Bucks from totally falling apart in Abdul-Jabbar's absence, but the team struggled and the franchise moved on to new head coach Don Nelson for the 1977–78 season. Winter's running mate Dandridge would also opt for Washington, D.C., in free agency.

With a new coach and a young team, little was expected out of the Bucks in the 1977–78 season, but they surprised everyone, even winning a first-round three-game playoff series over the Phoenix Suns. Leading the way, with the help of new friend Marques Johnson? Brian Winters. With Nelson's fast-paced lineups, Winters made a second All-Star appearance behind a career-high 19.9 points and 4.9 assists per game and eventually outdueled five-time All-Star Paul Westphal in the Milwaukee's playoff victory. In the second round, they fell to the Denver Nuggets in seven games, but had effectively put the basketball world on notice.

After falling at the hands of the Bucks, Suns guard Don Buse told *Sports Illustrated*, "The truth is, we weren't really prepared for them."

You might say that same thing of Winters throughout his career. With a full beard and light, floppy hair, Winters looked more burly lumberjack than sweet-shooting guard with the nifty footwork necessary to find small creases in a defense. Johnson, now a Bucks TV announcer, often discusses the beauty of Winters' jump shot during Bucks television broadcasts and it's no wonder why, as Winters was among the leaders in three-point percentage when the NBA introduced the three-point line in the 1979–80 season. Winters' shooting acumen and playmaking skills made him a useful fit for most any team, no matter what style of basketball they may employ.

Under Nelson, Winters found his groove as a regular contributor, but ended up coming off the bench more often than not in his final years as the innovative coach tested out different lineups that skewed less traditional than most teams around the league. No matter, Winters found a way to make a difference and often ended up closing games because of, according to Johnson, his "veteran, calming influence as primary ballhandler down the stretch." It said a lot about Winters that Nelson trusted him because those were some talented teams, with the Bucks winning 60 games in the 1980–81 season and 55 games the year after.

Fittingly, in Winters' final season in Milwaukee, the team made one last big run and made it all the way to the 1983 Eastern Conference Finals. With Winter's steadying play off the bench, the Bucks swept the Celtics in the semifinals to vanquish a foe who so often stood in their way. Winters would retire the following fall having never played in an NBA Finals, but his Bucks teams did reach the playoffs six times and compiled a .556 winning percentage over the eight seasons he spent in Milwaukee.

Winters likely won't end up in the Hall of Fame, but he was a huge part of why the Bucks didn't become irrelevant after being forced to trade the league's best player. With Winters leading the way, the Bucks played hard, competed, and executed their assignments. He buoyed the franchise in what could have been trying times and, for that, his number will hang in the rafters forever.

# 41 NellieBall

Around 2010, NBA teams started to tinker with utilizing smaller lineups to increase the speed with which they played and the efficiency with which they scored. The result of those experiments led to the popularization of something people called "small ball." In rushing to figure out who started the movement and revolutionized basketball forever, people failed to realize they had already seen something like this years before.

Many suggested Mike D'Antoni and his "Seven Seconds or Less" Phoenix Suns of the mid-2000s served as the motivation for the small ball revolution, but failed to acknowledge D'Antoni's predecessor. Someone who took the lessons of Red Auerbach in Boston and morphed them into something slightly stranger.

He's been called the man who invented the point forward, an innovator, a mad scientist of matchups, and a basketball genius, but if you ask him, he'll likely just tell you he was trying to put a winning product out on the floor.

Despite his objections, everyone knows exactly what you're talking about when you say "NellieBall" and its inventor, former Bucks coach Don Nelson.

When pressed by ESPN's Marc Stein, Nelson himself defined it as "small ball, fast and exciting, point forward, players playing out of position…all those kinds of things." Later, in an article he penned for the Players' Tribune, Nelson simplified his description to "unconventional basketball with an emphasis on the fast break."

When the Celtics signed Nelson before his fourth NBA season, no one would have guessed his number would hang in the rafters of the Boston Garden once he was done. At that point, he had made little impact in three underwhelming seasons in Chicago and Los

Angeles, but that was all before he met Red Auerbach. The coaching legend taught Nelson about something that would change his life: the fast break.

Auerbach insisted upon his teams playing fast. They would get up and down the floor quicker than anyone else in the league and it helped give Nelson a role on a number of beloved Celtics teams and find his place in the NBA. Under Auerbach, Nelson transformed into a double-digit scorer and a weapon for the Celtics off the bench, so it should come as no surprise Nelson decided to play the same way once he came to lead an NBA team.

Nelson took over as head coach of the Milwaukee Bucks 18 games into the 1976–77 NBA season. It was a rebuilding year. The team was still looking for its identity after Kareem Abdul-Jabbar had been traded away following the 1974–75 season and were unable to figure it out under Larry Costello, who was known for his deep playbook and exacting tendencies, which were helpful traits for a strong, veteran team, but not ideal for a young one. Enter Nelson, who was willing to try out some new ideas.

"You only play NellieBall when you don't have a very good team, or when you have a bunch of good small players and not many good big players," Nelson later told ESPN. "When you have bad teams, you've got to be creative to win games you're not supposed to win. I was innovative when I had to be, but I wasn't innovative when I didn't have to be."

So, in his first year, Nelson worked with what he had and tried to help them play good basketball. Bob Dandridge put together a strong season before leaving for Washington in free agency after the season. Brian Winters had one of his best individual seasons, but overall the team struggled, compiling a 30–52 record.

Through trades in-season and shortly after the season, the Bucks acquired the first, third, and 11ᵗʰ overall picks in the 1977 NBA Draft and the transformation in Milwaukee officially started. The third pick in that draft was talented, do-everything forward from UCLA Marques Johnson. He would battle for Rookie of the Year the next season, as he thrived in Nelson's fast-paced system while leading the Bucks to a 44–38 season and a first-round playoff upset.

For years, Nelson's teams pushed the pace and continued to win more and more games with Johnson leading the way, but the coach later wrote those teams weren't really playing NellieBall. That would take something special.

"It was the addition of Paul Pressey that brought a different dynamic that I had never seen before," Nelson wrote in the Players' Tribune. "Pressey was 6-foot-5, with long arms and ballhandling skills as good as some of the best guards in the league. He was naturally a forward, but with his great hands I had no problem playing him at guard. It was like having a point guard in a forward's body. He was just a matchup problem for defenders."

The Bucks drafted Pressey from Tulsa University with the 20th pick of the 1982 NBA Draft and that is when things started to get weird on the floor for the Bucks. Nelson wouldn't play a point guard and instead let Pressey run things with a variety of long-limbed athletes all over the floor. It was unlike anything else in the league and the Bucks won a number of games with their unique setup.

Unfortunately, the Bucks teams of the 1980s were never able to win a championship, despite winning a ton of games. As Nelson moved onto other teams using similar strategies, he never won a ring as a coach either, which became something many would hold against him. But his place as an innovator—Nelson was inducted to the Hall of Fame in 2012—is impossible to question and it all got started in Milwaukee.

# 42 Bucks Sweep Bird and the Celtics

Celtics great Larry Bird was swept only once in his entire career. It came at the hands of the Milwaukee Bucks in the 1983 Eastern Conference semifinals and nobody saw it coming.

"I know a lot of Boston fans are wondering what happened to their Celtics," Bucks forward Sidney Moncrief told the *Washington Post* after Milwaukee's series-deciding Game 4 victory, "but they just got beaten by a better team at the time."

Surely a difficult sentence for many to comprehend, but the Bucks had proven it was undoubtedly the truth. The Bucks dominated the series with an average margin of victory of almost 12 points per game. They opened the series with a 116–95 drubbing of the Celtics, in which the Bucks scored at will in the Boston Garden. Moncrief put up 22 points, eight rebounds and four assists, while his running mate Marques Johnson slapped up 17 points, eight rebounds, and five assists. Veteran center Bob Lanier scored an easy 21 points on 10-of-12 shooting.

On the other end, the Bucks confounded the Celtics with their impressive length. Rookie guard Paul Pressey, out of Tulsa University, displaced veteran point guard Brian Winters by season's end, which meant the shortest player in Milwaukee's starting lineup was Moncrief, a 6-foot-3 shooting guard who just happened to win the 1982–83 NBA Defensive Player of the Year award.

Pressey was the next shortest at 6-foot-5 followed by the 6-foot-7 Johnson, and then 6-foot-11 Lanier and 7-footer Alton Lister. There just weren't many teams with that sort of size on the floor, but the Bucks could afford to do it with the ballhandling skill of Pressey, Moncrief, and Johnson. Watching the game more than 30 years later as a member of the Bucks' broadcast team, Johnson pointed out Bucks coach Don Nelson was well ahead of his time with usage of length in all five positions.

Strangely enough, Game 2 was the closest game of the series despite Bird missing the contest with the flu. The Celtics banded together, knowing the importance of trying to keep a small portion of their home-court advantage, but failed to do it. With a 19-point contribution from forward Junior Bridgeman off the bench, the Bucks won 95–91 to take a commanding lead by stealing both games in the Garden to start the series.

"Nellie made sure we didn't poke the bear after [our] first two wins in Boston," Johnson tweeted during his game breakdown all these years later. "[He] wanted us to downplay wins and show respect for Cs."

With Bird returning from the flu and former Celtic Nelson at the helm, the Bucks would be ready for all Boston could throw at them in Game 3. The Celtics had inner-team turmoil the entire season with head coach Bill Fitch watching over the roster, but throughout the season, most observers expected them to flip the switch at some point. The Celtics would figure out whatever the Bucks were doing, it was believed, because they had Bird and had previously won an NBA championship. Eventually, the pedigree would take over.

Despite that common belief from folks around the league, the switch never got flipped, or possibly it did get flipped and the Celtics' lights just couldn't shine as bright as the lights produced by Milwaukee's long-armed, athletic squad. Milwaukee had it going again in Game 3 as Johnson and Moncrief each played more than 45 minutes and combined for 48 points in the Bucks' 107–99 win. This one was close though, as just two points separated the two teams after three quarters, but the Bucks' active, trapping defense was just too much for the Celtics.

Despite losing his starting job to Pressey, the veteran Winters often re-entered the game late in the proceedings to help close out the game. For the series, he averaged a rock-solid 12.8 points, 3.5

rebounds, and 3.5 assists in 26.8 minutes per game, and Johnson later credited him as a veteran, calming influence the team needed to finish off the Celtics late.

With the possibility of falling victim to a sweep for the first time ever in a seven-game series on the table for the Celtics, Game 4 seemed destined to be a battle for the ages, but it ended up feeling more like a coronation by the end of the game. The Bucks opened up a double-digit lead in the first half with a number of steals and dunks, a spectacular one coming on an alley-oop from Winters to Moncrief.

They quickly extended their nine-point lead after halftime with a 13–5 run, which gave them a 59–42 lead less than five minutes into the third quarter. The Celtics would be unable to pull within single digits the rest of the night and the Bucks won 107–93 to clinch the sweep as Bucks fans waved brooms in the stands. As folks reflected on the series, some wanted to give Bird an escape from responsibility for the loss by bringing up the flu and a finger he had dislocated earlier in the season, but he was having none of it.

"I've never been this embarrassed in my entire career and this is going to hurt for a long time because we didn't play to our potential," Larry Bird told reporters after the game. "When we were backed against the wall and challenged, we were supposed to come through like the champions I thought we were, and we didn't. We embarrassed ourselves and I'll live with that the rest of my life."

Having toppled the mighty Celtics, the Bucks' locker room in the Milwaukee Arena was filled with champagne, ready for the Bucks to revel in their monumental victory over the Celtics. The champagne would remain unopened, however.

"This is not a championship series," Johnson told reporters after the game. "It's not even a conference final series. They had champagne for us, but we told them to take it back. We'll save it. This wasn't our main goal, just a primary one."

The Bucks had trounced one of their regular foes in the Eastern Conference, only to run into another in the next round:

the Philadelphia 76ers. The Sixers were waiting for the Bucks in the Eastern Conference Finals and beat Milwaukee in five games to advance to the NBA Finals. It would be the only game Philadelphia lost that postseason, which ruined Moses Malone's famous "Fo, Fo, Fo" prediction for their run to a championship.

Milwaukee never went to an NBA Finals in the 1980s because of the Celtics and Sixers, but their sweep of the Celtics serves as a helpful reminder of just how good they were in those years and the constant threat they proved to be for both of those teams.

# 43 Bucks and Spurs Combine for 337 Points

One game. Two teams. Three overtimes. And a total of 337 points.

The Bucks lost to the San Antonio Spurs 171–166 on March 6, 1982, but the two teams combined for 337 points, the most ever scored in an NBA game at the time.

"I remember looking at the box score afterward and seeing guys made a tremendous amount of shots," Bucks guard Brian Winters later told Spurs.com. "It was one of those wild shoot-out affairs. Guys were making shots from everywhere. It was a highly entertaining game, and unfortunately we lost."

George Gervin, the league's leading scorer in the 1981–82 season, scored 50 points. His running mate Mike Mitchell scored 45 on the night. Combined, all five Bucks starters only tallied 88 points on the night, but that ended up being okay as the bench came through in a major way.

The aforementioned Winters led the Bucks with 42 points on 19-of-25 shooting off the bench, as well as six assists, five rebounds, and three steals. It was one of the best games of Winters' career (one short of his career-high 43), but it wasn't enough despite the Bucks guard hitting 13 straight field goals at one point. Next up in scoring for the Bucks was Junior Bridgeman, another bench player, with 31 points of his own.

Milwaukee's starters might not have been able to match the Spurs' production, but the Bucks tied it late. With two minutes and 43 seconds left, the Bucks managed to erase a six-point deficit. Milwaukee took a lead in each of the first two overtime periods but couldn't hold the Spurs down, allowing them to force extra periods each time. Finally, in the third overtime, Gervin scored eight straight points to give his squad a 165–161 lead, which the Spurs would not relinquish the rest of the night, eventually taking the 171–166 victory.

"It stands out in the sense the score was so high and it was a triple-overtime game," Winters told Spurs.com. "You don't play in that many triple-overtime games no matter how long you play. You might play in a few but I don't even remember another triple-overtime game in my career. I've played in overtime games but not too many. The score was so high and there were so many big shots made in regulation, in overtime, to keep extending the game. It was just unusual in that regard."

With a huge scoring night individually, it's no wonder Winters remembers the game, but even people just watching at home would come to remember it for decades. There wasn't just a lot of scoring; the scoring was close to equal throughout the entire game. It's often said basketball is a game of runs, but somehow even while the teams put together 337 points, neither team put together a big enough run to lead by more than six points, which seems impossible given such prodigious scoring.

"I want to go back and watch that game and see how and why so many points were scored with so few [three-pointers]," Spurs forward Matt Bonner told the *San Antonio Express-News* in 2017. "Was the defense awful? Did nobody help, nobody rotate? Did they let you go up the court and score? Were there no shot blockers at the rim? What is the explanation for that?"

Bonner's intuition was right in asking about three-point buckets. It was the third season of the three-point line in NBA play, but the game featured just four total threes. The Spurs were 1-of-3, while Winters hit 2-of-3 and Bridgeman hit his only attempt from behind the line. The defense would probably be viewed as what was lacking, as both teams scored more than 128 points per 100 possessions in the game, but with so many made shots neither team nor the fans watching the game complained.

"This has to be the most exciting game that I've ever played in, everybody on both teams was outstanding," Gervin told the *Chicago Tribune.*

The record for most points in an NBA game would stand for less than a year as the Detroit Pistons and the Denver Nuggets combined for 370 points in a 186–184 Pistons victory. No one has reached 337 points since, which puts the Bucks-Spurs game second on the all-time list.

# 44 Terry Cummings

In the end, Terry Cummings played just six of his 18 years in the NBA with the Bucks, but those years would be among his best in the league as he played a large role in the team's success during the 1980s. Unfortunately, with an early exit and long NBA career, his time in Milwaukee would not be honored with a jersey in the rafters, but that would not make his time in Milwaukee any less special.

Cummings was selected second overall in the 1982 NBA Draft by the San Diego Clippers, after a three-year career at his hometown DePaul University in Chicago. In his final season, he led the Blue Demons to a 26–2 record and a No. 1 seed in the NCAA Men's Basketball Tournament. Posting averages of 22.3 points and 11.9 rebounds per game, the 21-year-old was honored as a First-Team All-American. He was fantastic on the court, but many were fascinated by his story. Cummings grew up as a gun-toting teenager dabbling in drugs, surrounded by gangs in Chicago and Hammond, Indiana (a northern Indiana suburb in the Chicago metro area), before finding God as a 16-year-old and becoming an ordained minister.

He exploded on the scene as a member of the Clippers, averaging 23.7 points and 10.6 rebounds per game as a rookie and winning the 1983 NBA Rookie of the Year award, but the numbers weren't enough for him. During his time at DePaul, he had lost just six games in three years and told the Clippers he was having a really tough time. He wanted to go back to winning basketball and asked to be traded to the Bucks.

"I went into [Donald] Sterling's office and asked him to trade me," Cummings later told Clippers.com. "There wasn't any animosity. I told him I had a dream, and the dream I saw was to play for the Milwaukee Bucks and I wanted to be traded there. I felt like I needed to do something different for myself. He said he would not trade me, but a week later I was traded to the Bucks."

On September 24, 1984, the Bucks traded Junior Bridgeman, Marques Johnson, and Harvey Catchings to the Clippers for Craig Hodges, Ricky Pierce, and Cummings. The Bucks, coming off a trip to the Eastern Conference Finals, were seen by many as trading talented, established players for a trio of players who would shape the next version of a contending Bucks squad, but might take a little while to develop into winning players. That was not the case. Cummings quickly became one of the team's best players and a favorite of Bucks head coach Don Nelson.

"It's hard for me to fathom anybody much better at that [power forward] position than he is," Nelson told the *Los Angeles Times* midway through Cummings' first season in Milwaukee. "He's the most gifted player I've ever coached, but he's not the best. Someday, maybe. He's just beginning to learn the game."

Cummings made his first All-Star appearance in his first year in Milwaukee, averaging 23.6 points and 9.2 rebounds per game. Despite his impressive output, Nelson rode his young star hard, demanding he improve defensively and think through the game at a higher level. He did it so often Cummings joked he should throw a saddle on his back for Nelson, but he ended up enjoying the experience greatly.

"I've always had the talent. This year I sort of went to school and started to learn the game," Cummings said during his first year in Milwaukee. "I've always been able to learn from people who could teach me. In San Diego, I'd just go out and play. It finally got to the point where I didn't want to learn anything."

The Bucks played great basketball with Cummings on the squad, winning 59 games in his first season and making a trip to the Eastern Conference semifinals. They would go to the Eastern Conference Finals the next season and the semifinals twice more before Cummings was surprisingly traded to the San Antonio Spurs before the 1989–90 NBA season. He returned for one final season in Milwaukee in 1995–96.

Cummings' time in Milwaukee would be remembered similarly to that of many of his Bucks contemporaries. He put up big numbers—19.4 points and 7.8 rebounds per game across six seasons as a Buck—and they won a bunch of games. Ultimately, though, they were unable to secure an NBA championship or even an NBA Finals appearance, which means Cummings became just another one of the great players on the oft-forgotten great Bucks teams of the 1980s.

# 45 Retired Jerseys: Bob Lanier's No. 16

He was the final piece to the puzzle. Bucks coach Don Nelson had squeezed as much as he could out of his roster. No matter what defensive schemes he drew up or what players he called for offensively, the Bucks weren't going to go any further. They needed a star center and Bob Lanier was the man for the job. He played just four and a half seasons in Milwaukee, but still made such an impact that the organization hung his jersey from the rafters on December 4, 1984.

"They look for nobody else down the stretch," Celtics forward Larry Bird told *The New York Times*. "He does nothing but good things for the Bucks. Kareem's the best player in the league, but Lanier is second."

Bird said this during the 1980–81 NBA season. It was Lanier's 10th year in the league.

The Bucks traded for Lanier halfway through the previous season and he helped them close the season out with a 20–6 record in their final 26 games. At the time of the deal, Milwaukee was just 29–27. Instead of a middle-of-the-pack finish, Nelson's team made it to the playoffs and lost a seven-game series to the Seattle Supersonics in the Western Conference semifinals.

The next season, the Bucks won 60 games with Lanier on the squad for the entire year. His numbers weren't spectacular, but he was exactly what the team needed. In decreased minutes (26 minutes per game, down from 37.6 with Detroit in 1979–80), Lanier still managed 14.3 points and 6.2 rebounds per game, as well as more than one block and one steal per game. In Detroit, Lanier was expected to carry his team in every category and find a way to pick up wins, but that same pressure didn't follow him to Milwaukee.

"I don't have the emotional burden," Lanier told *Sports Illustrated* in 1980. "Here I help on defense, set picks and pass the ball, things I do well anyway. It makes life easier. My playing time has gone down but the Ws are up."

Those skills would be massively important as the team got ready to battle in the playoffs. With the Bucks now in the Eastern Conference, they needed size to compete with the Sixers and the Celtics, and Lanier gave them plenty of that. They also greatly appreciated Lanier's abilities defensively. In three of the four seasons the massive center spent in Milwaukee, the Bucks were among the league's top three defenses, including having the top defense in the 1981–82 season, and only fell to sixth in the remaining fourth season.

"Our strength is our flexibility," Marques Johnson told *Sports Illustrated* during the 1980–81 season. "Whatever matchup we meet, we have a lineup to counter it. Without Bob, we're not strong inside, and teams like Philadelphia, Boston, and Chicago can take advantage of us on the boards."

The Bucks would not end up winning an NBA title that season, despite winning 60 games. They didn't end up getting to an NBA Finals in any of Lanier's four and a half seasons either, which left him ringless for his entire career. Despite that disappointment, Nelson later told ESPN his Bucks teams with Lanier were the best he ever coached.

Lanier in a more limited role allowed Nelson's team to do all of the things he loved. They could pound the ball into the post with Lanier if they liked the matchup. They could defend with Lanier blocking shots or with their gang of versatile, athletic wings when he was on the bench. They could slow the game down with Lanier on the floor. He could rebound and start the break or they could take him off the floor and play even faster.

Lanier would not put up gaudy numbers in Milwaukee, both because of his relatively short tenure and restricted minutes. By the time he retired following the 1983–84 season though, his induction to the Hall of Fame seemed like a safe assumption and the organization honored him by retiring his jersey.

# 46 Saving the MECCA Floor

"Reclaimed Gym Floor in Panels" read the advertisement posted by Planet Reuse, an architecture reclamation company that helps companies track down building materials they could possibly re-use in their projects.

A friend emailed the advertisement to Bucks fan Andy Gorzalski in 2010 because the photos included in the advertisement appeared to show the MECCA floor.

"And lo and behold, it was Robert Indiana's MECCA floor," Gorzalski told *The New York Times*. "It shocked me, and it was so sad in a way because it just said, 'reclaimed gym floor.' It was almost like it was being thrown out."

Gorzalski acted immediately and put a $20,000 hold on the court with his credit card, knowing that he couldn't afford it but refusing to let the court fall into anyone else's hands, especially a company looking to chop it up for use in a different project. In the meantime, he reached out to anyone who might possibly be able to help him or have a way to let more people know the court needed a new home.

One of the first people Gorzalski thought to email was long-time Bucks television broadcaster Jim Paschke. Paschke immediately forwarded the email to his boss, Bucks vice-president John Steinmiller, who had been with the team since its inception in 1968. Steinmiller alerted Greg Koller, the CEO of Prostar Surfaces, the company which had installed the game floor in the Bradley Center, and maybe more importantly, a proud native Milwaukeean.

"We were at a very important meeting," Ben Koller, Greg's son, told ESPN. "My dad got an email on his phone and he said he had to go see about a basketball floor and left. The company's about to go bankrupt and me and my uncle [Greg's business partner at Prostar] are like, 'Dude, you're out of your mind. Like, we can't even make payroll right now and you're talking about buying the MECCA floor?'"

Koller, however, would not allow the floor to leave the city and bought the floor for $20,000 from Gorzalski. He had no idea what to do with it, but knew that he could not allow the floor to get destroyed or go anywhere else outside of Milwaukee. It was a piece of art that meant too much to him and the city that he loved. Sadly, just a week later, Greg passed away unexpectedly, just days before his 61st birthday.

Ben didn't immediately understand his dad's desire to purchase the floor, but Greg made it very clear before his passing that he knew quite a bit about the floor and why he felt so strongly about it staying in Milwaukee.

"He knew the story of the very turbulent 'floor wars,' as they called them then, when a group of very progressive Milwaukeeans in 1977 hired an openly gay New Yorker for the [modern-day] equivalent of a quarter of a million dollars to do a public art project using public funds," Ben told *The New York Times* in 2013. "He said, 'Not only do I want to celebrate that spirit of innovation and of history, I want to use it to inspire new entrepreneurs, new innovators, new people who want to rewrite policy and run for office. I want it to be a symbol of: you can do it. Take the risk. Go after it. Leave a dent in the universe.'"

With his father's passing, Ben became the owner of the MECCA floor and attempted, with the help of Gorzalski, to find a buyer willing to display the floor fully intact permanently and publicly. To try to create interest in the floor, the two worked together to have the court displayed at the MECCA, now the UWM Panther Arena, in August 2013 and invited people to come see it and revel in "the floor that made Milwaukee famous."

They did not find a buyer for the floor that night, but remain committed to finding a willing buyer and have opened up to the possibility of allowing someone to create a more functional piece out of the floor, possibly as a sculpture reimagined in a way which would allow it to be put on display. No matter what though, all parties involved feel strongly that the floor needs to remain together.

"I'm always struck that this significant piece of art in the least likely place was created here," Gorzalski told ESPN. "It wasn't in New York or Los Angeles. I love that it was the Bucks' floor. It wasn't the Knicks' or the Lakers'. And that was always a sense of pride to me as a Bucks fan, that we had the coolest floor in the NBA. No one could top that."

# 47 Eddie Doucette

Starting a basketball team from scratch is a difficult process. In addition to picking out players and a coach and an arena, you need to create an entire organization to support that team. For the Bucks' first year in 1968, the organization would be quite small compared to the large organizational flow charts you'll see for a modern NBA team, but there were still certain positions that needed to be filled. Play-by-play broadcaster was near the top of the list.

As Eddie Doucette tells it, he became the Bucks' radio announcer—a television broadcast would have been too much in the early days of the franchise—through pure happenstance.

Doucette was a radio DJ at the time in Milwaukee and was asked to emcee an event at a local pitch-and-putt. The crowd became a bit unruly, things started to go wrong, but the charismatic DJ was able to right the ship and keep the event from becoming a total disaster.

The owner of the pitch-and-putt requested to meet with the young DJ and ended up asking what he wanted to do with his life. Doucette informed him that he wanted to be involved in sports. As luck would have it, the owner was part of the organization trying to bring an NBA team to Milwaukee in 1967 and he hired Doucette to speak at events promoting the team, with the possibility of more work if they actually got a team.

A few months later, the group had landed a team and Doucette spoke in front of a group which, unbeknownst to him, contained the Bucks' team lawyer and team accountant. They were impressed by Doucette and soon he was made the team's public relations director, which he did in addition to his work as a DJ.

Eventually, the team decided they needed a broadcaster and thought about trying to get an experienced voice, but ultimately knew that would be unlikely. So, the Bucks went in the opposite direction, looking for a youthful voice to bring some excitement and enthusiasm.

The team lawyer immediately thought of that young guy who spoke to his group and asked around to find out more information about him, only to find out Doucette had been hired as the team's PR director. They suggested him to the ownership group as a broadcaster and they decided to go with the youngster, as long as he could get through a meeting with team president Ray Patterson.

"Hey, you weren't my choice," Patterson told Doucette, according to an article the broadcaster wrote on NBA.com. "I didn't know you were a broadcaster. But I'll tell you what. In the state of Wisconsin, we know high school and college basketball and nothing about the pros. I am going to give you one year to figure out how to sell these people on the game. At the end of one year, if you don't have it, you're gone."

With Patterson's words bouncing around in his head, Doucette decided to go for it.

"So I figured, what do I have to lose? I am just going to let it all hang out," Doucette wrote. "That is when I decided I was going to try and create something different and I created nicknames for the players."

Doucette had a nickname for everything. He spoke an intoxicating language so foreign to some fans they needed to create a dictionary for people to understand. Literally. Doucette and the team created the "Doucette Dictionary" and, with the help of sponsors, published it and distributed more than 1 million copies over the course of three or four years.

Here are some samples of his nicknames:

Bob Dandridge: "The Greyhound"
Greg Smith: "Captain Marvel"
Lucius Allen: "The Rabbit"
Jon McGlocklin: "Jonny Mac"
Dick Cunningham: "The Cement Mixer"
Paul Mokeski: "Speed Bump"
Flynn Robinson: "The Electric Eye"
Lew Alcindor, later Kareem Abdul-Jabbar: "The King"
Kareem Abdul-Jabbar and Oscar Robertson: "KO
    Combination"

"What happened was, I created a new lexicon for basketball which was kind of unheard of east of Chick Hearn or Bill King, who were doing the games in L.A. and San Francisco," Doucette wrote. "Every game was described with terms like 'north and south,' 'over the timeline,' 'in the lane,' the 'three-second area.' Well I changed all that stuff."

Some samples of his descriptions of the floor and gameplay:

"Bango": A long, exciting jump shot.

"Boulevard of Broken Dreams": Used in reference to an opposing player who attempts to drive down the lane with Kareem waiting to block the shot.

"Bulls eye/Cyclops": Midcourt circle.

"Doormat": Just in front of the basket.

"Forbidden Forest": The area around the basket when a little man tries to drive.

"Laying in the Weeds": Phrase describing a player who comes from nowhere to block a shot, get a pass, or cover a man on defense.

"Machine Gun Dribble": Hard, quick, staccato dribble.

"Pancake Jumper": Very flat jump shot, little arc or trajectory.

"Rings Up Another Sale": Scoring a basket, e.g., "Jonny Mac rings up another sale."

"String Music": A shot that never touches the rim—just the net.

"Sugar Cone": Another name for the hoop.

"Toaster": Area just in front of the basket where players are popping up and down.

"Zing Go the Strings": When ball goes through the hoop and hits nothing but the bottom of the net

With his one-of-a-kind delivery, Doucette more than impressed Patterson in his first year and went on to call some of the Bucks' greatest moments on radio (and eventually television) as he held down the job for the team's first 16 seasons. His description of Kareem Abdul-Jabbar's skyhook in Game 6 of the 1974 NBA Finals would be the basis of the name "skyhook" and one of Doucette's greatest calls.

Doucette decided to move on to bigger and better things in 1984, but his voice and style were synonymous with Bucks basketball.

# 48 Don Nelson

"Guys, I have no idea what I'm doing."

Those are the words Don Nelson says he uttered to his players when he called them together for a huddle during his first practice as head coach of the Bucks. It was the 1976–77 season, his first as an NBA assistant coach after a 14-year playing career, and his first season in Milwaukee. He didn't really know head coach Larry Costello, but his former teammate in Boston and then-Bucks general manager Wayne Embry thought a former player may work well as an assistant coach for Costello. After just 18 games, Costello resigned and left Milwaukee without a head coach.

"I turned the job down three times, but Fitz [then-Bucks owner Jim Fitzgerald] made me do it," Nelson later told ESPN. "Larry [Costello] resigned suddenly, but I just wasn't ready to be a head coach. I was 36 years old."

Nelson wanted to learn a little bit more about coaching before diving into it headfirst. He thought a few years with Costello would have been good before searching out basketball legend Jack Ramsay and learning a few things on his bench as an assistant, but Fitzgerald was persistent. He finally got Nelson to take the job after telling him that he could just take over in a handshake deal to try it out for a little bit and see if he liked it. If they needed to, they could move on after the season.

Coaching worked out for Nelson, to say the least. He didn't need to find something to do the next season or for the next 34 years of his life. Turns out, despite what he initially thought, Nelson did actually know what he was doing. So much so, he retired atop the career wins list for NBA coaches and his coaching contributions got him elected to the Hall of Fame in 2012.

Nelson struggled some in his first season as he found his footing and the Bucks attempted to figure out how to build a winner without Kareem Abdul-Jabbar, but Nelson had his team in the playoffs the next year with rookie Marques Johnson leading the way. The third year was a struggle, but that was the final season the Bucks would miss the playoffs with Nellie at the helm.

The Bucks made the Eastern Conference playoffs in eight straight years, beginning with the 1979–80 season. The roster largely didn't seem to matter as Milwaukee made the playoffs year after year. After compiling a 49–33 record in Nelson's fourth season, the Bucks won 50 or more games every season until Nelson left Milwaukee following the 1986–87 season, including a 60-win season in his fifth season with the Bucks.

Unfortunately, Nelson's Bucks played in the Eastern Conference in the 1980s, which meant they didn't have just one rival, but two. The Boston Celtics of the 1980s were among the greatest teams ever assembled and won three NBA championships while appearing in two more NBA Finals. The Philadelphia 76ers went to three NBA Finals in four years between 1979 and 1983. In 1983, the Bucks even swept the Celtics, only to get beat by the Sixers in the Eastern Conference Finals as Philadelphia went on to win the NBA championship.

"The only downside was we always had to go through Boston and Philly," Johnson later told CBS Sports. "Philly was a juggernaut themselves. Moses Malone, they picked him up, and it almost wasn't fair to put him on a team with Doc and Bobby Jones and Mo Cheeks and Andrew Toney and all the great players. It was kinda the way it was back in those days. It was just terrific basketball, high-level basketball being played."

During the Bucks' seven-year playoff streak, the Celtics and Sixers were the only teams to eliminate Milwaukee from the playoffs. Milwaukee put together more than a decade of winning basketball, but Nelson and the Bucks didn't even make an NBA Finals appearance. Despite being unable to collect the ultimate prize in Milwaukee, Nelson seemed more than content with his .611 winning percentage over his 11 seasons.

"They were great times," Nelson told the *Milwaukee Journal Sentinel* as he prepared to get inducted to the Hall of Fame in 2012. "It's when basketball was still fun. There's so much emphasis now on winning every game and not building...win now. With the talk shows and blogs, the industry has just really changed and not for the better. In those days you were able to have fun and enjoy yourself and work as hard as you can and kind of let the cards fall as they may. And as long as you were getting the best out of your team, everyone understood."

Ultimately, Nelson left Milwaukee after the 1986–87 season with rumors of regular disputes between him and new Bucks owner Herb Kohl, who bought the team in 1985. Despite the contentious divorce, Nelson's time will forever be fondly remembered as one of the most successful periods in the franchise's history.

# 49 The Inaugural McDonald's Open

The Cold War dominated global politics for decades following World War II, and slowly it seeped into any and everything that included the participation of multiple nations, including sports. For years, the Olympics served as the proving grounds for athletes around the world, but that never felt quite right in basketball, as the arms race on the hardwood between the United States of America and the Soviet Union was rarely a true measuring stick.

Surely, the USA had more talent, but a number of controversies over the years kept their dominance in question. In the 1972 Olympics, there was a massive controversy in the gold medal game between the U.S. and the Soviet Union, with the Soviets pulling out a last-second victory. The two teams didn't play in the 1976 Olympics before back-to-back boycotts, with the U.S. boycotting the 1980 Moscow Olympics and the Soviet Union in turn boycotting the 1984 Los Angeles Olympics. With little head-to-head action, both sides turned to their bravado to assert their basketball dominance during the 1980s.

With NBA players as the only professional players barred from international competition, the Soviet Union wondered just how well its national team would hold up against an NBA team. For years, the Soviets had sent their professional hockey teams to the States to play National Hockey League teams and they had fared well. In February 1987, the Soviet National Team even played a team of NHL All-Stars in lieu of the NHL's typical All-Star Game. Could they do likewise in basketball?

The NBA cooperated with the Soviets in the summer of 1987, as six Soviet players went on a barnstorming tour with the Atlanta Hawks. It was not a head-to-head competition; instead, the Soviets were intermingled with Dominique Wilkins and the rest of the Hawks with a chance to impress crowds that way. Their time to shine against U.S. competition would have to wait until the fall.

As part of NBA commissioner David Stern and FIBA secretary general Boris Stankovic's plan to make basketball more of a global game, the Bucks served as hosts to the Soviet national basketball team and Italy's Tracer Milano in the inaugural McDonald's Open, on October 23 through 25, 1987. Three nights, three teams, three games, with the Bucks facing off against the Soviets on Saturday night for the main event.

"It will be perceived as a giant game if we lose and just another game if we win," Bucks coach Del Harris told *Sports Illustrated* before the game.

The marquee said "Bucks vs. USSR," but this was USA vs. USSR. This wasn't about Harris' team winning a basketball game, but rather his country winning one. The Bucks would be the first team given a chance to display the country's basketball dominance against the best the Soviet Union had to offer...sort of. The Soviets' star 7-foot center, Arvydas Sabonis, who came to the NBA almost a decade later at age 31, did not make the trip because he was recovering from an Achilles tendon injury.

Nonetheless, there could not have been more pressure on Harris. Not only did he need to win the game for the entire country, it was his debut as head coach of the Bucks. Harris moved up from an assistant the previous season and needed to fill the monstrous shoes of the man he assisted, Don Nelson, who had won more than 60 percent of his games in his 11 years at the helm in Milwaukee. And Harris would be asked to do so without four of the team's best players—Sidney Moncrief, still recovering from off-season knee surgery; and Ricky Pierce, John Lucas, and Craig Hodges, who were all working out contract disputes with the team.

The moment and pressure would not affect Harris and his short-handed Bucks in the end as they easily dispatched the Soviets 127–100, with forward Terry Cummings taking home game MVP honors. Milwaukee led 98–50 with 4:20 left in the third quarter before taking out some of its starters and letting the game get away a little in the fourth quarter.

"My boys and I witnessed professional basketball today," Soviet coach Alexander Gomelsky told *Sports Illustrated*. "It is the best in the world. This is a chance for me to study. I can go home and improve my team after this."

And improve, they would. In 1988, the Soviets took home the gold medal in men's basketball at the 1988 Olympics in Seoul, South

Korea. Shortly after their victory, FIBA decided to repeal the ban on NBA players in international competition. The repeal had been discussed, but voted down in 1986 before the Soviets made the trip. In that way, the inaugural McDonald's Open was a part of the basketball diplomacy that helped open up the world and eventually allow the Dream Team to take the floor in the 1992 Barcelona Olympics.

# 50 Paul Pressey

"Nellie gets the most out of his players, whether they're All-Stars, stars, or role players, because he gets intake from all the players. If you have the ability to stay outside and shoot, he'll try to get you shots. He'll let you get a feel for what he wants you to do by allowing you the freedom to do what you do best."

Above is a quote from Paul Pressey to *The New York Times* on April 20, 1986. He was in the middle of another solid season as a professional basketball player and there were two reasons for his success: his talent and his coach.

In the entire history of the franchise, it would be difficult to find a more perfect basketball marriage than Don Nelson and Paul Pressey.

The Bucks selected Pressey 20th overall (out of 23 picks) in the 1982 NBA Draft out of Tulsa University, where Pressey was known as the "Rubber Band Man." He put up just 13.2 points per game in a third-team All-American senior season, but compiled the best steal and assist numbers in school history with single-game, single-season, and career records. There was no denying Pressey's production, but, at 6-foot-5 and neither really a guard or a forward, many teams struggled to place Pressey in their future plans. Nelson didn't share those concerns.

"Pressey was the guy we wanted all along," Nelson told reporters from the *Oklahoman* after the draft. "We thought he might go as early as 11th. We think he was the best defender in the draft, period. I said that there were some players, if they would drift [lower], we would take them. When Pressey slipped there was no question about it."

Where others were confused, Nelson was confident. Even if Pressey wasn't a great shooter or quite big enough to be a forward, Nelson wanted to work with someone who worked as hard and did as many things as well as Pressey. Despite his appreciation of Pressey's skills, Nelson used him primarily off the bench in his first two seasons, but finding minutes for him was not a priority as the Bucks went to back-to-back Eastern Conference Finals.

Pressey's role took on greater significance heading into the 1984–85 season because the Bucks traded star forward Marques Johnson, as well as Junior Bridgeman and Harvey Catchings, to the Clippers. Power forward Terry Cummings and guards Ricky Pierce and Craig Hodges returned to Milwaukee in exchange, which left an opening on the wing—and a new role—for Pressey.

Nelson, always a willing experimenter, decided to give Pressey the duties of a point guard, except from one of his two forward positions, thus creating the position of point forward. Now, Johnson will correctly tell you that Nelson already used him in that role, but Pressey was the first player Nelson used in that role fulltime. In fact, much of the Bucks' success was based on his ability to thrive in it.

"It allows us to start our offense from the forward spot," Nelson explained to *The New York Times*. "We did it to get the maximum out of Press' skills. It allows us to release our guards, who are not real quick, earlier, and alleviates some of the pressure on them and gives me a chance to play two non-ballhandling guards."

The new setup flummoxed other teams as they struggled to defend the Bucks because of the freedom Pressey playing point forward gave to the rest of the team, especially Sidney Moncrief. In his first season as a starter in the point forward role, Pressey doubled both his scoring and passing averages to 16.1 points and 6.8 assists per game. In the following three seasons, Pressey posted more than seven assists per game as he continued to work with Nelson in the point forward role. He also made three consecutive All-Defensive teams as he showed off the ability that originally drew Nelson and the Bucks to him in the first place.

By the time Pressey was traded to the San Antonio Spurs in 1990, he had racked up 3,272 assists, the most ever as a Buck and a number that still leads the franchise to this day. His number will never hang in the rafters. Aside from his assists total, it's impossible to pin down exactly why the "Rubber Band Man" was just so valuable, but when you reflect upon it, there's no doubt Pressey was one of the franchise's most valuable players of the 1980s.

# 51 Alvin Robertson's Playoff Performance

By the time the 1990–91 NBA postseason came around, Alvin Robertson and Michael Jordan knew each other well.

Robertson and Jordan were teammates on the 1984 United States Olympic Team. Robertson, who had been drafted seventh overall in the 1984 NBA Draft after a successful career at the University of Arkansas, was one of the few guys on the squad who relished going up against Jordan in practices as they prepared for the Olympics.

Robertson became a favorite of U.S. head coach Bobby Knight because of his dogged determination and his toughness. Knight even singled him out as the most impressive player on the floor during some of their workouts, even over Jordan. In fact, Jordan went on to call him one of the toughest competitors he ever played against.

After taking home gold in Los Angeles, Robertson began his rookie season with the Spurs, where he quickly earned a reputation as one of the league's best defenders.

"In the early 1980s, you could still hand-check guys and control where you wanted them to go," Robertson's Arkansas teammate Darrell Walker later told Bleacher Report. "Alvin had powerful arms, which helped. And he had the best, quickest hands you could possibly have. He could see the pass coming before the pass was thrown."

Robertson's package of strength, quickness, and athleticism made for an immediate impact defensively in the NBA. In his second season, Robertson led the league with 3.7 steals per game, a number that has not been matched in the history of the league. In fact, just six players in NBA history have recorded three or more steals per game in a season; Robertson was the only person to do it more than once. He did it three times with the Spurs and then once again in the 1990–91 season with the Bucks, the same year he was selected as an All-Star.

In the previous season, his first in Milwaukee, Robertson and the Bucks met up with the Chicago Bulls. The series was the second time the Bucks had met Jordan in the playoffs. Both teams had changed significantly since that meeting in Jordan's first playoff series during his rookie season in 1985.

The Bucks had moved on from their 1980s core, which won seven straight division titles between 1980 and 1986 under head coach Don Nelson, to a new-look team coached by Del Harris and led by Robertson and 1990 Sixth Man of the Year Ricky Pierce. The Bulls were one of the league's best teams with a trio of Jordan, Scottie Pippen, and Horace Grant leading them to a No. 3 seed.

Chicago took the first two games of the series, winning Game 1 by 14 and Game 2 by seven. In Game 3 of their first-round matchup, Robertson would lead the Bucks to victory, but it was his offense, not his defense, which helped keep his team from a sweep at the hand of Jordan and the Bulls.

Jordan went off in Game 3, scoring 48 points on 20-of-35 shooting and tallying nine rebounds and five assists. It didn't matter how good Robertson played defensively. The league's best player took over the game with his prodigious scoring ability and there was nothing the Bucks could do about it, except try to out-score him. And that's what they did.

Robertson led the way for Milwaukee and scored 38 points, while also putting up eight rebounds and seven assists. Never much of a shooter, the guard used the athleticism that propelled him to three All-Star appearances as a renowned defender to get loose offensively.

Most of his baskets came from in close, but how he scored once he got there was different. There was a pretty baseline spin move into a jump-stop finish. The Bulls lost track of him on an inbounds play and he got an easy layup. A couple tough finishes, where he used jump stops, pump fakes, and his impressive leaping ability. And then his jumper started to fall, which made for an even more dangerous offensive attack.

Robertson tallied 38 points, but his biggest play of the night might have been an assist in the closing moments. With the Bulls doing everything they could to slow him down, he found Fred Roberts streaking through the lane and the Bucks center hammered home a dunk that put the Bucks up four and helped seal a 119–112 victory.

The Bucks would lose the series in the next game as Jordan and the Bulls moved past them on their way to an eventual Eastern Conference Finals exit at the hands of the Detroit Pistons, but, for that night, Robertson found his scoring stroke and pushed the

Bucks to victory. There would be more of those nights the next season as Robertson made his fourth All-Star team and the Bucks made another playoff appearance, but the end of the Bucks' run as an Eastern Conference playoff team was not far off.

Robertson going shot-for-shot with Jordan for much of the night in a Bucks' playoff win would be one of the final positive moments for a franchise nearing the end of an era.

# 52 Retired Jerseys: Junior Bridgeman's No. 2

No one has played more games as a Milwaukee Buck than Junior Bridgeman. He started just 15 percent of his 711 games with Milwaukee, but the Bucks had little doubt about hanging his jersey from the rafters on January 17, 1988, after he retired following the 1986–87 season.

When asked why Bridgeman almost never started by *The New York Times*, Bucks head coach Don Nelson gave a simple answer: "Sidney Moncrief and Marques Johnson."

With two of the league's best at their respective positions on the squad, Nelson opted to bring Bridgeman off the bench in a role that Nelson knew all too well. Celtics coaching great Red Auerbach started using the "sixth man" in the 1940s as a way to empower players who might have been slightly duplicitous of teammates in the starting lineup and also find a way to get some scoring punch with the starters on the bench. By the time he got a hold of Nelson in the 1960s, he knew the perfect role for him in Boston.

So, when Nelson added Johnson to an already talented roster, he knew Bridgeman could excel in a role off the bench like he once had as a player. Bridgeman, along with Bobby Jones, Kevin

McHale, and Michael Cooper, ushered in a new era of sixth men in the 1980s. It became so commonplace the league even decided to start handing out a Sixth Man of the Year award following the 1982–83 season.

"The value of a sixth man is having someone who can immediately have a major impact on a game," Nelson told *The New York Times*. "Junior can do that. He can come in, hit three or four in a row and break a game wide open."

Bridgeman, however, wasn't keen on the idea when he was first introduced to it.

"In my first couple of years, it was an adjustment," Bridgeman said. "I didn't want to come off the bench. I don't believe anyone comes into the league wanting to do that, especially when you've been a starter most of the time you've been playing basketball."

This may have been especially true of Bridgeman, who came to Milwaukee in one of the most impactful trades in NBA history. He was one of three players, along with Brian Winters, Elmore Smith, and fellow rookie Dave Meyers, who arrived from Los Angeles in the Kareem Abdul-Jabbar swap. Meyers, a center out of UCLA, had been selected second overall in the 1975 NBA Draft, while Bridgeman, a guard/forward who led Louisville to the national semifinals, was selected eighth overall.

Bridgeman, never short on confidence, showed quickly he was not intimidated by being part of the package coming to Milwaukee for the league's best player.

"Frankly," Bridgeman told *The New York Times*, "I think the Bucks really got the best of the deal."

Though outsized, Bridgeman's confidence was warranted as he put together a fabulous career in Milwaukee. Mostly in a sixth man role, Bridgeman contributed to some of the Bucks' very best teams, including the 60-win team in 1980–81 and the teams that went to back-to-back Eastern Conference Finals in 1982–83 and 1983–84. Despite never averaging more than 30 minutes per game in any season, Bridgeman averaged more than 12.5 points per game in nine straight seasons.

For the better part of a decade, he was a rock in Milwaukee, both on and off the court. While with the Bucks, Bridgeman also served as the president of the NBA Players Association for four years during one of the largest periods of growth for the league. That experience would serve him well after his playing career, as he became an incredibly successful businessman as the president of Bridgeman Foods, which at one point owned 195 Wendy's, 125 Chili's, and 45 Fannie May Chocolate stores.

Bridgeman's time in Milwaukee ended in the same way it began—with a trade involving Los Angeles. He was sent to the Los Angeles Clippers, along with Johnson, as part of a swap in 1984. He would spend two years in L.A. before getting a more proper farewell from Milwaukee by spending his final season with the Bucks.

Like Nelson, who had his jersey retired by the Celtics despite rarely starting, Bridgeman would receive an honor befitting a franchise legend, despite rarely hearing his name called by the public address announcer during the starting lineups.

# 53 The Ray Allen Trade

"In terms of unfortunate moments, that was our most unfortunate moment, letting Ray Allen leave town."

Two years after selling the team, this was the move Herb Kohl singled out in a conversation with the *Milwaukee Journal Sentinel* reflecting on his time as owner of the Milwaukee Bucks.

"Well, he and [coach] George Karl got into it and it just didn't work so we traded him," Kohl said. "I didn't make the trade, but I let it happen. It became very much of a personality thing and so we traded Ray."

On February 20, 2003, the Bucks traded Ray Allen, Kevin Ollie, Ron Murray, and a conditional draft pick to the Seattle Supersonics for Gary Payton and Desmond Mason. The headliners of the deal were Allen and Payton, with Mason serving as the best of the rest of the players in the deal.

At the time, Allen was a 26-year-old shooting guard who had compiled a 20-plus point scoring average for three straight seasons and three straight All-Star Game appearances. Payton was a 34-year-old point guard who had been to eight All-Star Games. Allen had two and a half years left on his contract. Payton would be a free agent at the end of the season. Despite Allen's very clear potential as a franchise leader and Payton's unsure future in Milwaukee, the Bucks went through with the trade because of the strained relationship between Allen and Karl.

After falling just one game short of the NBA Finals in 2001, the Bucks took a major step backward in 2001 and missed the playoffs with a 41–41 record. Things started to go sideways between Karl and his players during that season.

"I think when we started to lose games, [Karl and I] kind of went away from each other," Allen told the *USA Today* after being traded to Seattle. "We didn't really communicate well. Last year, [Karl] wanted to blame me for certain things and blame it on other guys for certain things and there were times we wanted to blame him as well."

Allen was actually the second member of the Big Three—the trio of Allen, Glenn Robinson, and Sam Cassell that led the Bucks to the 2001 Eastern Conference Finals—to be traded out of Milwaukee. Robinson was traded to the Atlanta Hawks before the 2002–03 season even began, and if people were unsure of what was

*After he clashed with head coach George Karl, the Bucks traded Ray Allen to Seattle in 2003.* (Photo by Donald Miralle/NBAE via Getty Images)

bothering Karl before the trade, he made it very clear after trading Allen.

"I think it's more philosophically that maybe I'm fatigued by not playing defense for about four years," Karl told ESPN after trading Allen.

In the end, it came down to respect and neither side really felt like they were getting it. After the trade, Karl complained that he hadn't had many options with his offense-first bunch. He could tell them to play defense and sit them on the bench when he thought their defense wasn't good enough, but that was about it. Allen simply didn't agree with Karl's assessment of his defense.

"I think he was pushing a bad rap on me because I love playing defense," Allen told the *USA Today*. "I love playing team basketball. I love going out there to make sure we win basketball games."

In the end, the trade ended up being a massive mistake for the Bucks. Two years later, Allen was recognized as a second-team All-NBA guard and led the Sonics to the Western Conference Finals. On the other hand, Payton left the Bucks and signed with the Los Angeles Lakers in free agency after just two months in Milwaukee. And Karl was gone just two weeks later. Before he left, though, he was sure to approve a trade of Sam Cassell on the night of the 2003 NBA Draft.

Just two years after a magical run to the Eastern Conference Finals, the Bucks had traded away the three key players who led them in the postseason and galvanized the city around the team. Cassell and Robinson might have been entering the twilight of their careers, but Allen was just hitting his prime. The Bucks gave away their franchise player to appease a coach who would be gone two months later and they'll likely never stop regretting it. Kohl certainly won't.

# 54 The 2017 Comeback That Almost Was

Trailing 78–74 with 4:15 left and just half a second left on the shot clock, Bucks forward Giannis Antetokounmpo popped to the top of the key. Khris Middleton inbounded the ball and Antetokounmpo released the three before the shot clock expired. It ricocheted off the left side of the rim, off the backboard, and eventually to the hands of veteran guard Jason Terry on the left side of the floor. He dribbled out to the three-point line to line up a three of his own before Raptors defenders closed him out. He swung the ball to Antetokounmpo, who quickly flipped it over to Middleton.

With a quick flick of his wrist, Middleton let go a three that splashed through the net as a whistle blew for a shooting foul on Toronto Raptors guard Norman Powell. And with that foul, Middleton would have a chance to complete a four-point play and complete the Bucks' comeback.

Trailing 3–2 in their 2016–17 first-round Eastern Conference matchup against the Raptors, the Bucks had their backs firmly against the wall in a decisive Game 6. They gave up a 16–6 run to end the first half, heading to their locker room trailing 51–38. Then, they allowed the Raptors to rattle off a 20–10 run to start the second half and take their largest lead of the game at 71–46 halfway through the third quarter.

From that point, the Bucks clawed their way back into the game. Over the following 13-plus minutes, Milwaukee conceded just seven points on two made baskets, while forcing Toronto into 11 misses and nine turnovers.

"The one thing I said over and over when we were down, 'It's going to hurt if you want to win,'" Bucks coach Jason Kidd said. "I think they understood after the game what that comment meant.

I continued to say it as we came back. 'It's going to hurt, so just accept the pain if you want to win. If you don't want to accept the pain, then sit here on the bench and we'll put someone else in.' And those guys kept rising to the occasion."

That pain was no more apparent than in the man going to the free throw line to complete the four-point play to tie the game at 78–78 with 4:06 left. Before inbounding the ball to Antetokounmpo, Middleton's hands were on his knees. He had already played 38 minutes, despite being a game-time decision with a flu bug that made Kidd wonder if Middleton would play, robbed him of his voice, and hospitalized him after the game.

So, maybe it wasn't a surprise that he missed the free throw to tie the game. Or two other fourth-quarter free throws. Or that the tired legs extended to his running mate Antetokounmpo, who was the story of their entire season.

Antetokounmpo was a force throughout the series, leading both teams in points, rebounds, and steals. His stat-stuffing brilliance was similar to his performance in the regular season, in which he became the first player in NBA history to finish in the league's Top 20 in all five major statistical categories (points, rebounds, assists, steals, and blocks). As Antetokounmpo reached the fourth quarter in this game, you could see him getting close to his breaking point—having sat out just 81 seconds in the entire game—but that didn't stop him from willing the Bucks back into the game and putting on a playoff performance to remember.

After Matthew Dellavedova narrowed the score to 78–71, Antetokounmpo drew fouls on three consecutive offensive possessions when it seemed like he simply shouldn't have any energy left. In between attempts at the line, the 22-year-old put his hands on his knees and grabbed his shorts as he attempted to catch his breath, but ultimately the exhaustion got the better of him as he only hit three of his six free throws to cut the Bucks' deficit to four and set the stage for Middleton's potential game-tying four-point play.

Middleton ended up missing that free throw, by the way. The Bucks would gain the lead an offensive possession later on a Jason Terry three, but ultimately lose the game 92–89 after failing to match the Raptors offensively and defensively down the stretch. The potential four-point play served as an apt analogy for the entire series: great potential, not yet totally realized.

The four-point play capping a comeback in one of the most unlikely finishes in franchise history and ultimately inspiring an impromptu Eastern Conference Finals run would have made for an incredible debut in the spotlight for the Bucks, but they weren't quite ready for it. Outperforming two All-Stars and upsetting a 51-win Raptors team would have made for a loud declaration of Antetokounmpo's claim to the NBA throne, but he wasn't quite ready for that either.

"He's just starting," Kidd said. "He's only 22 years old. He's just starting his journey. And it's going to be a fun journey. He's going to take the state of Wisconsin and the city of Milwaukee on a ride that will be enjoyable. And we all should sign up. For those who signed up already, you got a front row seat. And he won't disappoint. He's going to get better. He always has big games, but he's going to have an impact in a game or a series and that's what makes him special."

The series did not end the Bucks' 16-year playoff series victory drought, but it did announce the arrival of Antetokounmpo and gave the city a new hope for a brighter future filled with relentless effort, magical comebacks, and hopefully a few playoff wins.

# 55 The Rest of the Big Three Bucks

Most Bucks fans have fond memories of the Big Three era in Milwaukee. Though they weren't able to sustain their run for long, the trio of Ray Allen, Sam Cassell, and Glenn Robinson played the best basketball the city of Milwaukee had seen in nearly two decades from 1999 to 2001. They took the Bucks to the 2001 Eastern Conference Finals and the franchise hasn't been back since.

The only problem is sometimes recounting the stellar play of the Big Three leads some to forget all the other players who helped those teams succeed. That leaves out a ton of great characters.

Let's start with Tim Thomas. The Bucks traded for Thomas during the lockout-shortened 1998–99 NBA season. He had fallen out of favor in Philadelphia after a solid rookie season, but was still just 21 years old. Bucks coach George Karl felt him out a little bit during his first season in Milwaukee before truly understanding the difference maker Thomas could be for his team.

The 6-foot-10 forward out of Villanova possessed a unique level of skill as a shooter and playmaker as well as plenty of athleticism and quickness. He could be hard to motivate at times, but Karl didn't have a problem with that in his first few years and Thomas' confidence and swagger fit right in with the Big Three when Karl unleashed him in his second season with the Bucks. Thomas quickly became the X factor for the Bucks as his potent playmaking could swing games for them off the bench.

(Fun fact: Thomas is one of the only NBA players to ever wear two headbands on his head during a game and he did it for three games with the Bucks before being forced to stop by the NBA.)

Scotty Williams was the other player traded to the Bucks in the deal with Philadelphia that netted Thomas and no one probably thought much of it. Williams had been little more than a role player during his nine NBA seasons before being traded to Milwaukee. The 31-year-old power forward/center surprised though, putting up career-highs in points (7.6) and rebounds (6.6) per game and starting 46 games in his first year in Milwaukee. Appropriately nicknamed "Tank," Williams quickly became one of the Bucks' enforcers, a tough guy who could give what some derided as a "jump-shooting team" a little edge when they needed it.

Ervin Johnson shared a similar-sounding name with one of the greatest basketball players of all time, but he wasn't quite bringing what "Magic" Johnson was bringing to the table. (In a cruel turn of events, when the Bucks visited the Los Angeles Lakers in the 2001 season, Ervin told the *USA Today*, "I was so bad in college they called me 'Tragic.'") Johnson was never the most gifted 7-footer, but he did serve a role for the Bucks as a physical presence and a shot blocker. In his first season in Milwaukee, Johnson started 74 games and averaged two blocks per game. Despite a move to the bench to make way for Jason Caffey in the 2000–01 season, Johnson still played in all 82 games and racked up 24 minutes per game, while focused on hitting the boards and blocking shots.

Before the 2000–01 season, the Bucks traded journeyman Billy Owens to Detroit for Lindsey Hunter, in what many considered a heist for Milwaukee. Hunter had started for the Pistons for nearly the entirety of his seven-year career, while Owens had struggled to catch on with six different teams. Hunter only played one season with the Bucks, but he was overqualified to come off the bench as a guard who could hit threes and defend an opponent's best player.

After opposing a move to Milwaukee during the 1999–2000 season, Jason Caffey became a member of the Bucks with a trade before the 2000–01 season and started 33 games for the team. Mark Pope, an unheralded former second-round pick who spent the previous season with the La Crosse Bobcats and a team in Turkey, became a super role player for the Bucks, scoring little but starting 45 games. And though he played in just 29 games, Darvin Ham started 13 contests and delighted fans in Milwaukee with "Ham Slamwiches."

Those years will always be remembered fondly in Milwaukee, but there was a lot more to the team than just the Big Three.

# 56 The 2001 Eastern Conference Finals Conspiracy Theory

Talk to a certain segment of Wisconsin sports fans about the NBA and you might hear one say, "I don't watch the NBA anymore. I can't believe you still watch that rigged league. I stopped watching in 2001."

While you might think that's a minority opinion, the 2001 Eastern Conference Finals did turn a number of Bucks fans away from the NBA.

When many fans recall the series between the Bucks and the Philadelphia 76ers that year, their minds go to Game 7, when the Bucks were forced to play short-handed because Scott Williams had been suspended. Those fans would point out the deck was stacked against them much earlier than that.

In Game 4, Glenn Robinson felt he was fouled on a late possession, which led to a fast-break layup for the Sixers' Allen Iverson, instead of the free throws Robinsons believed he had earned. Philadelphia went on to win Game 4, which tied the series at 2–2.

The Bucks traveled to Philadelphia for Game 5 and ended up feeling similarly about the calls and non-calls in that game. In the first quarter, Sam Cassell pump faked Iverson (his signature move) and the Sixers star whacked him across the arm. No foul was called. During Game 5, Robinson—who averaged four free throw attempts per game during the season—went to the line for the first time in the series.

Throughout the game there were touch fouls called on Cassell, early fouls on Ervin Johnson, and a moving screen called on Jason Caffey late in fourth quarter. Cassell ended up with a technical foul and Robinson and Tim Thomas both incurred flagrant fouls to give the Sixers extra points. After the game, the Bucks admitted those three mistakes likely cost them the game, but still offered an alternate suggestion.

"Nine times out of 10 when you have a referee you know there's no biases," Allen told ESPN. "But in the back of everybody's minds it's like Philadelphia and the MVP needs to play in the Finals. I used to always think the series were fixed when I was in high school, then when I got to the NBA I said there's no way they could be fixed. But even last year against Indiana in Game 5 [of Milwaukee's first-round series] it seemed like everything went against us."

Allen even went as far as saying his family members claim to have seen NBA commissioner David Stern jump up and stand to watch a replay of a foul Allen appeared to have gotten away with against Iverson that wasn't called.

"He jumped up real mad like he was cheering for Philly," Allen said.

Allen wasn't the only one to voice his complaints after Game 5. At first, Bucks coach George Karl dismissed any conspiracy theories as something people talk about during the summer, but then mentioned that he had three NBA coaches call him after Game 5 to raise their concern over a potential conspiracy against the Bucks.

"Sam Cassell said that Kevin Garnett and Rod Strickland had called him, so it's out there," Karl added to ESPN.

Karl and Allen racked up a combined $85,000 in fines for their comments, but things only got worse following Game 6. The Bucks won the game 110–100 behind a 41-point performance from Allen to force Game 7, but the Bucks would have to try to win the series short-handed because of a decision made after the game.

Two minutes into Game 6, Scott Williams fouled Iverson on a drive to the rim. He committed the foul by throwing his right forearm at Iverson. The forearm hit the Sixers star in the shoulder and across his neck, while Williams' bicep looked to go underneath Iverson's chin. In real time, the officials called Williams' foul a flagrant one. Both sides seemed fired up by the early, physical action. Williams scored 10 points in the first six minutes of the game and Iverson scored 46 points in the game.

The following day, the league notified Williams he would be suspended for Game 7. The suspension was not for the foul, but rather because of the accumulation of too many penalty points in the playoffs. NBA senior vice-president Stu Jackson reclassified the foul as a "flagrant foul penalty 2," which, when added to Williams' flagrant fouls against Orlando on April 22 and Charlotte on May 17, gave him too many penalty points and a one-game suspension.

"I wasn't trying to commit a flagrant foul or hurt him in any way," Williams told reporters after the game and before the suspension. "I have a knack for trying to get in the lane and draw charges when people come flying down the lane. And he's a little quicker than I thought he was and he's a little smaller than I thought he was."

The Bucks lost to the Sixers 108–91 in Game 7. After leading by nine in the second quarter, Philadelphia took control and Milwaukee was never able to get back within fewer than five points.

At the end of the series, the Bucks had been called for 186 fouls, while the Sixers had just 120 fouls. The Bucks had 12 technical fouls to just three for the Sixers, and the Bucks led in flagrant fouls five to zero. While the disparities could be explained through each team's tendencies—Milwaukee fouled a lot and rarely got fouled during the regular season, while the Sixers tried to avoid fouls and typically got to the line at a high rate—the conspiracy theory has persisted for nearly two decades at this point.

It was all just too juicy for Bucks fans: the regular feeling of rejection playing in a small market, the league MVP trying to get to the Finals, the comments from Karl and Allen, the foul discrepancy, the technicals. It was all right there in front of your eyes…if you looked at it from a certain angle in Milwaukee.

# 57 George Karl

A man in an emerald-green suit emerges from the tunnel at the Bradley Center. The building is packed and the entire crowd rises to its feet and begins applauding. A spotlight flashes onto him as he begins walking toward the court. He high-fives fans before eventually stepping onto the floor and taking his place along the home bench.

Bucks head coach George Karl has just stepped on the floor for Game 6 of the 2001 Eastern Conference Finals.

During the 2001 postseason, Bucks fans decided they would serenade Karl with a standing ovation during every home playoff game. They also decided he might not feel the same love if they waited for team introductions immediately preceding the game, so they found a time where he would fully understand the applause was for him. The tradition made Karl deeply uncomfortable, but he did always at least appear to enjoy the raucous reception.

It didn't take Karl long to become beloved in Milwaukee. After a seven-year playoff drought, Karl took the Bucks to the playoffs in his first year, the lockout-shortened 1998–99 season. He did the same thing the next season as well. Both years the Bucks were knocked out of the playoffs in the first round by the Indiana Pacers, but that would not be the case the following season, when the Bucks fell just one game short of the NBA Finals, falling to the Philadelphia 76ers in Game 7 of the Eastern Conference Finals.

Fans always felt a special connection to Karl because he was well-spoken, engaging, and unafraid to call out players publicly. While other coaches might avoid criticizing a player in the media, Karl did it regularly, which only endeared him more to Bucks fans. Often, when listening to Karl break down a game, some fans would hear a comment about a player's effort or a mistake they made and immediately think, "That is exactly what I said." When the Bucks started the 2000–01 season with a 3–9 record, Karl decided to go to the media to get his point across to players.

"I could've spun it," Karl told *Sports Illustrated*. "'Tough schedule, lost some close ones.' Yeah, I could've played that game. But that was the last place I wanted to go. So I called them everything [in the press]. Millionaire babies. Selfish bastards. Spoiled brats. But you know what really got the publicity? I called them 'employees.' I said, 'Hey, Senator Kohl pays you a lot of money.' That reached people. We don't think of players as employees, like everybody else."

Blunt public assessments of players quickly won over fans, but it took a toll on his relationships in the locker room. A defensive specialist in his previous NBA stops, Karl wanted his Bucks team to improve on that end of the floor, but that wasn't a simple task since the Big Three of Ray Allen, Sam Cassell, and Glenn Robinson were all players who excelled on offense, not defense.

"I didn't like it," Robinson told *Sports Illustrated* about the public criticism. "I don't think anybody liked it. We're supposed to be a family and address things here."

Asked whether or not Karl's public motivation tactics worked, Allen said, "Yeah, we came together. Against him."

Eventually, deteriorated relationships with Allen, Cassell, and Robinson would be the reason Karl left Milwaukee, but it should not cloud the contributions he made while with the Bucks. The team had the league's best offense in 2000–01, as well as the league's second-best offense the previous year.

While much of that had to do with the prodigious offensive talents of the Big Three, Karl allowed them to play with the freedom to make mistakes and gave them a framework that tried to leverage their skills. Allen was in the top five in three-point attempts per game. Cassell regularly worked from the middle of the floor with the chance to score or create for teammates. Robinson touched the ball regularly on the blocks and elbows. While always being a defense-first guy, Karl put his team in position to succeed offensively.

In five seasons with the Bucks, Karl posted a 205–173 record (.542 winning percentage) and went to the Eastern Conference Finals in 2001, the deepest the Bucks had gone in the playoffs since the 1985–86 season. He won over the fans and owner Herb Kohl to such an extent that he briefly became the highest-paid coach in all of professional sports when he signed a two-year, $14 million extension during March of the team's strong 2000–01 season. Rarely, if ever, does the highest-paid coach in all of sports reside in Milwaukee, but for a few years, that's exactly what happened with Karl and it is indicative of the massive turnaround he was able to pull off in Milwaukee in just a few years.

# 58 Robert Indiana's MECCA Floor

"It was a true home-court advantage."

Those were the words of Glenn "Doc" Rivers, who played on Robert Indiana's MECCA floor as a Marquette University basketball player before moving on to a long NBA career as both a player and coach. Normally when someone uses that phrase, they are referring to an incredible, raucous crowd that feels like it's sitting on top of the floor. Or a strange backdrop that is distracting to shoot against. Or some sort of physical advantage, like high altitude. They aren't literally referring to the court itself.

"It was amazing how many times we got opposing players to step out of bounds or to stay in the three-second lane," Rivers told ESPN. "That court did that to you."

The court didn't only confuse opponents; it also confused the entire community of Bucks fans. In 1976, the marketing committee of the board of the directors for the Milwaukee Exposition Convention Center and Arena (MECCA) wanted to try to find a way to draw attention to their entire facility. Committee chairman Steve Marcus learned the court in the arena needed to be resurfaced and proposed the idea of turning the floor design over to an artist.

Marcus and the rest of the committee talked to folks at the Milwaukee Art Museum and found a local gallery owner to help them find potential candidates to create the floor. In the end, they decided on Robert Indiana, the same pop artist who had created the LOVE Sculpture, which became extremely popular in Philadelphia and well-known nationally. Indiana would be paid $27,500 for his project.

The decision drew the ire of a portion of the public, who thought it was irresponsible to use public funds for such a project.

"Apparently MECCA board members under the guidance of Mayor Maier's henchman, ex-Alderman Robert Ertl, believe city property tax payers are a bottomless pit," wrote a Milwaukee citizen in an op-ed section of the *Milwaukee Sentinel*. "They are not satisfied with losing over a million dollars a year with their day-to-day operations. Now they have hired an artist named Robert Indiana from New York to paint the Arena basketball floor for $27,800. For this money, we should have something akin to the ceiling in the Sistine Chapel in the Vatican."

Citizens were concerned up until the very moment the court was unveiled on October 4, 1977, because Indiana refused to let anyone see it until the moment they lifted the cover off the floor before the Bucks' exhibition game against the Chicago Bulls. Unfortunately for the concerned citizen who wrote into the op-ed and those other citizens critical of the project, Indiana's MECCA floor was a masterpiece. If there can be a Sistine Chapel of basketball courts, his floor was it.

Like any basketball court, it had boundary lines, free throw lines, and lane lines. It had a midcourt circle and a halfcourt stripe.

*Unveiled in 1977, artist Robert Indiana's floor design for the MECCA eventually became a beloved part of Bucks history.* (Photo by Gary Dineen/NBAE via Getty Images)

But the MECCA floor had so much more. Every square inch of the floor was painted, something no one had done before or since. Indiana used yellow, orange, red, blue, and green paint. There were yellow Ms that started on each baseline. Their tops touched at halfcourt and when put together in that formation, they created a diamond. Inside the diamond, the word MECCA was written on each side of the court in a shade of blue that popped off the floor for fans (and television cameras) on each side to clearly see the name of the place that had a floor like no one had ever seen before.

"I was told that when the floor made its debut on television, someone from the New York Knicks immediately called and wondered how they could replicate this," Bucks television broadcaster Jim Paschke told *The New York Times*. "And they were told, 'I'm sure you have a few artists in New York and maybe you can find someone who can do a similar piece of work for you.'"

In the following days and weeks, a flood of stories about the floor was created. According to the MECCA board, it was featured in at least 48 different newspapers in the first month, which the board calculated was worth the cost of the project in marketing exposure many, many times over.

*TIME* magazine published a story on Indiana and his floor, including a color photo of Indiana on the floor with his arms outstretched, standing above the mark in the bottom corner of the floor with his name and signature on it. In his left hand, a paint can. His right hand is clenched in a fist prepared to be pumped into the air to signify a victory.

The photo ended up being a fitting symbol for the floor. It was an overwhelming success. It was well-received publicly. It became a unique piece of culture for the city and something the city became quite proud of. Most importantly, it was a winner. The Bucks went 555–347 (.615 winning percentage) and made the playoffs 10 of 11 seasons they played on the floor.

# 59 Listen to "Light It Up!"

In 1977, the Bucks unveiled the largest pop art painting in the world, Robert Indiana's MECCA floor.

In 2000, the Bucks released the greatest pop song of all time, "Light It Up!"

Okay, "Light It Up" might not be the greatest pop song ever recorded, but it did quickly become a favorite among Bucks fans and players and something that people still love nearly two decades later. Ask any Bucks fan from the era about it and they will remember the song, possibly even word-for-word. When former players Sam Cassell and Darvin Ham were asked about it while working as assistant coaches more than 15 years later, both immediately started to sing the chorus.

"We used to love it when it came on," Bucks point guard Sam Cassell said. "It was our song. It was our song for our team. The city enjoyed it too. Everybody that came to the game enjoyed it."

If you've never heard it before, you need to correct that immediately. Seriously, go to a computer and find it on the Internet. Or find a friend who burned it on a CD back in the day. It's a perfect piece of cheesy team-specific music commissioned and created by the team that helps explain exactly what George Karl's teams were all about. So, let's take a look at the lyrics.

### Yeah, yeah, yeah, yeah

This is where an audio book would really come in handy, but alas, I'll take you through it. The drums followed by the soulful, female voice with four straight yeahs to open the song is both iconic and unmistakable. You are undoubtedly preparing to light it up.

**Milwaukee, Milwaukee, Milwaukee**
These lyrics let you know exactly who this song is for. If you are a current resident of Milwaukee or a fan of the team that resides in Milwaukee (the Bucks), the song is for you.

**The word around town is that we're lighting it up / So who's gonna win it?**
Here a couple of things are established for you, the listener. First, people are talking about the Bucks, which means there must be something exciting or noteworthy about them. Second, the word is they're lighting it up, so they must be good. Putting these two facts together allows you to surmise exactly who will win it.

**The Bucks! The Bucks!**
Classic call and response here. You might not know it the first time around because it's your first time hearing the song, but you catch on quickly and the previous context clues give you a good hint for the proper response.

**The Purple and Green is exciting and tough / So who's gonna win it?**
See, the Bucks uniforms in the 1990s were purple and green. Purple and Green is just another way to refer to the Bucks.

**The Bucks! The Bucks!**
Now you're starting to get it.

**Straight from the Central Division, the team that's swishing / Running and dishing, the Bucks on a mission**
In both the 1999–2000 season and 2000–01 season, the Bucks had one of the best offenses in the league. Thus, the swishing, running, and dishing.

**Cassell and Ray hold it down in the back / Big Dog and Tim round out the attack**

At the time, the Bucks were starting Sam Cassell and Ray Allen at the two guard spots. And Glenn "Big Dog" Robinson and Tim Thomas were their starting forwards.

**It's the Bucks / Talented and tough, what's up? / The team from Milwaukee's about to erupt / We got the alley-oop, look away, hyping it up / The Bucks 2000 lighting it up**

These are more general descriptions of the teams under Karl. The Bucks had made a number of the moves leading up to the season that gave them the look of a team on the rise. Their talented scorers could put up points in a number of ways, including, yes, alley-oops and look-away passes.

**Ray Allen! Light it up! Light it up!**

Here is where the call and response begins for the team's key players. You hear a name. And then you hear, "Light it up! Light it up!"

**My man, Big Dog! Light it up! Light it up!**
**Tim Thomas! Light it up! Light it up!**
**So, who's gonna win it? / The Bucks! The Bucks!**

A callback to the start of the song and a great way to break up the list of players.

**Sam Cassell! Light it up! Light it up!**
**And the Tractor! Light it up! Light it up!**

Robert "Tractor" Traylor came to Milwaukee as part of a 1998 draft night trade. He was only with the Bucks for two years, but he still had a high-enough profile to make the first version of the "Light It Up!" video.

**Danny Manning! Light it up! Light it up!**
The Bucks' sixth man of "Danny and The Miracles" college basket-ball fame spent just one season in Milwaukee and struggled in that season, but a song doesn't get made overnight. They had to try to guess who might be valuable to the team. We all make mistakes.

**Who's gonna win it?/ The Bucks! The Bucks! / Milwaukee, Milwaukee, Milwaukee / Light it up! Light it up!**
And with that, the song comes to an end. Sixty seconds of perfection.

The song would be updated before the following season as new players came to town and started to have a major impact on the team. The love for the song, though, would not change. It would brighten up the Bradley Center every time it was played and leave an indelible positive impact on the quality of every Bucks fan's life.

# 60 Vin Baker

Vin Baker, a lottery pick from the University of Hartford? Wait, where is the University of Hartford? What state is that in? What conference do they play in?

Despite never scouting a player at the University of Hartford before Baker, the Bucks had no problem finding the place and scouting the 6-foot-10 center. In the NBA, he'd probably need to play one of the forward positions, but not at Hartford, Baker played center, putting up 28.3 points and 10.7 rebounds per game in his senior season on his way to North Atlantic Conference Player of the Year honors, despite double and triple-teams every night.

Even with some concerns over the level of the talent Baker played against in college, the Bucks made him the eighth selection of the 1993 NBA Draft. The underdog from the small school quickly became a fan favorite among Bucks fans.

"He's humble, honest, caring, hardworking, and he has a deep faith in God," Bucks center Andrew Lang told *Sports Illustrated* in 1996. "How can you not like him? He's not just a good guy, he's one of the great people in this league."

Baker, the son of a minister, made it plenty easy for fans to like him off the court, but that rarely matters if a player struggles on the floor. Baker didn't have to worry about that part though, making the NBA All-Rookie Team with 13.5 points and 7.6 rebounds per game in his first year. As a rookie, he weighed just 220 pounds, which wasn't enough for an NBA center—or power forward for that matter—so the Bucks worked with him to gain some weight and get stronger.

In his second season, Baker showed off a toughness some questioned he had. He added four points to his scoring average and almost three rebounds per game to average a double-double and earn NBA All-Star recognition. At All-Star Weekend, he was joined by rookie and No. 1 overall pick in the 1994 NBA Draft Glenn Robinson, and it served as one of the moments that helped solidify their friendship.

"When I was sitting on the bench at the start of that game, Glenn was sitting right behind me, telling me I better go out and show them what I can do," Baker told *Sports Illustrated*. "In any kind of important situation each of us knows he can depend on the other for support."

Part of the reason they grew close might have been their vast differences. Robinson grew up in the urban decay of Gary, Indiana. Baker grew up in picturesque Old Saybrook, Connecticut. Robinson was the first pick and National Player of the Year out of Purdue. Baker's college experience was nearly the opposite at

Hartford. Robinson signed the largest rookie contract in the history of the league. Baker just signed for what the Bucks offered.

Through all of that, they grew and supported each other and ended up being interesting counterbalances on the floor. In Baker's third season, both he and Robinson averaged more than 20 points per game. Though it was easy to think of the two forwards as an outside-inside combo with Robinson's jumper and Baker's work on the block, they ended up being nearly interchangeable. Robinson could also post up, while Baker was more than talented enough to knock down a midrange jumper.

"If we've gone to Glenn three or four times in a row on offense, he'll make sure to tell me to go down on the blocks because the ball is coming to me," Baker said. "We'll call his favorite inbounds play, but he'll say, 'No, let's run yours.' We try to make sure that everything stays in balance, because then it's harder to stop either one of us."

Before Baker's fourth season, the Bucks decided to make a coaching change. Mike Dunleavy moved from the bench to the front office and hired Chris Ford to take over for him as head coach. One of Ford's very first moves upon taking the job was making Baker and Robinson co-captains and making it very clear to each of them that they were the players responsible for the team's success. They took the role very seriously, but the Bucks' record didn't improve all that much, ending the season 33–49, despite adding impactful rookie shooting guard Ray Allen.

After three years together, the Bucks decided to split up Baker and Robinson by moving Baker to the Seattle Supersonics in a three-team trade that brought Tyrone Hill, Terrell Brandon, and a first-round pick to Milwaukee. In his final three seasons in Milwaukee, Baker averaged 20 points and 10 rebounds per game and went to three straight All-Star Games. Until Giannis Antetokounmpo's 2017–18 season, Baker was the only Buck other than Kareem Abdul-Jabbar to average 20 points and 10 rebounds per game in a season.

Unfortunately, Baker battled substance abuse issues throughout his NBA career. Baker later recounted the first time he played under the influence was January 5, 1996—the night he'd score a career-high 41 points for the Bucks against the Portland Trail Blazers. Baker said he would drink before, after, and sometimes even during games. By the time he found himself on the Boston Celtics, head coach Jim O'Brien suspended Baker three times during the 2002 season before the team cut him with $35 million remaining on his contract.

His drinking would eventually force him out of the league, but Baker eventually fought his way back to sobriety with the help of former Sonics owner and Starbucks founder Howard Schultz. With Schultz's help, Baker started working at Starbucks in its management training program and moved his way up through the ranks as he continued to stay sober. Eventually, Baker got a chance to return to the NBA when Bucks coach Jason Kidd asked him to help the team at NBA Summer League in 2014. With his foot in the door, Baker joined the broadcast team for the Bucks and began working on player development. Despite a circuitous path, Baker was finally back where it all began.

# 61 Del Harris

Larry Costello coached the Milwaukee Bucks for eight seasons and compiled a 410–264 record. He also put together a 37–23 record in playoff games and won the 1971 NBA Finals, the only championship in franchise history.

Don Nelson coached the Bucks for 11 seasons and led the Bucks to a 540–344 record. Over the franchise's first 19 years, the team had just five losing seasons. Whoever followed Don Nelson in the coaches' box was going to have a very difficult legacy to uphold.

After a feud with Bucks owner Herb Kohl that began nearly the moment he took over ownership of the team in 1985, Nelson resigned as Bucks coach on May 27, 1987. A week later, his long-time assistant, Del Harris, signed a three-year contract to take over as head coach of the Bucks. Taking over for the coach who got to 500 wins faster than any other coach in NBA history would be no easy task and Harris seemed well-aware of that fact.

"I always figured I was a filler-in guy between Nellie and the real guy," Harris later told the *Chicago Tribune*. "In the meantime, I was going to do everything that I could to help our team win ball-games. But I never expected to be accepted as coach of the Bucks when Nellie had been here for 11 years and established himself as one of the two or three top coaches in the history of the game."

Despite some initial misgivings, Harris and the Bucks managed to surge into fifth-place in the Eastern Conference in mid-March with a 35–26 record, just a game out of fourth-place and the right to host a playoff series. But the Bucks finished the season with a 7–14 slump to finish just two games over .500, an ending which left a bad taste in everyone's mouth.

With the poor finish, Kohl thought it might be best to fulfill Harris' expectation and look for a new coach. *Chicago Tribune* reporter Sam Smith even wrote that is exactly what would have happened had Kohl not decided to run for senate. Instead, Harris was given a chance and it paid off.

Serving as both coach and vice-president of basketball operations, like Nelson before him, Harris was able to give his team a makeover heading into this second season. He cut ties with vet-erans John Lucas, Jerry Reynolds, and Pace Mannion and moved Randy Breuer to the bench to make room for Larry Krystkowiak in the starting lineup. Jay Humphries, who had been acquired the previous year for Craig Hodges, found a groove and helped the Bucks find a better tempo.

Most importantly, though, Harris reached Ricky Pierce and Terry Cummings. Both players were standouts for Nelson, but didn't fully believe in the message Harris was sending in his first year at the helm in Milwaukee. Before assisting Nelson, Harris had been a head coach and even led the Houston Rockets to the NBA Finals in 1981, but his message just didn't seem to resonate in his first season.

"Del has got us playing defense, but mostly using the abilities of the players on the team," Cummings told the *Chicago Tribune*. "If a player can't do something, Del doesn't expect him to. We also have a better understanding of what he wants now. It always takes time to get used to a new coach."

There were still rough patches between Cummings and Harris, including an in-game argument between the two over rebounding, but something clicked as Cummings went to his second All-Star Game during the 1988–89 season and played some of the best basketball of his life. A similar thing happened to Pierce as he struggled in his first year with Harris, improved in his second, and erupted for his second Sixth Man of the Year award in Harris' third season.

Despite some individual success stories, the team just couldn't seem to find playoff success and picked up just one victory—a 3–2 series win over the Hawks in the 1988–89 postseason—in Harris' four full seasons as Bucks coach. The team compiled a 191–154 record under Harris, but a month into his fifth season with the Bucks at 8–9, the Bucks' third coach ever decided to give up the coaching part of his job description and move to the front office.

"The bottom line is that in today's NBA I believe that it is most difficult for one person to fulfill the dual role of head of basketball operations and head coach," Harris told reporters when announcing the move. "Since I felt it necessary to choose one, I have decided to let the one go that I know I can do well and pursue the other which I hope I can do well."

Harris hired his assistant Frank Hamblen as the new head coach for the remainder of the season. No one really knew it at the time, but the move would be one of the first steps on a long journey the team would take looking to regain the stability the franchise had under its first three coaches in its first 25 years.

# 62 Mike Dunleavy

It was all sort of convoluted. Del Harris stepped down as head coach a month into the 1991–92 season, but remained the Bucks' vice-president of basketball operations. Harris' assistant Frank Hamblen took over as the head coach for the remainder of the season. Later in the season, Harris was removed as vice-president of basketball operations. Then after the season, the Bucks relieved Hamblen as their head coach, but asked him to stick around the organization and he did.

The Bucks found their next coach in Los Angeles, hiring Mike Dunleavy. Dunleavy, a former Bucks player (1983–85) and assistant coach (1987–90), had been hired in Los Angeles just two years earlier and went to the 1991 NBA Finals in his first season with the Lakers. He was hired to be the Bucks' head coach, but eventually he too wound up being both head coach and vice-president of basketball operations.

"I was really put into the job by necessity," Dunleavy told the *Sun-Sentinel.* "When I was not coaching during the off-season, I enjoyed [the personnel role]. Now the big question is how it will go during the season."

Many coaches who take on both positions do their best to stay on top of their front office duties, but end up spending most of their time coaching. That's what they know best, so that's what they focus on. Not Dunleavy. He did everything he could to fulfill both roles, even elevating Frank Hamblen to head coach for a late December game against the Orlando Magic so that he could fly to Hawaii to scout a college basketball tournament featuring some of the nation's top prospects.

It truly was a new generation of Bucks basketball with Dunleavy at the helm. He wasted little time making significant changes to the roster. Jay Humphries and Larry Krystkowiak were moved to Utah on draft night for Blue Edwards, Eric Murdock, and the 23rd pick of the draft. The Bucks selected Todd Day and Lee Mayberry, teammates at the University of Arkansas, with the eighth and 23rd picks, respectively. A week later, Dunleavy traded Dale Ellis for Alaa Abdelnaby. A month later, Lester Conner was moved to the Magic for Sam Vincent. In just over a month, Dunleavy had totally turned over his roster.

Despite working incredibly hard on both roster construction and coaching, the Dunleavy years would not be kind to the Bucks. In his four years as coach, Dunleavy would lead the Bucks to a 107–221 record. The new players he brought in simply didn't get the job done, but the team's struggles did lead to a couple of picks at the top of the draft, which ended up being a large part of Dunleavy's legacy.

After a 28–54 season in his first year at the helm, the Bucks took a chance and selected Vin Baker, a forward out of the tiny University of Hartford. Despite a strong rookie season from Baker, the Bucks finished Dunleavy's second season with a 20–62 record, which gave them the first pick in the 1994 NBA Draft. With that pick, Dunleavy selected the nation's leading scorer, Glenn Robinson out of Purdue University. Robinson would eventually star on one of the franchise's most memorable teams in 2001 and

Baker was a four-time All-Star, with three of those All-Star appearances coming as a member of the Bucks.

After putting up a 25–57 record in the 1995–96 season with both Baker and Robinson averaging more than 20 points per game, Dunleavy decided he would be better suited in a front office role and hired Chris Ford to take over for him in the 1996–97 season.

# 63 The MACC Fund

Jon McGlocklin's basketball career was over. He had played more than 20,000 minutes and scored more than 9,000 points in his 11 NBA seasons, the final eight of which he spent in Milwaukee. He won an NBA championship in 1971, and the Bucks celebrated his retirement during halftime of their game in the Milwaukee Arena on December 10, 1976.

It was a night McGlocklin would never forget, but not because of anything to do with his retirement.

Little of the ceremony actually focused on McGlocklin stepping away from the game because of a much bigger announcement he had to make. McGlocklin and Bucks radio announcer Eddie Doucette had founded the Milwaukee Athletes Against Childhood Cancer, a foundation focused on making a difference by "Giving Hope Through Research" to children with cancer.

Among the many folks on the court with him during halftime for the ceremony was the inspiration for the charity, Eddie's two-year-old son, Brett. Brett was diagnosed with leukemia in 1975; since that moment, Eddie, and his wife, Karen, attempted to learn as much about the disease as possible and quickly found out that survival rates were very low for children. Their son faced a five-year survival rate of just 66 percent.

Eddie couldn't believe how slim his son's chances were and set out to learn as much as possible about the disease and how children with cancer were treated. He met with several members of the medical staff at the Milwaukee's Children Hospital and eventually developed strong relationships with them. They helped connect him with Dr. Donald Pinkel, the first director and CEO of St. Jude Children's Research Hospital, and Dr. Jim Casper, a pediatric hematologist-oncologist at Children's Hospital.

Both experts helped explain some of the biggest challenges in combating childhood cancer, especially a lack of funding. Doucette found this out directly when the National Leukemia Society reached out to him shortly after hearing about his son's battle and his connection to the Milwaukee Bucks. It pointed out that though the organization did a lot of great work, only a small percentage of the money donated to them would ever reach the Milwaukee area.

Doucette realized an organization to help with childhood cancer was needed in Wisconsin. Throughout the process, he talked with his friend McGlocklin about what he was learning and they eventually came to believe they needed to do something about the problem and started making plans for a charity. McGlocklin's retirement ceremony served as the moment they announced their charity's foundation and as a springboard forward.

With their connections in the area, McGlocklin and Doucette were able to put together a group of athletes, business leaders, and celebrities to support the charity. The charity took off rather quickly and just a few years later, they changed the meaning of the acronym of the MACC Fund to Midwest Athletes Against Childhood Cancer.

"When we started the MACC Fund in 1976, only 20 percent of the children that developed any form of cancer survived," McGlocklin said. "The cure rates were very low. Today, we've reversed those numbers. Today, about 80 percent of our kids are surviving, so the success is in that, not in the amount of people, the events, and the money we've raised only, but in the results."

In June of 2017, the MACC Fund announced it had raised more than $60 million since its founding in 1976. MACC Fund–supported scientific research is now conducted in the six-story MACC Fund Research Center of the Medical College of Wisconsin and the MACC Fund Childhood Cancer Research Wing of the Wisconsin Interdisciplinary Medical Research Center at the University of Wisconsin.

"It means so much to open up a center like this [MACC Fund Research Center] and to see what we've come from when we started the MACC Fund," said McGlocklin. "Children's Hospital and the Midwest Children's Cancer Center was located on Wisconsin Avenue, near Marquette, in the old facility and it was an antiquated warehouse at the time. To see this is remarkable."

On the night of the ceremony, the Bucks became the very first major sponsor of the charity, creating an annual event called the MACC Fund Bucks Game. Unsurprisingly, the event has become an annual affair with the team offering a limited number of special ticket packages for a one-of-a-kind game experience. In 41 years, the MACC Fund Game has raised more than $1.4 million and continues to be a highlight of each season.

# 64 Ricky Pierce

The first Sixth Man of the Year award was given to Bobby Jones of the Philadelphia 76ers following the 1982–83 season. Five players have won the award more than once: Kevin McHale, Detlef Schrempf, Jamal Crawford, Lou Williams, and Ricky Pierce.

When the Bucks traded Marques Johnson before the 1984–85 season, Bucks coach Don Nelson bemoaned the fact he had to include his beloved sixth man Junior Bridgeman in the deal. Not only would he lose his star player, he would lose the guy who gave his team a boost off the bench, a role he loved. Nelson knew he needed to find a new muse with Bridgeman gone.

Nelson didn't know much about Pierce, but acquired him in the deal that saw Terry Cummings come to the Bucks at the urging of his assistant Mike Schuler. He had coached Pierce at Rice University, where Pierce averaged 22.5 points per game despite double and triple teams from defenses night in and night out. Schuler insisted Pierce could be a difference maker even though he had produced little in his rookie year in Detroit or his second season with San Diego.

Pierce arrived in Milwaukee while working through a knee injury and missed the start of the season, but he caught the eye of Nelson as he ran 100 laps around the MECCA during the winter as part of his rehab. Nelson quickly used him in the sixth man role and Pierce rounded into form, scoring 10 or more points in 23 of his 44 appearances as the Bucks won 59 games. It didn't take long for Pierce to figure out exactly what Nelson was looking for him to do.

"My job is to come in and score," Pierce told *Sports Illustrated*.

Like Bridgeman before him, Pierce was overlooked by many coaches because he was a tweener. Often those type of players can struggle to find a role, but that was never the case with Nelson in Milwaukee. It didn't necessarily matter what size or shape you were as long as you performed, and Pierce didn't have any problem with that when he was given the chance.

Pierce broke out in a major way as a scorer, tallying 19.5 points on 53.4 percent shooting off the bench in almost 32 minutes per game, which eventually led to him taking home the Sixth Man of the Year award for the first time. (He started 31 games, but that wasn't enough to disqualify from sixth man eligibility.)

Unfortunately for Pierce, his breakout season corresponded with Nelson's final season in Milwaukee. Del Harris, Nelson's lead assistant, took over the next season, so Pierce's role would remain largely the same, but he would miss the start of the season with a contract issue. Pierce was among the Bucks' best players the previous season and didn't believe his contract reflected that. Eventually, the deal was worked out and Pierce got back to work.

He had a down year, appearing in just 37 games for Harris, and followed that up with another down season by his standards before exploding in the 1989–90 season. Pierce scored 23 points per game in just 29 minutes per night, which meant he scored a career-high 28.6 points per 36 minutes—a number only bested by Michael Jordan and Karl Malone that season.

"Ricky has the outside shot and he's strong down low, but what makes him really difficult is that he has the in-between game," Atlanta Hawks guard Doc Rivers told *Sports Illustrated*. "He can take the ball into the lane on one or two dribbles and pull up for the short jumper. That's the hardest shot to make, and it's his best shot. Then, he's so mentally tough. Against some guys you go into the game with one plan to stop them, and you can get them frustrated. With him that may work for five minutes, but then you have to change the plan. When I do summer camps and I get asked who's the hardest guy for me to guard, I don't hesitate. It's Ricky Pierce."

Pierce terrorized opponents throughout the season and won his second Sixth Man of the Year award. Get through the first five minutes with a lead, and you had to fend off Pierce trying to take it from you. Fall behind early against the Bucks, and one of the league's most feared scorers was going to try to put you away in the first half. With Pierce coming off the bench, there was no reprieve for Bucks opponents.

Eventually, the Bucks couldn't seem to come to agree with their sixth man about his value and what he deserved to be paid. He was traded to the Seattle Supersonics after his second Sixth Man of the Year award and the Bucks would struggle to fill the scoring void he left for a few years. Pierce was one of the few Bucks who impacted both the Nelson and Harris eras and he did so by doing the one thing both coaches asked him to do: get buckets.

# 65 Chris Ford

From 1990 to 1995, Chris Ford oversaw the Celtics as they fell from the heights of the Larry Bird era back to the middle of the pack. A few years after he left, the franchise hit rock bottom before coming back to life.

In Milwaukee, the franchise's decline came a little bit quicker. There were fewer middling years and a more immediate fall from a perch once high atop the Eastern Conference. In back-to-back drafts, the Bucks found impact players in Vin Baker and Glenn Robinson. By the time, Ford took over the Bucks in 1996 for Mike Dunleavy, who remained as general manager in Milwaukee, both of his young stars were scoring 20 points per game.

One of his first actions as head coach was naming Baker and Robinson co-captains to allow both players to take ownership of the team. It also gave the two young forwards—Baker was 25, while Robinson was 23—a partner to challenge along the way as they improved their individual skills. It ended up working perfectly because both of them wanted to share the experience and leadership burden with someone else.

The relationship between Baker and Robinson grew under Ford and seemed to be working better than it did under Dunleavy, who became frustrated with his forwards' struggles on the defensive end, Robinson especially. Ford improved those defensive numbers in his first year, getting the squad out of the 20s in Defensive

Rating, but the Bucks were still a middle-of-the-pack defense and they would remain that or worse for the rest of the decade.

While the defense might have been a struggle, the same could not be said for the offensive talent on the roster. In addition to Baker and Robinson, Ford had the pleasure of coaching a rookie out of the University of Connecticut, Ray Allen. The Bucks acquired the 6-foot-5 guard through a draft night trade with the Minnesota Timberwolves and he started 81 games, scoring 13.4 points per game. Despite two 20-point-per-game forwards and a sharpshooting youngster, the offense couldn't lead them to victories and Ford's Bucks finished his first season with a 33–49 record.

During that summer, Dunleavy resigned from his role as general manager to become the head coach in Portland. The Bucks appointed Bob Weinhauer, one of Ford's assistant coaches, as their new general manager. In September of 1997, Weinhauer decided to move Baker to Seattle in a three-team deal. In return, the Bucks received point guard Terrell Brandon, power forward Tyrone Hill, and a 1998 first-round pick.

So, for a second straight season, Ford was asked to adapt to a new roster and find ways to produce winning basketball. Milwaukee was just out of the playoff picture at 28–26 before injuries hit. Robinson suffered a knee injury that forced him to miss the final 26 games of the season and both Hill and Brandon missed games in the second half as well, which was a major factor in the team posting an 8–20 record in the final 28 games for a 36–46 record on the season.

Because of the injuries and the general success before the ailments, Ford likely would have gotten another season at the helm for the Bucks, but Herb Kohl decided to make a drastic decision at the urging of his friend (and coach) Rick Majerus, who insisted George Karl always knew how to make teams better. With that recommendation (and maybe a few more), Kohl decided to make Karl one of the league's highest-paid executives and made him both the general manager and the coach. With the hiring, Chris Ford became one of the shortest-tenured Bucks head coaches of all time and finished his time in Milwaukee with a 69–95 (.421) record.

# 66 Terry Porter

For the second time in his life, Terry Porter sat in a Milwaukee Bucks facility waiting for his name to be called, but this time it actually happened.

"I'm glad they didn't pass on me this time; '85 was a tough year for me," Porter told reporters at the news conference introducing him as the next Bucks head coach on August 6, 2003.

After dismissing George Karl with one year left on his contract on July 20, the Bucks worked quickly to find their next coach and decided on Porter, a Milwaukee native. Porter played his high school basketball at South Division High School and stayed in the state for his college hoops at the University of Wisconsin–Stevens Point.

After going through pre-draft workouts across the country, the Bucks invited him to the Milwaukee Arena on the night of the 1985 NBA Draft. Although he played at a small NAIA school, many expected Porter to be drafted late in the first round. The Bucks selected 22nd overall, which seemed like a solid spot for the hometown hero, but Bucks general manager and head coach Don Nelson opted for LSU wing Jerry Reynolds instead, leaving Porter sitting in the Bucks facility waiting for his name to be called. He would not wait long, as the Portland Trail Blazers selected him two picks later, but it certainly made for an unusual situation.

Nineteen years later, there was no doubt Porter was the Bucks' man.

If Porter had entered the fray a year earlier, he might not have been well received by fans. Karl might have simply had a bad year in 2001–02 , but any lingering doubts were dispelled the following season when the Bucks imploded and the Big Three were gone. First, Glenn Robinson. Then, Ray Allen. Next, Sam Cassell. After that, general manager Ernie Grunfeld. And finally, Karl. By that point, Bucks fans were ready for a fresh face and that is what Porter ended up being.

And it would have been difficult to find a face much fresher than Porter. After a 17-year playing career that ended with the San Antonio Spurs after the 2001–02 season, he started his coaching career as an assistant for the Sacramento Kings in the very next season. Despite only one year of experience coaching on an NBA bench, the Bucks (and truthfully, many other folks around the league) believed in Porter's ability as a head coach in the NBA and hired him.

In his first season, Porter led the Bucks to a 41–41 record and a surprise playoff appearance with an unheralded group of players. They were led by a 24-year-old Michael Redd, who was just beginning to figure out exactly what he would be as the No. 1 option of an NBA team, and a savvy group of veterans—Keith Van Horn, Toni Kukoc, Joe Smith, and Desmond Mason. Like the Karl-led teams before them, they struggled defensively, but managed to be one of the league's top five offenses despite not having household names as their lead offensive options.

As a former player himself, Porter quickly came to be known as a player's coach. He wasn't the type of coach who would berate his players on the sidelines or in a practice, but rather talk them through some things and work on those things in practice.

"He doesn't beat you up," Bucks guard and co-captain Erick Strickland told *Sports Illustrated*. "He allows you to make your mistakes and then learn from them. He knows when it's time to rest, what you're going through, and all the mental aspects of the game."

In the postseason, the Bucks fell in five games to the Detroit Pistons, their lone victory coming in a 92–88 Game 2 win.

Porter's second season would not go as well, with the Bucks falling to 30–52 on the year. The offense dropped down to around league average and the defense remained weak.

In a major stroke of a luck, the Bucks won the 2005 NBA Draft lottery and then the off-season started to get a little strange. Obviously, the Bucks needed to make a selection between a couple quality prospects (ultimately opting for Andrew Bogut), but they also decided they would need to pick a new coach as well. Porter still had another year on his original three-year deal, but the Bucks made it clear they were not interested in offering him a contract extension.

There were two prevailing rumors about why they let Porter go after two seasons. Some believed the Bucks desperately wanted to make a play for Flip Saunders or Nate McMillan to be their head coach. Others thought the Bucks knew Porter wanted a chance at the Trail Blazers job, the team with which he spent the first 10 years of his playing career.

At the end of his two seasons as coach of the Bucks, Porter had compiled a 71–93 record, which ultimately doesn't seem all that bad for a coach tasked with replacing one of the franchise's most respected coaches and an unproven roster. Nevertheless, Porter was out and the Bucks were on the search for a new coach just two years after hiring Porter.

# 67 Terry Stotts

After the Bucks moved on from coach Terry Porter in the summer of 2005, most assumed their replacement targets would be veteran coaches such as Nate McMillan, Flip Saunders, or Doug Collins. Ultimately, though, Collins took his name out of the running. McMillan signed a five-year deal to move from Seattle to Portland. And Saunders made the Bucks wait longer than they would have liked, which eventually forced Bucks owner Herb Kohl to go with a face that was there for the franchise's most recent playoff success.

On July 8, 2005, the Bucks announced the hiring of Terry Stotts, the ninth head coach in franchise history. He had previously been with the Bucks from 1998 to 2002 as an assistant coach on George Karl's staff. He missed out on Karl's last season in Milwaukee, as he went to Atlanta to be an assistant for Lon Kruger before taking over midseason as head coach. Stotts eventually stuck around for two full seasons before being removed from the position and heading to Golden State for a season as an assistant before being hired in Milwaukee.

Stotts inherited a team that went just 30–52 in the previous season, but an off-season full of splashy moves meant expectations would be higher in his first season. The Bucks selected center Andrew Bogut with the first overall pick of the 2005 NBA Draft. They re-signed Michael Redd to a six-year max contract, despite the Cleveland Cavaliers offering a five-year max contract for him to become LeBron James' running mate. They also signed 2004–05 NBA Most Improved Player Bobby Simmons from the Los Angeles Clippers to a five-year, $47 million deal.

With expectations higher than they maybe should have been, the Bucks still managed to improve by 10 wins and sneak into the playoffs as the eighth seed. It was the first time in NBA history a team made the playoffs despite having four new starters from the previous season's roster.

Redd took another step forward, averaging 25.4 points, 4.3 rebounds, and 2.9 assists as the Bucks' leader on the floor. Stotts was an assistant in Milwaukee in Redd's first two seasons and the two had the opportunity to work hand-in-hand during Redd's development. The team's lone playoff win in their series against the top-seeded Pistons came in Game 3, when Redd scored 40 points on 14-of-21 shooting against one of the league's best defenses.

Stotts' second season in Milwaukee did not go as well as his first and he was not even allowed to see it all the way through as Kohl decided to let go of him after 64 games. The decision seemed harsh, as he didn't have any control over the injuries his players sustained and the 2006–07 season was a rough one for the Bucks when it came to injuries. Redd went down with a knee injury in mid-January and ended up missing 20 games, which added to an already very serious list of injuries. With his absence, the Bucks were then playing without four of their starters from the beginning of the season and things started to unravel.

On March 12, 2007, the Bucks hosted the Raptors on a Monday night with Redd back in the lineup. (He had returned from his 20-game absence a month earlier.) They lost 108–93 that night and Bogut was ejected for committing a flagrant foul on Toronto's Chris Bosh. As the center left the court, he made an obscene gesture toward the fans. Stotts was informed of his dismissal two days later before the Bucks played their next game against the Spurs.

"I'm obviously saddened by the fact that he's not going to be here anymore," Redd told the Associated Press. "I hate to see anyone lose their job. Terry did the best he could with what he had for our team. It just didn't work out."

Even in the official press conference, general manager Larry Harris mentioned just how difficult it had been in that season for Stotts with all of the injuries, but the team still decided to let him go and immediately sign Larry Krystkowiak, one of Stotts' assistants, to a multi-year deal.

Stotts was gracious leaving Milwaukee, thanking the Bucks for the opportunity, and eventually catching on with Rick Carlisle in Dallas as a Mavericks assistant. After four years as an assistant, Stotts got another chance with the Portland Trail Blazers, which is where he finally found a true home as an NBA coach.

In the fourth of his six seasons thus far with the Blazers, Stotts hand-delivered a check to Jon McGlocklin for the MACC Fund during their December 15 game against the Bucks. During the broadcast, McGlocklin and Jim Paschke mentioned how Stotts delivered his check personally every single year, which helped show just how much the city of Milwaukee meant to Stotts, even if his time as head coach didn't end how he would have liked.

# 68 Larry Krystkowiak

After firing Terry Stotts on Wednesday, March 14, 2007, Herb Kohl did not wait until the end of the season to look for the 10th coach in his franchise's history. Milwaukee hired former Buck Larry Krystkowiak just a few hours later.

At the time, rumors connected Krystkowiak as a candidate for the open coaching position at the University of Utah, so the Bucks moved quickly to make sure they were able to keep their guy.

Krystkowiak became an assistant in Milwaukee after Stotts finished up his first season. Before that, Krystkowiak led the

University of Montana, his alma mater, to the NCAA tournament in each of his two seasons as head coach.

"Becoming an NBA head coach was my No. 1 goal when I went into coaching and I welcome the challenges that lie ahead of me," Krystkowiak told the Associated Press when he was hired. "This team has a great deal of potential and I'm eager to move forward."

Krystkowiak played in Milwaukee from 1987 to 1992 and many Bucks fans still remembered him because of the way he pumped his fist as he was carted off the Bradley Center floor after suffering a horrific knee injury against the Pistons in a playoffs series in the spring of 1990.

Krystkowiak employed the same fighting, never-give-up spirit as a coach, but it just didn't much matter during the 2007–08 season, his first full season on the bench. Michael Redd had a bounce-back season after missing some games the previous season with a knee injury and former first overall pick Andrew Bogut started to come into his own offensively in his third NBA season, but it just wasn't enough.

The Bucks were also unable to fix their defensive problems under Krystkowiak. After underperforming defensively for Stotts, much of the same occurred with their new coach in tow. In fact, it got slightly worse, as the team finished the season as the worst defensive team in the league. After going 8–8 in their first 16 games, the Bucks never got back to .500 and went just 18–48 the rest of the way to finish the season with a 26–56 record.

On March 19, 2008, with a month still remaining in the season, the Bucks announced they would not renew the contract of general manager Larry Harris. About a month later, on April 11, they announced John Hammond would take over as GM. There likely wasn't much doubt in Krystkowiak's mind at that moment he would not be returning as Bucks coach since a new general manager often wants to hire a new coach. And he was right. Hammond and the Bucks announced the decision to relieve Krystkowiak of his duties on April 18, a day after the season ended.

"The bottom line on this decision is that this is a results-driven league," Hammond told the Associated Press after deciding to fire Krystkowiak. "Sometimes it comes down to wins and losses. Once again, the man that Larry was and the effort he put forth had little to do with the decision."

With Hammond in charge, Krystkowiak might have received the short end of the stick, but it largely felt like everyone involved understood it was a part of the business they had chosen. The Bucks had moved quickly to sign Krystkowiak to a deal originally because they were concerned about him potentially taking the job at Utah, and their concern ended up being valid because he took the job at Utah in 2011 and remains there to this day.

Just four days after letting Krystkowiak go, Hammond inked Scott Skiles to a four-year, $18 million contract to become the next head coach of the Milwaukee Bucks with the hope of bring some stability to an organization that had just gone through three coaches in five years.

# 69 Marques Johnson

"I wasn't looking at him like [Larry Bird] was better than me at that point, I was just as good if not better than him. That was my attitude. I felt I could score and do everything he could do against me. I could respond tit for tat. Same thing with Julius Erving coming in…You didn't really look at it with the kind of reverence for Larry Bird or Dr. J that fans have now. At that point we were kinda the top three forwards in the league, and battled accordingly."

That is what former Milwaukee Bucks forward Marques Johnson had to say about playing against former Celtics great Larry Bird when asked about it in 2017 by CBS Sports. And it serves as a great place to start any conversation about Johnson's time in Milwaukee.

The Bucks selected Johnson third overall in the 1977 NBA Draft out of UCLA. He immediately set the league on fire, averaging 19.5 points and 10.6 rebounds per game in his rookie season, as he helped lead the Bucks to a surprising 44–38 record and a first-round playoff victory in Don Nelson's first full season as head coach.

Johnson would make his first All-Star team and earn First-Team All-NBA honors in his second season. He was already recognized as one of the best forwards in the game because of the profound impact he had on each game he played. While a number of players of his era put up gaudier scoring numbers—Johnson averaged just around 20 per game—but his coach was quick to remind anyone who would listen his forward could easily put up those numbers if they'd ask him to do so.

"Doc's the Doc," Nelson told *Sports Illustrated* of Erving and Johnson in 1980. "But Marques is the best all around. We ask him to do more and he does do more. I never want to limit his abilities to one or two areas. There's no doubt I could get 30 points a night from him if I went to him more. But he's got to work his butt off on the D, so I limit him to 35 minutes or so. I could play him at guard if I wanted to, he's that versatile."

In Johnson, Nelson had found his perfect superstar. With an ability to handle the ball uncanny for a player his size, floor vision befitting of a point guard, and athleticism that would make Dr. J blush, Johnson could do everything Nelson needed and more. He gave the effort Nelson demanded defensively and served as the offensive hub who could play well with others. The league's most versatile forward would make the All-Star team four times with the

*The third overall pick in the 1977 NBA Draft, forward Marques Johnson played seven seasons in Milwaukee and returned as the team's TV analyst in 2015.*

Bucks and receive three consecutive All-NBA nods in 1979, 1980, and 1981, but individual success would not be the only thing he'd find in Milwaukee.

The Bucks won 49 games in Johnson's third season before catapulting to 60 wins in the 1980–81 season, the franchise's first back in the Eastern Conference. They'd win 50 or more games in the next three seasons and make two trips to the Eastern Conference Finals, but never got all the way to the NBA Finals. It was the curse of the Bucks of the 1980s, as each and every year they would need to beat both the 76ers and the Celtics, but typically could only beat one in a given postseason.

Despite the stellar play on the floor, Johnson's relationship with the Bucks was rocky through the years. Before his third season, Johnson held out in an attempt to renegotiate the six-year deal he signed when he was drafted in 1977. The Bucks gave him a modest bonus, but refused to do a full renegotiation.

"A contract is a contract," Johnson told *Sports Illustrated* in 1980. "My mistake was signing for six years. Now I realize I was betting against myself. But I just saw that million dollars. I wouldn't have cared if it was spread over 30 years. They told me six years would go fast, but...wow, I still have two more to go."

The relationship was patched up briefly, but Johnson's desire for a more lucrative contract did not change, nor did his preference for the city of Los Angeles over Milwaukee. In the summer of 1981, Johnson asked the organization for a trade, citing his contract once again, as well as an inability to leverage his talents off the floor (television, movies, commercials, etc.) in Milwaukee. Again, though, the Bucks were resolute in keeping him in Milwaukee, especially Nelson, and the two sides would eventually come to an agreement on a new contract in December of 1981 after Johnson had held out for the first month of the season. The contract would pay him $8 million over eight years and once again, it appeared as though both sides could move forward. They did just that until the summer of 1984.

Johnson was traded to the Clippers on September 29, 1984, along with his teammates Junior Bridgeman and Harvey Catchings, for Terry Cummings, Craig Hodges, and Ricky Pierce. The Clippers later tried to get the deal nullified because the Bucks did not tell them Johnson went through treatment at St. Mary's Drug Rehabilitation Center in Minneapolis for cocaine use in the summer of 1982.

The trade was not nullified, but the damage had already been done to Johnson's reputation. With the contract disputes and the public reveal of his drug problem while in Milwaukee, Johnson's relationship with the Bucks became complicated. Although his résumé would stack up favorably to a number of the other players who have their jerseys hanging from the rafters, the organization opted not to give him such an honor when he eventually retired from the NBA in 1990.

In 2015, the former Bucks forward returned to Milwaukee as a color commentator on the team's television broadcasts. One can only wonder if enough time has passed for Johnson to be honored by seeing his jersey raised above the floor in the Bucks' new arena.

# 70 The MECCA

People tend to romanticize their first homes. In hindsight, things that may have bothered them at the time, such as small closets or a leaky faucet, pale in comparison to all of the incredible memories they created there.

The Bucks might have some of the same feelings about their first home, the Milwaukee Arena, which was later renamed the MECCA as part of the larger Milwaukee Exposition, Conference Center and Arena.

The MECCA was dedicated on April 9, 1950. It was part of a much larger post–World War II project in Milwaukee to construct new sports and entertainment venues, as well as cultural institutions. Along with the arena, Milwaukee also built a new art museum and baseball stadium.

It was one of the first arenas in the United States built to accommodate the new medium of television, but that ultimately didn't affect the appearance of the building from the outside or ability for patrons to see whatever event they attended from the inside. On the outside, the building is characteristic of post-war modernism, featuring stainless-steel curves common of the era (think of a local drive-in restaurant of the time).

Inside, you'd have to work incredibly hard to find a bad seat. There are no obstructed-view seats and there isn't a balcony, which would create any "nosebleed seats." So, almost every seat felt like it was on top of the floor and fans acted that way when opposing teams came to town.

"It was always capacity," Bucks forward Marques Johnson later told CBS Sports. "We had the smallest venue in the league. We'd catch these teams coming into Milwaukee like the Lakers. My buddies Norm Nixon and Jamaal Wilkes would be coming in with their fur coats and cowboy boots and hats and all that, and we just knew that if we jumped on 'em early, and really put the pressure on 'em early, they'd be ready to get back to the warm weather in a hurry. It would be in the dead of winter, it might be 30 below or whatever, but our fans were there in full force, and completely behind us. It was just a great, great time to play professional basketball in Milwaukee for me."

With a seating capacity of 10,938, the Milwaukee Arena was the smallest venue in the league from nearly the moment the Bucks entered the NBA for the 1968–69 season, but that never seemed to bother them. In fact, it created a strong home-court advantage for a young team without necessarily having the requisite success for a full house every night.

"It was ideal for us starting out, because we had a lot of full houses and that made it feel big," former Bucks general manager Wayne Embry told NBA.com.

It didn't take long though for the Bucks to become a big-time team because of the coin flip they won for Lew Alcindor. In just their third year of existence, the Bucks won the NBA Finals and the Milwaukee Arena was the home of a champion.

The Bucks even knew some of the smaller advantages they could pull from their 20-year-old building. In the northwest corner of the building, there is a large garage door that can open up on the loading dock right outside the building. The door is no more than a couple hundred feet from an opening in the lower bowl that allowed players to get from the court to the locker rooms. With things going in and out of the arena on game days, cold winter winds from the streets of Milwaukee might blow across the court during a shootarounds. (This also affected Bucks players, who often practiced in hoodies and sweatpants, but at least they knew about it ahead of time.)

In 1974, when the Milwaukee Arena was folded into the MECCA complex, the MECCA board of directors decided the arena almost a quarter century hold could use a bit of a facelift and tried to figure out a bold new way to show off the arena and the city. Ultimately, they decided on commissioning an artist to create a new floor that could draw people's eyes to any game played there and the city of Milwaukee. They did just that with the MECCA floor created by pop artist Robert Indiana.

"It accomplished its goal," Johnson told NBA.com. "It became a talking point, whether it was 'the crazy floor,' 'the colorful floor.' A lot of guys back in those days from opposing teams would say, 'What's it like to play on this psychedelic floor?'"

Whether on the exciting Robert Indiana floor or the original floor, one thing was almost always true of any game played at the MECCA: the Bucks won. Milwaukee's all-time regular season record on the floor was 582–209 (.736). Much of that credit obviously goes to the great coaches and players the organization put in that arena, but as the Bucks look back on their first home, maybe the arena had something to do with the wins they racked up.

# 71 The Wisconsin Entertainment and Sports Center

When Herb Kohl sold the Bucks to Wes Edens and Marc Lasry in June 2013, both he and the new ownership group had just one thing on their mind: a new arena in Milwaukee.

It was their focus for two reasons. First, the Bradley Center had grown outdated by NBA standards, so the new ownership group wanted to make sure to keep the franchise among the league's best in every facet, which would include the arena in which it played. Second, it was literally a provision of the purchase agreement they signed with Kohl in buying the team.

The provision stated if the construction of a new arena did not start in 2015, the NBA would buy back the team from Edens and Lasry's group for a $25 million profit and move the team to a city that would have a proper facility. When speaking in front of the Wisconsin legislature's Joint Finance Committee in July 2015,

Bucks president Peter Feigin mentioned Las Vegas or Seattle as cities that might be able to host the team in the event of relocation.

With this provision disclosed, the arena's funding immediately became a major topic of public discussion as the public vs. private funding debate has intensified over the years in the United States. The Bucks were in a slightly better position than a number of teams lobbying for public funding because of the generous $100 million gift from Kohl and the $150 million pledged by the new ownership group.

After some very public debate, Wisconsin governor Scott Walker approved a $250 million commitment in taxpayer money to help pay for a new arena in Milwaukee on August 12, 2015. The public money would come from the state, the city, and Milwaukee County.

And with that, the Wisconsin Sports and Entertainment Center (WSEC) was born. Scheduled to open by the fall of 2018, the arena has a totally unique look with an arched design and a rising wall that pulls up and over the top of the arena. The rising wall is covered in pre-patina zinc shingles and broken up by six vertical glass "ripples," which allows for a closer look at the activity in the arena from the outside, as well as a way for natural light to flow into the arena.

Inside the arena, fans will experience a totally different viewing experience. Unlike the Bradley Center, which put more of its seating in the upper level than the lower level, the WSEC will feature a wider and larger lower level to go along with a smaller upper level that will be closer to the action. In all, the WSEC will feature 17,500 seats for fans with 65 percent of them on the lower level.

All of the action may be on the floor, but the eyes of fans may also be drawn to the state-of-the-art scoreboard hanging from the ceiling. Made up of four high definition screens on each side, the $10 million scoreboard weighs more than 71,000 pounds. Each of the side panels of the cube-shaped scoreboard is 29 feet tall by 25 feet wide. When the new arena opens, it will be the largest center-hung scoreboard in the NBA.

"It's going to be a blow-away experience beyond expectations for anybody that's been to a pro sporting event in the state of Wisconsin, that's for sure," Bucks president Peter Feigin told The Post Game. "We really want it to be a model around the world. We've made it intimate with a 17,500-person crowd. We've made it really authentic and localized with what our food and beverage offerings are going to be. It's really best of class."

Along with the arena, the Bucks are working on a 30-acre district surrounding the arena, which is the largest development project ever undertaken in downtown Milwaukee. The new district will include entertainment, residential, and commercial spaces with the possibility of bars, restaurants, apartments, and space to hold events.

"We want to attract residents down here, and we want to spur retail spending in a big way," Feigin told the *Milwaukee Journal Sentinel*. "We should be getting an additional million or a million and a half to visit downtown."

Feigin and the Bucks would love for the team to be the biggest attraction downtown, but just in case the team struggles, they'll be more than ready to entertain Milwaukee with their arena and the surrounding area.

# 72 Bango

When you purchase a ticket to a Bucks game, there is no guarantee exactly who you will see on the floor. Players get injured, suspended, and traded. Coaches can sometimes get ejected. But one thing that will always be there is the Bucks' mascot, Bango.

Everyone's favorite furry, cartoonish deer has been delighting fans for more than 40 years since his debut on October 18, 1977.

It was the Bucks' season opener against the Los Angeles Lakers, and with former Bucks legend Kareem Abdul-Jabbar in the building, it could not have been a bigger regular season game for Bango's debut. His first game was hardly a surprise because people had voted on his name, which wasn't the first time the Bucks had left naming rights up to the people.

The first time the Bucks allowed their fans to have a voice was when they selected their nickname. At the time, teams throughout the fledgling league were desperate to try to get fan participation and the new team in Milwaukee was no different in 1968. So, the board of directors decided to sponsor a contest and let fans (or potential fans) contribute their ideas.

More than 14,000 fans submitted entries to name the team and there was a clear winner: "Robins." Yes, fans in Milwaukee believed the team should be named after the popular bird with the orange breast that typically appears shortly after the end of winter. Despite winning the popular election, the team decided to go with the fourth-most popular response, "Bucks."

Contest judges wanted to choose a name that reflected the fish and game area of Wisconsin with GM John Erickson explaining the "Buck" was a good choice "because it is indigenous to Wisconsin." The team also ended up selecting R.D. Trebilcox as the contest's winner. Trebilcox explained the name would make sense for basketball players because Bucks are "spirited, good jumpers, fast, and agile."

Less than 10 years later, the team put the name of the mascot up for a vote as well, but actually decided to listen this time around. Again, thousands of votes were received and "Bango" was the most popular option by far. "Bango" was actually a phrase used by the original voice of the Bucks, Eddie Doucette, as a way to punctuate a shot from deep.

Bango hit the floor on opening night of the 1977–78 season. He didn't do a jump that evening, but over the years, jumps would

*Bango, the team's mascot, has become a must-see attraction during any Bucks home game.*

become a big part of his career. In the early days, the costume was surprisingly tall and NBA mascots were only expected to walk around the floor and greet guests. Over the years, many mascots morphed into high-flying stuntmen and that's no different in Milwaukee. Tune into a Bucks game now and you will likely see Bango get on a skateboard, jump off a trampoline for a dunk, and shoot a ball over his head from halfcourt.

Despite some alterations to his look over the years, Bango has always been roughly the same. Even if his eyes are slightly different and his muscles are bigger and his antlers are not quite as high as they used to be, one thing about Bango will never change: he's going to put a smile on your face, no matter what he has to do.

# 73 Bogut Goes Down

With less than two weeks remaining in the 2010 NBA season and two playoff teams on the floor, the Bradley Center was packed for a game between the Bucks and the Phoenix Suns on a Saturday night. Bucks center Andrew Bogut had somehow gotten out front of the entire Phoenix defense in transition for a dunk and yet the entire arena had gone silent.

After the dunk, Bogut took a fall, a disastrous fall that would change the entire trajectory of his career, the Bucks' season, and the franchise's next five years. Nothing would be the same after that moment.

It was a strange play from the start. Suns forward Amar'e Stoudemire missed a long two from the right wing, which Bogut had challenged. Bucks shooting guard Carlos Delfino ended up rebounding Stoudemire's miss in the lane, while Bogut streaked up the floor, inverting action typical of an NBA fast break.

Throughout the season, Bogut had made a habit of hitting his guards all over the floor with outlet passes, which ultimately freed them for layups. This time, it would be Delfino who would get Bogut an easy bucket with a high-arching, two-handed chest pass flying from the middle of the lane over the defense and into Bogut's hands at the opposite free throw line.

Bogut leapt off his left foot at the dotted line, a distance maybe slightly further away than on an ideal dunk. In addition to jumping from slightly too far away, Stoudemire had caught up to Bogut and given him the slightest of forearm bumps in the back. Bogut still slammed home a two-handed dunk, but his hands slipped off the rim and he fell to the floor.

With his 7-foot, nearly 260-pound body perpendicular to the floor around four feet off the ground, Bogut reached back with his right arm to brace his fall. His arm would not be able to withstand the pressure, though, and slipped under his back and took the entire brunt of the fall. Almost 250 pounds down on top of his right arm left Bogut with a broken hand, a dislocated elbow, and a sprained wrist.

The injury to Bogut would not end the Bucks season, but it did mar what could have been a magical run. At the All-Star break, Milwaukee was just 24–27, good for ninth in the Eastern Conference. Less than two months later, after they beat the Suns 107–98 on the night of the injury, they had won 18 of 25 and taken over sixth place in the East with a 42–34 record.

At the trade deadline, the Bucks made a few moves, most notably a trade which brought journeyman shooting guard John Salmons to town. The 30-year-old Salmons slotted into the starting lineup shortly after joining the squad and put up the best numbers of his career, averaging 19.9 points, three assists, and three rebounds per game in Milwaukee. Salmons and Bogut shepherded what would come to be known as the "Fear the Deer" Bucks into the playoff picture, but the Bucks would be forced to go into the playoffs without their leader and fell in a seven-game series to the fourth-seeded Atlanta Hawks.

It's impossible not to wonder what would have happened in a playoff series with Bogut, but that pales in comparison to what would have happened if Bogut had never fallen at all. The 2009–10 season was the year Bogut had put it all together, showcasing the total package of skills that made the Bucks select him with the first overall pick in the 2005 NBA Draft. He was named Third Team All-NBA, despite missing the final six games of the season.

On the defensive end, he was the anchor of one of the league's best defenses and was second in the league in blocks with 2.5 per game. On offense, he scored a career-high 15.9 points per game, but also helped serve as one of the team's offensive hubs as an initiator at the elbow and an elite screener.

After the injury, Bogut was a shell of himself. Once known for his touch around the rim and deft passing, Bogut's right arm and hand took years to recover and never really came back around to what it was in that one magical season. After a few more years in Milwaukee, he was traded to the Golden State Warriors, where he eventually won a championship. The Bucks, on the other hand, received Monta Ellis, Ekpe Udoh, and Kwame Brown for him, all of which were gone in three years. All the Bucks and their fans could really do was ask "What if?"

# 74 Scott Skiles

The Bucks were tired of losing. So, Herb Kohl hired a general manager, John Hammond, who had been a part of one of the league's most successful franchises of the 2000s, the Detroit Pistons. And Hammond wanted a coach who could give his team some toughness and help scrape them off the bottom of the league's defensive rankings, so he hired Scott Skiles.

On April 21, 2008, Skiles took over the Bucks and all parties involved seemed to want Skiles to be the guy everyone thought he was. Before taking the job in Milwaukee, people saw him as a coach who demanded a lot of his players, and when he was questioned about it during his introductory press conference, he made sure to let everyone know he wasn't planning on changing.

"I always feel like I'm supposed to apologize for that," Skiles told the assembled media. "And I'm not sure that's the tack I want to take. Anybody that is going to come to work with enthusiasm, concentrate, and play hard will never have a problem with me. I don't care if they throw the ball in the seats 25 times a game."

After being in the lower third of defensive rating in the NBA for nine consecutive seasons and having the league's worst defense in the 2007–08 season, Skiles helped turn the Bucks into the league's 15th-best team in the 2008–09 season. Now, there are any number of people who contributed to the turnaround, but Skiles' demanding style was certainly a large part of the drastic improvement. In his first season, Skiles made it clear players would not be able to skirt their defensive duties with him in town.

In his second season, Bucks players were not just trying marginally harder to help the team get to the middle of the league on defense; they were dominating. In just two years, Skiles transformed the defense from one of the league's most pathetic units to a nearly impenetrable one that shut down teams on a nightly basis. Andrew Bogut manned the middle as a Defensive Player of the Year candidate in the 2009–10 season, which would have been a sentence impossible to believe for most when he was first drafted as an offense-first center.

With Bogut's leadership, the Bucks surged in the season's second half. At the trade deadline, Hammond swung a trade for Bulls swingman John Salmons and saw him improbably become one of the league's most important additions. After averaging 12.7 points per game in the season's first 51 games of the season with Chicago, Salmons came to Milwaukee and averaged 19.9 points, 3.2 rebounds, and 3.3 assists per game. Hammond added veteran guard Jerry Stackhouse off the waiver wire after he had played just 10 games in the previous season with the Dallas Mavericks because of foot and knee problems.

The Bucks won 22 of their 31 games after the All-Star break and surged up the Eastern Conference standings, but ended up getting a sizable hurdle thrown into their path with just two weeks left in the season. Against the Phoenix Suns, Bogut was knocked off the rim on a fast-break dunk attempt by Amar'e Stoudemire and took a gruesome fall, which resulted in significant arm and shoulder injuries. It was the turning point of the season and quite possibly the turning point of Skiles' time in Milwaukee. Bogut would miss the rest of the season and the Bucks fell to the fourth-seeded Atlanta Hawks in a seven-game series in the first round of the Eastern Conference playoffs.

The following season, the Bucks were great again defensively, but the offense cratered. Bogut only averaged about three fewer points per game, but he just wasn't the same offensive player after his fall and he couldn't finish around the rim quite as well as he once could. Salmons returned to playing more like himself than the super-efficient scorer he was after the All-Star break the previous season. And without the same success they had found the previous season, Skiles' hard-pressing tendencies began to grate.

One year later, it all started to fall apart. The Bucks dropped all the way down to 16th in the league defensively, while their offense bumped up to middle of the pack. The bump came at least partially because of a trade at the deadline in which Hammond moved Bogut and Stephen Jackson's contract to the Golden State Warriors for Monta Ellis, Kwame Brown, and Ekpe Udoh. Jennings and Ellis could always find a way to score, but often struggled defensively, which drove Skiles crazy.

Skiles entered his fifth season in the last year of his contract, but he would not make it all the way to the end of that contract because the Bucks parted ways with him in the beginning of January. After Skiles' departure, multiple sources reported the Bucks had actually approached Skiles about a contract extension, but he was not interested and had actually wanted out for months.

When Jim Boylan took over for Skiles on January 8, 2013, an all-too-familiar story could be told: he got his players to work hard and they became a good defensive unit…until his players tired of his demanding style and their patience wore thin. And then he left.

# 75 Larry Drew

No Bucks head coach without an interim tag has served in the position for a shorter period of time than Larry Drew. Drew was given just 82 games, and they were among the most forgettable games the team has ever played. Strangely enough, that is not really an indictment of Drew's coaching, but rather the reality of a convergence of a series of bad events with a flawed roster to cause the Bucks to lose a ton of games.

The Bucks won just 15 games in the 2013–14 season, the fewest in franchise history. The roster that struggled throughout the year was completely different than the previous season's. In the 2012–13 season, the team removed Scott Skiles as head coach and turned to one of his assistant coaches, Jim Boylan, to serve as interim head coach for the final 50 games of the season.

After a 38–44 season, general manager John Hammond decided to remake the roster. His work started with two draft picks: Giannis Antetokounmpo, a forward out of Greece, and Nate Wolters, a senior guard from South Dakota State University. On July 10, 2014, his work continued, sending guard J.J. Redick to the Los Angeles Clippers for two future second-round picks in a three-team trade. One day later, he traded the rights to Szymon Szewczyk for Luke Ridnour and a future second-round pick in another three-team deal. He wrapped up his off-season trades the following day by moving Luc Richard Mbah a Moute to the Sacramento Kings for two future second-round picks.

Hammond then moved on to free agents. The day after trading Mbah a Moute, he signed free agent shooting guard O.J. Mayo. Four days later, he signed veteran free agents Carlos Delfino and Zaza Pachulia. Two weeks later, he added Miroslav Raduljica and Gary Neal.

On July 31, Hammond was able to pull off a trade for restricted free agent Brandon Jennings. The sign-and-trade deal of the former star of the Bucks netted Brandon Knight, a young point guard from the University of Kentucky, and Khris Middleton, a former second-round pick. Finally, at the end of August, Hammond shipped Viacheslav Kravtsov and Ishmael Smith to the Phoenix Suns for Caron Butler.

On opening night, only four players remained from the previous season's final roster: John Henson, Ersan Ilyasova, Larry Sanders, and Ekpe Udoh.

Little went according to plan for Drew. Delfino didn't play a game in the 2013–14 season because of a foot injury. Sanders played just 23 games thanks to various injuries and a suspension. Mayo played just 52 games, and Ilyasova missed almost 30 games. With injuries all over the roster, Drew turned to his young players, which happened to be a blessing in disguise for the franchise as Antetokounmpo and Middleton played big minutes which helped foster their development, but didn't help the Bucks win many games in Drew's lone season.

Despite the bad luck, Drew likely would have gotten a second season with the Bucks, but new owners Wes Edens and Marc Lasry took over the team in April 2014 and decided to go in a new direction. Unfortunately for Drew, they didn't decide to tell him they wanted to go in a new direction and it ultimately became the most memorable part of his tenure in Milwaukee.

The Bucks selected second in the 2014 NBA Draft because, despite having the best chance at the first overall selection, the Cavaliers snuck in front of Milwaukee in the draft lottery. With the second pick, the Bucks selected Jabari Parker, a forward out of Duke University. On June 27, 2014, the Bucks held a press conference at the Milwaukee Public Market to introduce Parker to the city and the world for the first time as a Milwaukee Buck. Drew sat on Parker's right and Hammond sat on his left during the press conference and they discussed a bright future together.

The next day, reports began to surface suggesting the Bucks' new owners were trying to get permission from the Brooklyn Nets to interview their head coach, Jason Kidd, for a position in Milwaukee. Drew was fired the next day and Kidd was hired as the Bucks' next head coach on June 30.

"The whole Jabari thing, putting me in that position, I don't think it was very professional," Drew told the *Milwaukee Journal Sentinel*. "I wish it wouldn't have happened that way, but it did."

Nothing went right for Drew in his lone season in Milwaukee and the same was somehow true of his exit, as he was discarded with little thought to make way for a flashier new coach.

# 76 Jason Kidd

Fair or unfair, how the Bucks perform under Mike Budenholzer will almost certainly affect how people judge the Jason Kidd era in Milwaukee. Because of the ups and downs and ambiguity of the team's performance during Kidd's time at the helm, it's tough to judge until more is learned about all of the involved parties. Let's start at the beginning.

Kidd replaced Larry Drew as head coach on June 30, 2014. Coming off a 15–67 season, the move in and of itself would not have been all that difficult to defend. However, the switch was not executed well. Three days earlier, Drew sat on stage with the No. 2 overall pick in the 2014 NBA Draft, Jabari Parker, and discussed the future and what it might hold for him, Parker, and the Bucks. While he was doing that, ownership was discussing the possibility of Kidd replacing him as coach.

Despite a controversial start to his time in Milwaukee, Kidd put together an impressive first season. With the help of a couple of veterans (Jared Dudley and Zaza Pachulia), some long-armed wings (Khris Middleton and Giannis Antetokounmpo), and an aggressive defensive scheme, the Bucks became one of the league's stingiest teams in Kidd's first season. By helping aggressively and forcing teams to pass the ball as much as possible, the Bucks forced more turnovers than anyone else in the NBA and made teams shoot the ball late in the shot clock.

In fact, the Bucks won eight of their last nine games before the All-Star break to enter the hiatus with a 30–23 record. In the closing moments before the trade deadline, the Bucks decided to break up the team that had been so hot by trading Brandon Knight and Kendall Marshall to Phoenix in a three-team deal that netted them Michael Carter-Williams from the Philadelphia 76ers, as well as Tyler Ennis and Miles Plumlee from the Suns. They would go just 11–18 to close out the season and ultimately fall to the Bulls in six games in the first round of the Eastern Conference playoffs.

During the off-season, the Bucks made a huge splash by signing one of the biggest free agents on the market in Greg Monroe. The big man took meetings with a couple other teams, including the New York Knicks and the Los Angeles Lakers, yet he decided to sign with the small-market Bucks. In accordance with that move, the Bucks moved Dudley and Pachulia to give more opportunities to their own young players.

Kidd's second season did not go as well as the Bucks struggled to find the same success defensively. With their trusty veterans gone and Monroe, a slow-footed center, in the middle of the defense attempting to learn what to do, the rotations and execution were simply not where they needed to be to find success. The Bucks missed the postseason as their record fell to 33–49 and much of the blame for the defensive struggles was attributed to Monroe and the lack of veterans who knew the system.

In Kidd's third season, the defense improved slightly—up from 23rd in defensive efficiency to 19th—while the offense took off with Antetokounmpo developing into a star in his fourth NBA season. His ascendance was validated with his first career All-Star appearance and start. On the season, he led the Bucks in each of the five major statistical categories with 22.9 points, 8.8 rebounds, 5.4 assists, 1.6 steals, and 1.9 blocks per game. The Bucks would make the playoffs for the second time under Kidd with a 42–40 record, but again lost in the first round of the Eastern Conference playoffs, this time to the Toronto Raptors.

Heading into this fourth season in Milwaukee, Kidd and the Bucks did not shy away from expectations. After a rousing six-game series against the Raptors and the logical next developmental steps from Antetokounmpo and Middleton, the organization was openly discussing 50 wins, a top-four seed, and a playoff series win. On January 22, however, the Bucks were just one game over .500 at 23–22 and ownership decided to fire Kidd and replace him with interim head coach Joe Prunty. Bucks general manager Jon Horst cited the team's performance, as well as a desire to increase the team's chances to win games in the current season, as reasons for the firing, which left a complicated puzzle to piece together in Milwaukee.

In Kidd's first season, the Bucks were an absolute terror for teams to play against because of their unrelenting defense, but that same defense grew stale over the following three seasons. Antetokounmpo grew into one of the five best players on the planet, but it's difficult to know what he would or would not have done with a different teacher. Middleton developed into a 20-point scorer, but did so through a large number of midrange jumpers, instead of a more modern offensive approach. While the defense was creative and different before growing predictable, the offense was boring and rarely fostered a synergistic attack.

If the Bucks improve and become contenders, Kidd will likely be seen as someone who was unequipped to help the team make that leap. If they continue to be a playoff bubble team, perhaps Kidd will be vindicated as someone who did the best he could with a flawed roster. As the Bucks move forward, history will be the judge of Kidd's time in Milwaukee.

# 77 John Erickson

He was the Bucks' general manager for just two years, but it is difficult to find many people more impactful in franchise history than John Erickson.

In 1968, Bucks owners Marvin Fishman and Wes Pavalon were looking for the perfect people to run their expansion basketball franchise. They looked around the country for the greatest basketball minds, as well as around the state of Wisconsin. Early in the process, they targeted renowned Marquette University basketball coach Al McGuire as a potential head coach. Marquette would not allow him to leave, so the owners moved on to Alex Hannum, who had won a championship a year with the Philadelphia 76ers. The 76ers also kept him from taking on a new job and Hannum himself suggested Larry Costello.

The Bucks signed Costello to be their coach, but still needed a general manager and went about it the same way, looking around the country for the best basketball minds before ultimately circling back to the state of Wisconsin. In Madison, they found Erickson, who had just completed his ninth season as head coach of the Wisconsin Badgers.

"It was a little strange," Erickson later told Bucks.com. "The Bucks actually hired Larry before they hired me. We were announced at the same time. It was only a matter of a day or so. They actually had tried to get Al McGuire to be the general manager, but Marquette wouldn't release him."

Customarily, teams will select a general manager to run their franchise and then, the franchise will allow the general manager to select a coach, but the Bucks owners did it in the opposite order. Nonetheless, Erickson seemed more than happy to accept the position.

"Just about the same time, I accepted the offer to be general manager. I didn't meet Larry until the day we were announced. I knew of him, of course. I didn't have any problem with that, and I had a great relationship with him in the years I was there."

Erickson had his work cut out for him. Since the Bucks were an expansion franchise, he didn't just need to find a couple of players or make a trade or two to firm up the bench; he needed to find an entirely new roster from the draft and the NBA's expansion draft.

"I think what I really enjoyed was the building of the franchise," Erickson told Bucks.com. "We had an expansion draft and a player draft to get going. Tom Nissalke had been hired as an assistant coach by Ray Patterson, our team president. Tom was scouting college players. Larry was very much involved in the expansion draft."

For the expansion draft, teams left unprotected those players they were willing to lose, which typically means over-the-hill veterans or unproven young players. Erickson used his college experience with young players and Costello's pro experience with the veterans to find a happy balance of young and old for the team's inaugural roster. The creation of that roster, though, would pale in comparison to the job Erickson had to get done in his second off-season as general manager.

The Bucks went 27–55 in their first season of NBA competition, which wasn't terrible but still bad enough for them to get entered in a coin flip for the first overall pick in the 1969 NBA Draft. The prize of that draft was obvious: Lew Alcindor. Alcindor dominated the competition at UCLA under head coach for John Wooden for three straight years. UCLA went 88–2 and won three national championships during Alcindor's three years in the middle, as he collected three First-Team All American honors and two National Player of the Year awards.

Both the Bucks and the Phoenix Suns got on the phone and waited for NBA commissioner J. Walter Kennedy to flip the coin to determine the first pick of the draft and only the Bucks came away from the conversation happy. The team's selection with the first pick was obvious, but there was still plenty of drama surrounding adding Alcindor to Milwaukee's roster.

The American Basketball Association desperately wanted Alcindor to join them and make them true competitors with the NBA. Instead of allowing the two leagues to get into a bidding war, Alcindor told both leagues he would solicit one offer from both sides and make a decision.

"We were in New York for what I thought was a get-acquainted session," Erickson later told the *Kansas City Star*. "[Alcindor] and his agent, Sam Gilbert, walked into the hotel room and asked us for an offer. Well, we didn't have an offer. But I noticed that Lew appeared hungry, so I said, 'We've got a plan in mind, but we'd like a little time to work it into a firm offer. Let's go have lunch. Then, give us a couple of hours, come back, and we'll present it to you.'"

So, Erickson and the Bucks took Alcindor out for lunch and let him go shopping for a couple of hours afterward, while they put their offer together. Ultimately, they decided on something that hadn't been done before and presented the UCLA star with a range of guaranteed packages ranging in length from one to five years. The salary went as high as $1.5 million, which was the highest ever offered. Not only had the Bucks gotten creative with the options, they also guaranteed all of the contracts, which was unheard of at the time.

"Lew liked [the offer] because it gave him some options," Erickson said. "He wasn't sure that he wanted to play in Milwaukee. He'd said that he preferred to play in Los Angeles or New York."

A few days after their meeting, Alcindor informed the Bucks he would be signing with them and joining the NBA. He would immediately turn the team into a contender, leading the Bucks to 56–26 record in his first season and an NBA championship in his second season.

Erickson left the Bucks after Alcindor's first season for a run at a United States senate seat, so he didn't get a championship ring in 1971. Despite that, Bucks fans should never forget the job Erickson did in helping create the franchise's best team.

# 78 John Hammond

After nine years at any job, it would be tough to have a single decision define your entire time with the organization, but that might be how fans view John Hammond's contribution to the Bucks.

After all, Hammond is the man who drafted Giannis Antetokounmpo.

He served as the general manager of the Bucks for five years before making that selection, but everyone will circle the chance he took on the rail-thin 18-year-old from Greece when reviewing his time in Milwaukee and his career in NBA front offices. Hammond has been asked about the selection many times since Antetokounmpo has blossomed into a star and each time he has been quick to dismiss any sort of special premonition he had of a skinny Greek kid becoming one of the league's best players.

"I wish I could say we knew he was going to be an All-Star at 22 years old," Hammond later told *The Sporting News*. "I wish we had known he was going to be this, but I don't proclaim to be that smart."

Despite his continued dismissal of the idea, it is hard for people to believe that Hammond finding an All-NBA player with the 15th overall selection of the 2013 NBA Draft was blind luck. He insists, however, that they just went through their typical process and Antetokounmpo built on the skills he flashed less frequently at a younger age.

His explanation makes quite a bit more sense when considering the entirety of his résumé as general manager in Milwaukee. While Antetokounmpo was a great pick, Hammond also had some misses in the draft, including his very first selection, Joe Alexander. Overall, Hammond did pretty well in the first round with some misses in the second round, which is no different than most other general managers.

Hammond's other biggest hit came on a trade during the summer of 2013. After a disappointing 2012–13 season, Bucks point guard Brandon Jennings entered restricted free agency and Hammond had a decision to make. Sign him? Let him walk? Neither. Hammond decided to move Jennings to the Detroit Pistons, the team he worked for before coming to Milwaukee, in a sign-and-trade deal for point guard Brandon Knight and Khris Middleton.

The deal looked good quickly as Knight put together a solid 2013–14 season, leading the Bucks in scoring. The team as a whole struggled with just 15 wins, but Knight looked good, as did Middleton. The 6-foot-8 shooting guard appeared in all 82 games and averaged 12 points per game, while shooting 40 percent from behind the three-point line. As the years went on, the Bucks moved on from Knight and ultimately traded him before they had to extend his contract, but Middleton stuck around and developed into a much better player. In Middleton's sixth season (his fifth in Milwaukee), the player many saw as just another guy turned into a 20-point scorer for the Bucks.

Both the selection of Antetokounmpo and trading for Middleton were moves that brought talented players to Milwaukee who could help a future version of the team as they developed, but even combined they might not be Hammond's most complete season performance.

In 2010, John Hammond won NBA Executive of the Year, deserved recognition after the Bucks improved from 34 wins to a playoff appearance with a 46–36 record in Hammond's second season with the organization. To start the off-season, Hammond selected Brandon Jennings with the 10th pick of the draft and he ended up being the team's starting point guard and one of the league's best rookies. In January, veteran Jerry Stackhouse joined the squad and revived his career with solid play throughout the second half.

At the trade deadline, the Bucks traded for veteran guard John Salmons, who ended up adding nearly 20 points per game in the second half of the season and helped the Bucks put together an 18–8 record to close out the regular season. They were hit with serious injuries—season-ending injuries for Michael Redd and Andrew Bogut—during the season, but they kept winning and used their depth to adjust throughout the season.

Hammond's tenure was not without misses. In the draft, first-round picks were spent on non-contributors like Alexander and Rashad Vaughn. In the summer, Hammond gave overstuffed contracts to marginal contributors such as Drew Gooden, O.J. Mayo, and Miles Plumlee. In trades, there were multiple times where the Bucks took on questionable pieces—Corey Maggette, Stephen Jackson, and Greivis Vasquez, to name a few—or gave up too soon on young players like Tobias Harris or draft picks in general.

Yet, in the end, a championship from an Antetokounmpo-led Bucks squad would earn John Hammond a very special place in the hearts of all Bucks fans.

# 79 The "Fear the Deer" Court

Look good. Feel good. Play good.

A number of NBA players subscribe to the theory and the Bucks took it to new lengths in 2015 with their alternate court. That's right—a second court painted with a different color scheme used only for certain games.

"The idea has always been to take the fan experience to the next level," Bucks vice-president of marketing Dustin Godsey told ESPN. "We rebranded with the alternate uniforms, but other teams have done that."

No one else had ever done it before the Bucks decided to do it in 2015. And they fully committed to the new idea, with alternate jerseys that matched the alternate court as part of "Fear the Deer Nights." The announcement came as a surprise to fans because the Bucks had already unveiled new jerseys over the summer.

In June 2015, the Bucks revealed the sixth iteration of their jerseys in franchise history at the team's annual Summer Block Party. This version would change up the color scheme and utilize Good Land Green, Cream City Cream, and Great Lakes Blue, with black and white also included in the official color palette. Green would remain as it has throughout the entirety of Bucks history, but the secondary colors have changed over the years.

In 1968, the Bucks started with green, white, and red. Green with white numbers and red trim on the road, white with green numbers and red trim at home. The uniforms utilized a basic all-caps font style, but the NBA was still getting a foothold and extravagant jerseys were not something the rest of the league did very often.

The Bucks' first jersey change came for the 1973–74 season as the team decided to use a script font to spell out MILWAUKEE on the road jerseys and BUCKS on the home jerseys. They also opted to use red numbers, which used green trim at home and white trim on the road.

Those jerseys lasted just three seasons before the Bucks moved back to an all-caps font style and also added an Irish rainbow—a color-block pattern on the side of the jerseys adorned with three different shades of green, as well as white. The away jerseys were green with red numbers and white trim with the Irish rainbow on the side, while the home white jerseys further incorporated the green by using green numbers and light-green trim with the red removed completely.

In 1993, the Bucks veered in a totally different direction by replacing the red with purple and also added silver to their color scheme, along with the classic forest green. The Bucks also unveiled a new logo, a realistic deer torso and head in front of a purple triangle and a MILWAUKEE BUCKS wordmark in front of everything. Then-head coach and president of basketball operations Mike Dunleavy was inspired by the purple-and-green combination he saw at Wimbledon. The road jerseys were purple with green numbers and silver trim, while the home jerseys were white with green numbers and purple trim and side piping. They also featured a third, alternate jersey with an actual deer on the front of them in the most 1990s way possible.

The purple disappeared again in 2006 when the Bucks brought back the red. The Bucks' fifth batch of jerseys was a return to a very traditional look, with green away jerseys featuring white numbers and red trim, and the home jerseys getting green numbers and red trim. The third, alternate jersey was red with white numbers and green trim.

Because alternate jerseys had swept through the league almost a decade earlier, it was no surprise to Bucks fans when the Bucks announced an alternate jersey to go with their new set unveiled in October 2015. The surprise came in them being black. It was the first time in team history the Bucks had a black jersey and they even splashed the new deer head logo on the front of the uniform to create an entirely different look.

To match black jerseys, the Bucks needed a new court, so they made one. And thus, the first NBA alternate court was born.

# 80 Bucks in the Olympics

While players are proud to throw on their Bucks jersey each night they step on the floor, they feel an even greater level of pride when they are able to wear the colors of their country.

These 19 Bucks players all competed for their respective countries in at least one Olympic Games: Ray Allen, Vin Baker, Andrew Bogut, Bob Boozer, Quinn Buckner, Adrian Dantley,

Carlos Delfino, Matthew Dellavedova, Jeff Grayer, Ernie Grunfeld, Richard Jefferson, Yi Jianlian, Toni Kukoc, Gary Payton, Miroslav Raduljica, Michael Redd, J.R. Reid, Alvin Robertson, and Oscar Robertson.

The first Bucks at the Olympics were Bob Boozer and Oscar Robertson. Boozer actually waited a year to turn pro after being drafted by the Cincinnati Royals in 1959 in order to maintain his eligibility for the 1960 Olympics. It would be a worthwhile decision for Boozer as he took home a gold medal before playing with the "Big O" again in Cincinnati. Ultimately, both players would become Bucks late in their careers and win the 1971 NBA Finals together.

Buckner, Dantley, and Grunfeld all won their gold medals in the 1976 Olympics. It was an important victory for the U.S. after the team had controversially dropped the gold medal game to the Soviets in 1972. Buckner and Grunfeld were each first-round draft picks by the Bucks, while Dantley spent just 10 games with the team at the end of his career.

Allen, Baker, Payton, and Redd took home gold in their respective Olympics, with Allen and Redd being the only two of the four to be members of the Bucks at the time they went to the Olympics in 2008.

Unfortunately, Grayer, Jefferson, and Reid were all members of American teams that fell short of their ultimate goal of a gold medal. Grayer and Reid were both members of the bronze medal winners in 1988, with Grayer going 13th in the 1988 NBA Draft to the Bucks and Reid not becoming a member of the team until the 1999–2000 season. Jefferson won bronze in 2004, when the United States fell to an Argentinian team led by future Hall of Famer Manu Ginobili.

Delfino, one of the many Bucks players to play for a team other than the United States in Olympic competition, was also on that Argentinian team. He ended up participating in four Olympics

(2004, 2008, 2012, 2016), while also winning a second medal in 2008 as he helped lead Argentina's "Golden Generation" to a bronze medal. Though he added a bronze to his collection, Delfino is the only non-American Bucks player to win a gold medal.

Kukoc cut his teeth in international competition as he prepared for life in the NBA as a 19-year-old playing for Yugoslavia in the 1988 Olympics. Yugoslavia won the silver medal in that year's competition. Kukoc also won silver in 1992 playing for the newly independent Croatian team. He would participate in his third Olympics in 1996, all of which happened before he became a member of the Bucks in 2002.

No Bucks player has participated in more Olympic basketball tournaments than Jianlian, as he managed to rack up four Olympics appearances for China in 2004, 2008, 2012, and 2016. The Chinese team did not win a medal in any of Jianlian's appearances, but his 24 games played in the Olympics is the most by any Bucks player.

Raduljica is rare among the rest of the Bucks' non-American Olympians in that he has only appeared in one Olympics, appearing for Serbia in 2016.

Finally, the Bucks' most famous Olympic participants might be their pair from Down Under, Bogut and Dellavedova. Both are unabashedly Australian and actually got the chance to play together in the 2016 Olympics and forged an impressive bit of chemistry together, with Dellavedova finding Bogut on alley-oops throughout the tournament. The elder Bogut has played in three Olympics, with his only missed tournament coming because of an injury.

# 81 Shoot a Skyhook

Just about any time two people get together to get a few shots up, a game of H-O-R-S-E breaks out. Inevitably, someone will grab the ball, place their shoulders perpendicular to the rim, extend their arm out as far as possible, and give it a try.

The Skyhook.

It'll likely clank off the rim and that's okay, maybe even expected, because only one person has ever perfected the shot. Aside from any variation of the dunk or the layup, it's the most unstoppable shot in the history of basketball, and Kareem Abdul-Jabbar is the only player to ever master it.

"I've worked on it," Memphis Grizzlies All-NBA center Marc Gasol told Yahoo Sports. "It's hard to be that consistent with it. And I have good touch. It's hard to stop, but it's just such a hard shot. For him to be that consistent and that efficient with it, there's a reason he's the only guy to do it that well."

With NBA All-Stars struggling to figure out how to shoot it, it should come as no surprise that Abdul-Jabbar didn't just add it to his repertoire overnight. He adopted the shot around the fifth grade when he started to play because as he got better at the game in his hometown of New York City, he started to play older players. With taller and stronger players, he somehow needed to find a way to get shots off, and thus, he started using the Skyhook.

"It was the only shot I could shoot that didn't get smashed back in my face," Abdul-Jabbar told ESPN. "So I learned to rely on it early, and it was always something that I could get off, even in traffic."

Quickly, Abdul-Jabbar found it to be a powerful weapon. And he used and practiced it for pretty much the entirety of his time on a basketball court. Eventually, he told reporters he credited George Mikan for the ability to shoot the shot because of all the time he spent on the Mikan Drill—consisting of shooting a hook shot from the right side with the right hand, then a hook from the left side with the left hand, and repeating while slowly moving further away from the basket—throughout his childhood.

Abdul-Jabbar dominated the high school and college ranks before joining the Bucks in the 1969 NBA Draft, and it was in Milwaukee where the Skyhook actually got its name. What everyone knows as the Skyhook now was once just a hook shot until Bucks announcer Eddie Doucette got a hold of it.

Known for his fanciful turns of phrase and ability to nickname just about anything on a basketball court, Doucette soon came to call Abdul-Jabbar's most powerful weapon the Skyhook. As he tells it, the first time he used the term came in Game 6 of the 1974 Eastern Conference Finals on the shot that won the Bucks the game, quite possibly the most famous Skyhook ever made. The truth is Doucette had used the term for years before that game, but describing that particular Skyhook as a divine moment of inspiration just felt right. It was an unbelievable shot in an impossible situation with Celtics defenders surrounding Abdul-Jabbar.

"When you shoot it, you force people to wait for you to go up," Abdul-Jabbar later told ESPN. "And if they wait until I started to shoot it then they'd have to judge the distance and time it, and it's gone before they can catch up to it. That's, for me, the beauty of it. You're in control because of when you're gonna release it and where. The defense has to see that and calculate everything before they get an opportunity to block it."

In that moment, none of the Celtics on the floor could touch it and it went through the basket to win the Bucks the game. That is how it would go for defenders for the 15 years that followed. No

one could block it. And no one has ever successfully replicated it…
except you, in the driveway or at your local gym.

Go ahead. Grab a ball and put one up.

# 82 Larry Harris

It was a long-time coming for Larry Harris in Milwaukee.

In 1990, he got his start with the Bucks as a scout and the team's video coordinator under his father, Del Harris, the team's head coach at the time. A few years later, he transitioned into a position as a scout only. Eventually, that led to Harris taking over as director of scouting in 1996, then director of player personnel in 1998, and finally all the way up to assistant general manager in 2001 for then-general manager Ernie Grunfeld.

When Grunfeld left for the general manager positions with the Washington Wizards, Bucks owner Herb Kohl tabbed Harris as the man to serve as acting general manager on June 29, 2003, before making it official on July 1. Harris lasted five seasons as Milwaukee's GM before being let go on March 19, 2008.

"I don't want it to be forgotten what Senator Kohl did for me," Harris told the assembled media after his release, while struggling to keep his composure before and after the statement.

Even though Kohl was the man to relieve Harris of his duties, he couldn't help but get emotional when speaking of the man who hired and fired him. It wasn't just that Kohl had given him the chance as general manager; Kohl was the man signing his checks for the entirety of his career in basketball.

But it just didn't work out for Harris as general manager as he attempted to steward the Bucks through some tough times after the best team in more than a decade—the Big Three Bucks—came and went with Grunfeld and George Karl, who would leave (as expected) three weeks after Harris took over.

After Karl left, Harris continued the house cleaning and requested waivers on Anthony Mason and Jason Caffey, two of the big men Grunfeld unsuccessfully brought in to help the Bucks move to the next level. Harris also moved Tim Thomas and Joel Przybilla in his first season on the job at the trade deadline in February 2004, which essentially removed just about every major contributor to the 2000–01 team that made the Eastern Conference Finals.

The cuts and trades clearly showed Harris wanted to move on from the previous era, but he would not make the moves that defined his time as general manager until the summer of 2005. In a great stroke of luck, the Bucks won the 2005 NBA Draft lottery and the opportunity to draft a franchise-defining player with the first pick in the draft. Harris selected University of Utah center Andrew Bogut.

Michael Redd spent the first week of free agency chatting with other teams before Harris signed him to the maximum contract permitted, a six-year, $91 million deal, which kept him from joining LeBron James and the Cleveland Cavaliers. Along with Redd, Harris made an unexpected splash by signing Bobby Simmons. Simmons had just won the Most Improved Player of the Year award for the Los Angeles Clippers and appeared poised for an even bigger breakout season.

The same could be said of center Dan Gadzuric. He started 81 games in his third NBA season in the 2004–05 season and averaged just seven points and eight rebounds in 22 minutes per game, but plenty of people, especially Harris, were excited about what the future held for the 26-year-old big man.

Each of the signings ultimately defined Harris' time as general manager and the 2000s in general. Nobody could fault Harris for taking Bogut, but Deron Williams and Chris Paul would be selected third and fourth overall and go on to have much bigger impacts early in their careers. Bogut would end up playing great in 2009 and 2010, but Harris was already gone by the time he did.

Redd simply couldn't stay healthy during the rest of his time in Milwaukee. Redd played in just 266 of a potential 492 games during the length of his six-year contract with the Bucks with much of his effectiveness in those games sapped because of his chronic knee problems. After a strong first season in Milwaukee, an ankle injury cost Simmons his second season with the Bucks and eventually stalled out his career. And Gadzuric started just 44 games during the entirety of his contract.

The Bucks signed other free agents, drafted other players, and executed other trades, but the summer of 2005 helps explain why the Bucks were unable to find success in the first decade of the 21st century and why Harris ultimately made way for John Hammond as general manager.

# 83 Mo Williams' Game-Winner

The call from Jim Paschke and Jon McGlocklin on the Bucks' television broadcast wasn't incredibly clear. Over the years, McGlocklin has apologized to Paschke, his play-by-play man, for getting too excited and yelling too much over the top of his buzzer-beater calls. He was certainly guilty of just that on this night, but after the cacophony of competing calls, one statement was clear as Jim Paschke declared the Bucks' win "a masterful use of the foul-and-chase."

With seven seconds remaining, Pacers guard Fred Jones stepped to the line with the game tied at 100–100. He hit his first free throw, but missed his second attempt. Jermaine O'Neal was able to tip it at the basket, but it missed everything before Bucks forward Bobby Simmons corralled it on the baseline. He took a dribble up the floor before passing it to guard Mo Williams. Williams dribbled up the left side of the floor and released a three from about 30 feet out. It plunged through the net as time expired and gave the Bucks a 103–101 victory.

"I felt like they would play for the drive," Williams told reporters after the game. "Rather than shoot the tough shot, I tried a shot I know I can make. That's a lot of credit to us that we came back on a great team like that."

With 3:39 left in the game, the Bucks trailed 95–82 after a Jones dunk and it looked like all was lost, but they kept fighting and managed to come back. Indiana gave them a major assist by hitting just 6-of-16 from the free throw line in the final two minutes, but the Bucks still made the shots they needed to down the stretch and stole one from the Pacers.

In the summer of 2004, Bucks general manager Larry Harris signed Williams, a restricted free agent, to an offer sheet and the Utah Jazz decided not to match the offer on their 2003 second-round pick. It came somewhat as a surprise, as Williams had appeared in 53 games as a rookie and showed a couple flashes of being a capable NBA player, but the Jazz decided the offer sheet was too rich and allowed him to come to Milwaukee.

T.J. Ford was the Bucks' starting point guard in the previous season, but missed the entire 2004–05 season with a spinal cord injury. Williams could have just been nice insurance for the lightning-quick Ford, but ended up starting all 80 games he appeared in and putting together a really solid season. In his first year as a Buck, the 22-year-old point guard averaged 10 points and six assists per game.

Williams' big shot against the Pacers didn't end up being a legendary, one-time occurrence either, as he hit a number of big shots during his time in Milwaukee. He quickly became one of the success stories during the middle of the 2000s as he continued to grow as a player. Ford was back from his injury in the 2005–06 season and Williams became part of a point guard tandem in Milwaukee, but new Bucks coach Terry Stotts became more fond of Williams by season's end. With playing time dwindling for Ford, Harris opted to trade Ford to Toronto for forward Charlie Villanueva.

With Ford out of the picture, Williams became the starting point guard and put up career highs in the 2006–07 season, averaging 17.3 points, 4.8 rebounds, and 6.1 assists per game. The following season Williams became a free agent but ultimately came back to Milwaukee on a six-year, $52 million deal. The Bucks' main competition in signing Williams was the Miami Heat, which could only sign him to a mid-level exception for roughly $5.3 million per year.

It was an overpay on Milwaukee's part, which is part of what makes Williams such a useful example of a Bucks player from the

*Mo Williams reacts after hitting a game-winning three-pointer at the buzzer to beat the Pacers in 2005.*

era. He played great in the next season, putting up nearly identical numbers, but new general manager John Hammond traded him to the Cleveland Cavaliers the following season in a three-team deal, which netted Milwaukee four players, two of which were on expiring contracts.

His time in Milwaukee was incredibly useful until his salary became too much for the team to swallow, and then he was traded away by new management. It was a story far too common while the team continued to try to put together a winner to pick up its first playoff series victory since 2001.

# 84 The Game That Just Wouldn't End

"I don't remember much other than at the time thinking, 'Good grief. Somebody please make a shot, or not make a shot, and end this stupid game,'" Bucks center Randy Breuer told VICE Sports.

In the end, that's essentially what happened on November 9, 1989. The Bucks beat the Seattle Supersonics 155–154 after five overtimes, the longest NBA game of the shot clock era. Even before the advent of the shot clock, only the Indianapolis Olympians and Rochester Royals put together a longer game, a six-overtime 75–73 "thriller" on January 6, 1951.

No matter how hard the Bucks and Sonics tried, they couldn't end the game, which is part of what made the game so compelling. After 48 minutes, the game was tied at 103–103. Five minutes later, it was tied at 110–110. Then, 120–120 after the second overtime period. Up to 127–127 after three overtimes. And finally, they were tied at 138–138 after four overtimes. The leads fluctuated throughout and each team had a couple chances to end the game.

The Bucks led 102–97 near the end of regulation, but the Sonics rattled off six unanswered points to take a 103–102 lead. Bucks forward Fred Roberts was fouled late and went to the line with a chance to give the Bucks a lead. He only hit one of his free throws to tie the game at 103–103 and send it to overtime.

With five seconds left in the third overtime, the Bucks were up 126–125 and the Sonics fouled Bucks center Jack Sikma. In his five seasons in Milwaukee, Sikma hit 88.4 of his free throws and had yet to miss a free throw (9-of-9) in the 1989–90 season. He went to the line and hit just one free throw. The Sonics went down to the other end, got the ball to Dale Ellis, and he hit a jumper to tie it and send it to a fourth overtime.

Ellis was incredible for the Sonics. He scored 53 points on 18-of-39 shooting and played 69 of a possible 73 minutes of the night. Sonics forward Xavier McDaniel played 68 minutes and scored 37 points. To this day, they remain atop the NBA leaderboard for most minutes played in an NBA game. Bucks point guard Jay Humphries is fifth with 62 minutes. Alvin Robertson is tied for 14th with 59 minutes on the night.

In the fourth overtime, the Sonics ran out to a five-point lead and looked to have a chance to finally end it, but Sikma made up for his earlier transgression with a three and Bucks wing Troy Brown hit a 20-footer to tie it back up at 136–136. Brown followed with another jumper to give the Bucks a 138–136 lead, but Ellis once again would bank in a 15-footer to knot it back up and send it to a fifth overtime.

Somehow, the two teams traded baskets for the first few minutes of the fifth overtime and rattled off a combined 16 points. With the game tied at 146–146, the Bucks went on a 9–0 run to take a 155–146 lead with 36 seconds left, which surely signaled the end of the marathon game.

Not so fast.

Seattle guard Dana Barros quickly hit a three. His teammate Nate McMillan was fouled after picking off a Jay Humphries pass and hit one of his two free throws with just over 15 seconds left. On the ensuing play, the Bucks inbounded the ball to Sikma, who threw it away with 12.7 seconds remaining. The Sonics missed a layup and two more tip-ins before Sedale Threatt hit an eight-foot jump shot to cut the Bucks lead to just 155–152 with 5.1 seconds left.

The Bucks called a timeout, which advanced the ball to the frontcourt. Brown inbounded from the sideline and turned it over. The Sonics rushed up the floor, but Humphries poked the ball out of bounds on the Sonics baseline with 0.8 seconds left. McDaniel caught the ball on the left wing and got a three-point attempt off, but missed the shot off the back rim.

The Bucks fouled him on the shot, but it didn't matter. Not because he couldn't hit free throws, but because players fouled on three-point attempts shot just two free throws until the NBA changed the rule in the 1994–95 season. If the game had been played 10 years later, it may have continued to a sixth overtime, but instead McDaniels hit his two free throws with no time remaining as the players walked off the floor and the game had finally ended.

Bucks 155, Sonics 154. Final (5OT).

On the night, eight Bucks players scored in double digits. Six of them played 40 or more minutes. Sikma tallied 23 points and Robertson had 28 of his own. Bucks sixth man Ricky Pierce led the way for the Bucks with 36 points on 15-of-21 shooting in 42 minutes on the night.

"I didn't even eat after that game," McDaniels told VICE Sports. "I went straight to my room and passed out. I was tired for seven days, it felt like we played for 24 hours straight."

It wasn't quite that long, but no one has played a longer game than those two teams on that night in the shot clock era.

# 85 Quinn Buckner

The first 20 years of Bucks basketball featured a whole lot of wins, even as they transitioned between coaches. That isn't always the easiest thing to do, but even as the Bucks moved from the Larry Costello era to the Don Nelson era, they managed to keep it together despite losing more games than normal.

To weather those storms, teams need to find players who can fit into a specific role and be counted on to execute their duties at a high level. In the latter portion of the 1970s, Bucks point guard Quinn Buckner served that position, keeping the Bucks consistent with steady play and leadership.

Despite being the seventh overall pick in the 1976 NBA Draft, Buckner didn't have quite the same cachet as his University of Indiana teammate Scott May, who was selected second overall. And the level of excitement for the Bucks just wasn't there either because they had just gone through their first season without Kareem Abdul-Jabbar.

Expectations for the team had changed and a point guard, even a national champion like Buckner, wasn't going to help the team get back to the same level of basketball they played when Abdul-Jabbar was around. In Buckner's first season, the Bucks won 30 games. In his second season, their win total increased to 44 in large thanks to No. 1 overall pick Kent Benson, No. 3 pick Marques Johnson, and No. 11 pick Ernie Grunfeld.

Much of the credit for the Bucks' improvement went to Johnson, who burst onto the scene as one of the league's young stars, but Buckner was there as well, contributing 9.3 points and a team-leading 5.6 assists in 25 minutes per game off the bench.

In his third season, Buckner's averages would remain modest, but he also added 1.9 steals per game as Nelson began finding a way to better use him as someone who could make it tough for opposing point guards off the bench. As the Bucks turned into one of the most feared defensive units in the league and began rattling off wins, Buckner was one of the major reasons why.

"Two years ago when Quinn pulled a hamstring and missed about 20 games, we nearly fell apart," Johnson told *Sports Illustrated* regarding the end of the 1979–80 season. "Until then I took him for granted, but it was obvious without him we were severely hurt."

Buckner was often taken for granted, but his impact could never be diminished. In his final four seasons in Milwaukee, Buckner led the Bucks in steals with over two per game and formed a dastardly, defensive combination with Sidney Moncrief after the Bucks drafted him with the fifth overall pick in the 1979 NBA Draft. Buckner also remained among the team's leaders in assists, finishing either first or second in each of his final four seasons in Milwaukee. He was never the star, but always an impactful player.

Before the 1982–83 season, Don Nelson decided to trade Buckner to the Boston Celtics for forward Dave Cowens, who had been retired for each of the previous two seasons. The move was met with much criticism, as no one knew what Cowens could still do, while Buckner had been a consistent contributor for years. Nelson even admitted the risk inherent in the move, but insisted on getting the Bucks more bulk in the middle.

When he was traded to the Celtics after six seasons with the Bucks, Buckner was the franchise leader in assists and steals. He has since moved down to fourth on the career assists list, but still remains the franchise's leader in steals. He was never viewed as a star, but Buckner ended up being one of the most important parts of the teams that set up the Bucks' success in the 1980s.

# 86 Jon Horst

On June 16, 2017, the Bucks named Jon Horst their 11th general manager. He would be taking over for John Hammond, who had left the organization on May 23, 2017, to join the Orlando Magic as their general manager.

Despite the announcement and confirmation Horst would be taking over, many fans were left to wonder exactly who Horst was and why he was chosen as general manager. He was not one of the six finalists the team interviewed 10 days earlier, and he was not one of the three finalists the team brought to Milwaukee the following week for further discussions.

As the week leading up to June 16 came to an end, one of the three finalists took another job, which left even less doubt the Bucks would hire Justin Zanik. He was the team's assistant general manager who had reportedly been hired the previous summer to take over for Hammond at the end of his contract in the summer of 2018. But on June 15, the Bucks interviewed Horst for the position and one day later decided he was the man for the job.

"The process may look like it's a little bit sloppy but at the end of the day, the result is what matters," Bucks owner Wes Edens said at Horst's introductory press conference. "We got the right guy for the job and there's not a lot of hand-wringing about what we could have done differently."

Though the interviewing and hiring of a general manager in just one day may have felt rushed, Edens assured fans they knew the 34-year-old Horst incredibly well and thus felt very comfortable with the hiring, even if things looked strange from the outside. Horst had been with the organization for nine years, joining the Bucks in May 2008 when he was brought in by Hammond.

Horst was used to working his way up the ladder. For three years in Detroit before Hammond came to Milwaukee, Horst worked for the Pistons' basketball operations staff. To help entice him to come to the Bucks, Hammond offered Horst the position of director of basketball operations. Horst accepted the job and spent the next nine years in that position.

During his time in that role, Horst developed into one of the most trusted members of the team's front office. Horst took part in many of the biggest decisions, including participating in scouting, draft room discussions, contract negotiations, and personnel evaluation.

He would be tested almost immediately because the 2017 NBA Draft was set to take place just six days after he was hired, and free agency just a week after that.

The first year as general manager ended up being very busy for Horst. In the draft, he selected Michigan forward D.J. Wilson with the 17th pick before selling the 48th selection in the draft and buying the 46th pick (for less than he sold the later pick) and selecting Southern Methodist University guard Sterling Brown. Wilson appeared in just 22 games for the Bucks for a total of 69 minutes and struggled to find time on the floor for much of his rookie season. Brown played nearly 800 minutes in 54 appearances.

In free agency, the Bucks didn't really have the ability to make many moves because of a lack of cap space, but did have the rights to restricted free agent Tony Snell. Horst signed Snell to a three-year deal with a fourth-year player option worth $46 million.

Horst's biggest player personnel move came less than a month into the season when he moved center Greg Monroe, a first-round pick, and a second-round pick to the Phoenix Suns for point guard Eric Bledsoe. After a month or so of integration, the Bucks and Bledsoe grew accustomed to each other and the team's new point guard became more efficient as his comfort with his teammates grew.

Before all of that could happen, though, Horst and the Bucks fired head coach Jason Kidd. With 50-win expectations for the season, the organization did not believe they were doing well enough for their lofty goals with Horst saying, "It just felt like we were standing still when we should be climbing." The Bucks were 23–22 at the time of the firing.

Through a year of work, Horst made a couple serious moves in drafting two players, completing a significant trade, and firing a coach, but only time will tell just how productive Horst can be in the role. In the summer of 2018, he hired former Atlanta coach Mike Budenholzer to take over on the bench and also had a serious decision to make on Jabari Parker's next contract. Welcome to the life of an NBA general manager.

# 87 Ernie Grunfeld

Sometimes, winning isn't enough. At least it wasn't for Ernie Grunfeld in New York.

Grunfeld served as the Knicks' general manager from 1993 to 1999, when the Bucks hired him to be their new GM on August 13, 1999.

Oddly enough, the Knicks team Grunfeld had assembled went to the NBA Finals in the lockout-shortened 1998–99 season, but he had been fired with eight games left before any future result could coalesce. Grunfeld caught considerable flack for signing Allan Houston in 1996, as well as a number of his other acquisitions, which resulted in a team full of what many viewed as big egos who eventually put it together to go to the NBA Finals. He also didn't have the best relationship with Knicks head coach Jeff Van Gundy, which surely didn't help the situation.

Grunfeld replaced Bob Weinhauer in Milwaukee, who had been fired earlier in the week after two years as general manager. It was a déjà vu scenario in Milwaukee, as the Bucks actually hired coach George Karl before hiring a general manager instead of vice-versa. (The team had done the same thing in the past, hiring Larry Costello to be its inaugural coach before hiring John Erickson to be the GM.) Karl was given the opportunity to serve in both positions but declined, preferring to not be held responsible for general manager duties. However, multiple sources reported he would retain final say on all personnel matters.

Being able to retain full personnel power without the day-to-day duties of an NBA general manager allowed Karl to avoid a common pitfall among those who have tried to do both jobs, as Mike Dunleavy did in the 1990s in Milwaukee, while still wielding maximum power. The distinction would also be important when later on Karl could deflect some of the blame for poor decisions.

For example, during the 2001–02 season the Bucks decided to trade Ray Allen. Karl did not get along with his star and wanted to trade him. It ended up being the most regrettable trade of Herb Kohl's time as owner. When asked about it nearly 15 years later, Karl shifted at least partial responsibility to the other two notable men in the front office.

"When the Senator and [general manager] Ernie Grunfeld decided that would be the best thing for our team, at that moment I was okay with it," Karl told the *Milwaukee Journal Sentinel* years later. "It wasn't one of those feel-good trades."

With just a single answer, Karl cast doubt on who exactly made the move, even though his poor relationship with Allen was well documented. It's also the type of quote that gets at the larger tension of Grunfeld's time with the Bucks: he was the general manager and helped put together a strong roster, but his work is hard to grade without knowing exactly who was pulling the strings.

With Grunfeld working together with Karl, the Bucks made a number of the moves that led them to an Eastern Conference Finals appearance in 2001. After the 2000 season, they moved Vinny Del Negro, J.R. Reid, and Robert "Tractor" Traylor in a three-team deal for Jason Caffey and Billy Owens. Caffey would go on to appear in 70 games and start in 33 of them as the Bucks won 52 games in the 2000–01 season. During that same off-season, they traded Owens, a career journeyman, to the Detroit Pistons for Lindsey Hunter, who ended up becoming one of their most essential players off the bench. Each of those moves helped make the Bucks a contender.

Grunfeld and Karl wanted to find a way to make a move to push the team over the top in the Eastern Conference. For that, they turned to someone Grunfeld knew extremely well, Anthony Mason. In the 2000–01 season, Mason made his first All-Star appearance as a member of the Miami Heat, but Grunfeld knew him from his days with the Knicks and thought he'd be the perfect guy to give the Bucks a little more toughness and an extra edge.

It didn't work out.

Mason didn't find the same level of success and became a problem in the locker room. The team went just 41–41 and missed the playoffs and the Bucks started making moves. On August 2, 2002, Karl decided to trade away one of the members of the Big Three, Glenn Robinson. At the trade deadline in February 2003, they traded away the second member of the Big Three, Ray Allen. And after the season, they finished the job by trading away Sam Cassell.

With rumors of Kohl selling the Bucks to Michael Jordan reverberating around the basketball world, Grunfeld opted for a new job as general manager of the Washington Wizards. When he left, Grunfeld had been a part of assembling and disassembling the best Bucks team in decades.

# 88 Play as the Bucks in *NBA Jam*

In 1993, *NBA Jam* took the world by storm—or at least the arcade world.

American video game developer and publisher Midway Games released *NBA Jam*, an over-the-top basketball game featuring actual NBA players from each NBA team somersaulting in the air for fantastical dunks, shattered backboards, and a basketball that caught on fire if you hit three shots in a row. It featured the actual names and likenesses of real players playing two-on-two with an imaginative form of basketball and people loved it.

Well, maybe just people who didn't feel obligated to play with the Bucks.

The first version of *NBA Jam* was released in April 1993. In the 1992–93 season, Mike Dunleavy's first as head coach, the Bucks went just 28–54 and finished the season with the league's sixth-worst record. On top of that, their pair of highly drafted rookies from the University of Arkansas, Todd Day and Lee Mayberry, had yet to make an impression on the rest of the league. So, the game's developers assigned the team's leading scorer, Blue Edwards, and one of its big men, Brad Lohaus, to be the Bucks avatars.

The 1992–93 season would be Edwards' best in the NBA, as he put career highs in points (16.9), rebounds (4.7), and assists (2.6) per game. Before breaking out with the Bucks, Edwards had put together three solid, if unspectacular, seasons in Utah, but nothing like he did in the 1992–93 season.

Lohaus, on the other hand, is an even more surprising inclusion. The 6-foot-11 forward out of the University of Iowa was in his seventh NBA season and ended the season sixth in scoring average for the Bucks. He led the team with 0.9 blocks per game, but hardly seemed like a large enough impact maker to make the game's roster. Now, there may be some credence to the theory that developers were just trying to find a big man to include, but even if that was the case, Frank Brickowski was putting together a better season with 17 points and six rebounds per game.

In the end, any criticism of player selection from the Bucks roster should be minimal because the Bucks simply didn't have a great roster that season.

So, the thing you need to do is play *NBA Jam: Tournament Edition*. Though you are more than welcome to play with Edwards and Lohaus, finding the second edition of the game might lead to a more enjoyable experience for Bucks fans.

*NBA Jam: Tournament Edition* came out a year later with the Bucks' squad composed of three new players: Vin Baker, Todd Day, and Eric Murdock. Baker, a rookie out of the tiny University of Hartford, didn't end up winning Rookie of the Year in 1994, but he was named to the All-Rookie First Team on 13.5 points and 7.6 rebounds per game averages, which was more than enough to earn inclusion in the game.

While Day might not have been quite strong enough to warrant inclusion in the game the first time around, improving to 12 points and four rebounds per game impressed the developers enough for Day to see a digital version of himself shattering backboards and ripping nets.

Like Edwards, Murdock came to Milwaukee in a trade from the Utah Jazz before the 1992–93 season. He didn't score quite as much as Edwards in that season, but he did put together a solid year, starting 78 games in his second NBA season. He made a jump for his career-best season the next year, with 15.3 points and 6.7 assists per game and a spot on the Bucks squad.

On top of those three, *NBA Jam: Tournament Edition* also featured the man the Bucks selected with the first pick of the 1994 NBA Draft, Glenn Robinson. Robinson is not a member of the

Bucks—he is just on the larger squad of Rookies placed in the game—but at least he's there.

So, go find your local arcade or dig your gaming console out of the attic and spend the next couple hours playing *NBA Jam: Tournament Edition.*

# 89 Take a Trip to the Basketball Hall of Fame

If you're reading this book, you are probably a big fan of the Milwaukee Bucks. If you're a big fan of the Milwaukee Bucks, you are probably a big fan of the game of basketball. If you're a big fan of the game of basketball, you probably need to go to the Naismith Memorial Basketball Hall of Fame in Springfield, Massachusetts, at some point in your life.

While there, you should track down every piece of Bucks memorabilia you can find and also attempt to find every connection to the team that you can. (In case you're curious, there is a pair of size-22 shoes from Bucks center Bob Lanier among any number of Bucks-related pieces throughout the Hall.) Here is a quick rundown of every player, coach, and contributor officially inducted into the Hall of Fame.

Let's start with the headliners:

**Kareem Abdul-Jabbar,** one of the greatest basketball players in the history of the game, spent his first six seasons in Milwaukee and led the Bucks to their lone NBA championship in 1971, as well as another Finals appearance in 1974. Three NBA MVP awards. Named one of the NBA's 50 Greatest Players in 1996.

**Oscar Robertson** ended his career in Milwaukee and partnered with Abdul-Jabbar to help the Bucks win the franchise's lone NBA championship. He spent the first 10 seasons of his career in

Cincinnati, but because of the success he found in Milwaukee, many people remember him as a Buck. Named one of the NBA's 50 Greatest Players in 1996.

**Don Nelson,** the winningest coach in NBA history, compiled the first 540 of his 1,335 all-time wins in Milwaukee. With the Bucks, Nelson became the fastest NBA coach to 500 wins (a mark later beat by Pat Riley). His winning percentage in Milwaukee was .611 in 11 seasons.

**Wayne Embry** became the first African American general manager in the history of the NBA when he was hired by the Bucks in 1972.

**Ray Allen** made more three-point baskets than anyone in NBA history and he got started in Milwaukee when the Bucks acquired him in a draft night trade. Allen played for the Bucks for the first six and a half years of his career before being traded to Seattle.

Next, the legends who spent a brief period in Milwaukee:

**Nate "Tiny" Archibald** made his name with the Kings, won a championship with the Celtics, and ended his career in Milwaukee.

**Dave Cowens** retired following the 1979–80 season after 10 years with the Boston Celtics before ultimately deciding to return to the NBA for a season with the Bucks two years after initially retiring.

**Adrian Dantley** made his way to the Hall of Fame thanks to his time with the Utah Jazz and Detroit Pistons, but ended his career with 10 games in the 1990–91 season with the Bucks.

**Alex English,** one of the most prolific scorers of the 1980s, played his first two seasons with the Bucks before being traded to Indiana and then to Denver, where he developed into a Hall of Famer.

**Bob Lanier** eventually got his jersey retired by the Bucks despite playing just four and a half seasons for them in the twilight of his career.

**Moses Malone** played the 18th and 19th seasons of his 21-year career in Milwaukee.

**Gary Payton** played just 28 games in Milwaukee in the 2001–02 season after he was traded to the Bucks for Ray Allen. He signed as a free agent with the Lakers after the season.

**Guy Rodgers** served as the one of the league's most potent playmakers of the 1960s with the Warriors, but ultimately ended his career with two years in Milwaukee after the Bucks selected him in the 1968 NBA Expansion Draft.

And finally, the coaching connections:

**K.C. Jones** is known around the world as a Celtic because of his time in Boston as both a player and coach, but few remember he served as an assistant coach for the Bucks in the 1976–77 season with his former Celtics teammate Don Nelson. Nelson took over as head coach 18 games into the season and Jones moved back to Boston to be Bill Fitch's lead assistant.

**Jason Kidd** coached the Bucks for three and a half seasons before getting fired during the 2017–18 season, but his inclusion in the Hall of Fame was clearly based on his skills as a player.

**Hubie Brown** served as a Bucks assistant coach from 1972 to 1974. Eventually, he'd be honored as a contributor to the game for all of the work he did as a player, coach, and broadcaster.

# 90 Alton Lister

When announcing his retirement following the 1983–84 season, Bucks legend Bob Lanier joked with reporters that he was leaving because the Bucks finally found someone who could fill his shoes.

He was speaking both metaphorically and literally.

Lanier famously wore size-22 shoes, the same size as his assumed heir apparent, Alton Lister. The Bucks were hopeful that Lister would provide a reasonable facsimile of the player Lanier had played in the final few seasons of his career.

The Bucks drafted Lister with the 21st overall pick of the 1981 NBA Draft, three years before Lanier's retirement. The 22-year-old center from Arizona State University was an insurance policy of sorts for Lanier, who they knew had bad knees. In fact, on the day Lister was introduced to the Milwaukee media, Lanier underwent successful knee surgery. Bucks coach and general manager Don Nelson thought Lister could serve as an apprentice to Lanier as the rookie learned from one of the best in the business.

"[Lister] has a tremendous amount of ability and talent," Nelson said during Lister's introductory press conference. "Through the years of learning the pro game, he will develop and be a big part of what we're trying to do in Milwaukee."

In his rookie season, Lister appeared in 80 games on a 55-win Bucks team and actually contributed to an Eastern Conference contender, which cannot often be said of a young player, especially one drafted to a team as talented as the Bucks. Lister averaged just 4.5 points and 4.8 rebounds per game, but he blocked 1.5 shots per game, which is where he would end up making his biggest impact as a Buck.

In Lister's second season, Nelson used him even more and he started almost half the season at center, with Lanier appearing in just 39 games because of injuries. Lister improved his rim protection skills and bumped his tally up to 2.2 blocks per game, a top-10 NBA mark. He even received an MVP vote as the Bucks went to the Eastern Conference Finals.

With his success in the 1982–83 season filling in for Lanier, Nelson moved Lister into the starting lineup the following season— not in front of Lanier, but alongside him. The young center did not enjoy playing power forward and openly complained to Nelson about it. The coach dealt with it for a while before benching Lister and inserting Randy Breuer into the starting lineup for a month. In spite of his irritation at starting at power forward, Lister managed to put together another solid season and posted the best defensive rating (points per 100 possessions) in the entire league.

Lanier retired after the season, which finally opened a starting role for Lister at center, his preferred position. Again, the Arizona State product blocked a whole bunch of shots as the starter in a three-man rotation that included Breuer and Paul Mokeski. He started 80 games for Nelson and blocked 2.1 shots per game, seventh-most in the league.

He played one more season in Milwaukee, averaging 10 points, seven rebounds, and 1.8 blocks per game, before Nelson packaged him with a couple of first-round picks for Seattle Supersonics center Jack Sikma. By the time Lister left Milwaukee, he was the franchise leader in blocks with 744.

Now, this can be a contentious distinction for many franchises around the league because blocks were not officially recorded until the 1973–74 season and that is no different in Milwaukee. Kareem Abdul-Jabbar posted 495 blocks in just two seasons, a number good for seventh on the all-time list, so it's fair to assume Abdul-Jabbar would be the team's leader if blocks had been recorded officially for the entirety of his career.

Lister returned to Milwaukee in the 1994–95 season after a season abroad in Italy and found himself in the opposite role he'd served during his first Milwaukee tenure: as a mentor and veteran presence. While he was not a future Hall of Famer like Lanier, he did put together a solid career and came to Milwaukee at least partially to help a young Vin Baker. A month into his second season, Lister was added to a trade that sent Todd Day to Boston and brought Sherman Douglas back to Milwaukee. In just over a year, Lister had served his role as a veteran leader, but also added 60 more blocks to get to 804 blocks in his Bucks career, a number no one has been able to match quite yet.

# 91 Get to Know Mike Budenholzer

On May 21, 2018, the Bucks introduced Mike Budenholzer as the 16th head coach in franchise history at their brand-new arena. Both figuratively and literally, it was the start of a new era of Bucks basketball.

"Since the moment we all said yes to each other, nothing's felt more right," Budenholzer said at the introductory press conference. "I think there's a genuine excitement about where we can go, a genuine understanding of how much work we have to put in to get there, and that focus on getting better every day individually and collectively."

Budenholzer joined the Bucks after five seasons with the Atlanta Hawks. In his first head coaching gig in Atlanta, Budenholzer put together a .520 winning percentage and made three playoff trips. The highlight of his time in Atlanta was a 60-win season in the 2014–15 season, highlighted by four Hawks making the All-Star Game and a trip to the Eastern Conference Finals.

Before getting hired in Atlanta, Budenholzer spent 17 seasons in San Antonio, where he won four NBA championships as an assistant to Spurs head coach Gregg Popovich. Much like the Spurs, the Hawks under Budenholzer found contributions from players up and down the roster and developed young players into difference-makers. Using some of the things he learned from Popovich, Budenholzer and his staff quickly developed "Hawks University," the term coined for their player development work, which seemed to churn out starters and role players regularly in Atlanta.

"I was very, very fortunate to be so close to a coach who's done so much for the league, done so much for so many coaches, and has shared so much with me," Budenholzer said of his time with Popovich while accepting the NBA Coach of the Year award after the 2014–15 season. "And I can't even begin to articulate how thankful I am and all the things I've learned."

One of the other things Budenholzer learned from Popovich was a focus on defensive fundamentals, something he demonstrated clearly in Atlanta. The Hawks finished in the top seven of defensive efficiency in three of his five seasons and it was something Budenholzer emphasized throughout his introductory press conference in Milwaukee, even going so far as to mention creating an elite defense in his first season.

When asked why he felt so confident about his new team's defensive potential, his optimism started with one man: Giannis Antetokounmpo.

"I think if you just look at some of the individuals and if you want to just single out a few of them...Giannis," Budenholzer said. "I think what Giannis can do defensively, the uniqueness of him, it's on that end of the court that I think the potential for him to be an elite defender is obvious to everybody, but especially me."

In his introductory press conference, Budenholzer made it clear he expected Antetokounmpo to not just improve defensively. He would demand Antetokounmpo lead his team on the floor and help Budenholzer guide the Bucks into a new era.

"There's a lot of reasons to be excited about coming to Milwaukee, but there's no doubt Giannis is one of [the biggest]," Budenholzer said. "He's so important to our success. I think he embraces his leadership role and how he needs to grow and improve and get better along with all of the rest of us. So the excitement level is through the roof."

*Mike Budenholzer was named the 16th head coach in Bucks history in 2018.*

In his final two years under previous head coach Jason Kidd (and Joe Prunty, who took over for Kidd in the 2017–18 season), Antetokounmpo received Second-Team All-NBA honors, so Budenholzer's excitement and expectations were well-warranted.

Entering the 2018–19 season, the Bucks have not won a playoff series since the 2000–01 season and have not had an NBA MVP since Kareem Abdul-Jabbar won the award in the 1973–74 season. If his team and star live up to his expectations, Mike Budenholzer just might be able to change both of those things.

# 92 A Stop in Milwaukee for Moses Malone

Some think of Moses Malone as a Philadelphia 76er. After all, it was there that he made his famous "Fo, Fo, Fo" prediction. Others think of him as a Houston Rocket, because it'd be easy to argue those were his peak years. Others might even think of him as the teenager who became the first high schooler to go straight to the pros with the Utah Stars of the ABA.

Few, if any, would think of him as a Milwaukee Buck, but it happened.

Before the 1991–92 season, Bucks coach and general manager Del Harris signed Malone to a two-year contract. It would be Malone's 16th season in the NBA and 18th season as a professional basketball player.

In fact, Harris went back to the beginning with Malone. After coaching in Europe and Puerto Rico, Harris became an assistant coach for the ABA's Stars in the 1975–76 season. Malone was named an ABA All-Star for the Stars the previous season, but Harris only got to coach him for a couple months, as the team folded just 16 games into the season.

Harris and Stars head coach (and former Bucks assistant) Tom Nissalke went without a job for the rest of the season before Nissalke was hired as the head coach of the Houston Rockets at the start of the 1976–77 season. The Rockets had serendipitously just traded for one of the biggest stars to enter the NBA during the ABA-NBA merger: Moses Malone. Nissalke lasted through the 1978–79 season before being removed as head coach and replaced by Harris. Harris coached Malone for the next three years, his most dominant in the NBA, so it came as no surprise he was interested in bringing him to the Bucks a decade later.

"Moses is an intense competitor with the heart of a lion and the spirit of a thoroughbred," Del Harris told the *Washington Post*. "He will give us a big lift in our rebounding and inside game."

Malone was coming off the most statistically insignificant year of his storied career, averaging just 10.6 points and 8.1 rebounds in 23 minutes per game with the Atlanta Hawks, but he did play in all 82 games.

Malone rebounded from that down season and served the workhorse role Harris envisioned, starting 77 of the 82 games he played in the 1991–92 season and playing more than 30 minutes per game. Scoring 15 points and grabbing nine rebounds a night, Malone became an impact player, but he wouldn't end up having a huge impact on the season as the Bucks went just 31–51. Harris would end up coaching Malone for just 17 games before moving exclusively to the front office and putting Frank Hamblen in charge on the bench.

After such a strong first year, Malone felt destined to put together another great season, no matter how much logic would seem to suggest that it couldn't be done. But as a wise man once said, Father Time is undefeated. As Malone prepared for his second season as a Buck, he struggled with a back problem that just would not go away. When he let doctors examine it, they found a herniated disc. Malone opted for surgery to fix the problem and missed a majority of the season. He ended up playing in just 11 games. With his two-year contract up, he moved on to a homecoming with the Sixers for his 20th professional season, but his relationship with Harris did not end there.

"We remained close the rest of his life," Harris later told the *Houston Chronicle*. "We stayed in contact. In fact, I talked with him on the Thursday and Friday of the weekend that he died at the Hall of Fame. I'll miss him."

Indeed, Malone passed away suddenly at the age of 60 in 2015 due to cardiovascular disease. Harris and Malone shared a special connection that went back to the start of each of their NBA careers and that connection brought the Hall of Famer to Milwaukee, even if it was only for two years.

# 93 Bango's Backflip

On his way to work, Kevin Vanderkolk picked up a 16-foot ladder from the hardware store. He thought he may end up needing it for work that night. When he pulled up to his work site, he still wasn't sure he would need it, but brought it in with him anyway.

Vanderkolk's work site was the Bradley Center. But it wasn't 1986, when the arena was being built. And he was not a member of a construction crew in need of some extra equipment. It was April 26, 2010, the afternoon before Game 4 of the Bucks' playoff series against the Atlanta Hawks. And he needed the ladder for a stunt he was going to try for the first time that night.

See, Vanderkolk would be playing his typical role as Bucks mascot Bango for the night and he needed something fresh and exciting to pump up the fans for this crucial contest.

He got his start as Bango at the end of the 2000–01 NBA season. As the Bucks made their way to the Eastern Conference Finals, Vanderkolk was in the stands studying how Bango mingled with fans during a game and entertained them during the breaks in the action. He had been informed by the organization he would be taking over the role for the Bucks and needed to figure exactly how one went about being an NBA mascot 250 days a year.

Vanderkolk originally got his start as a mascot by coaching gymnastics in Phoenix. Through his gymnastics work, he was put into contact with the Arizona Cardinals, who eventually asked him to be their mascot "Big Red." His impressive performance quickly earned him the opportunity to audition for the Bucks. At the end of the 2000–01 season, he was given the job and started his life as Bango.

"It was my responsibility to develop the skits and in-game repertoire," Vanderkolk told the *Milwaukee Journal Sentinel.* "I didn't have the background or know how important it was. In the beginning, it was pure passion. I was creating stuff out there and performing and getting reactions from the crowd. As I matured, you realize you are a pretty big piece of the brand."

Although he was part of a larger brand, it took actually becoming Bango for Vanderkolk to realize everything he did was up to him to imagine, create, and then execute. Parts of his performance certainly needed to integrate larger promotional campaigns and team-specific ideas, but the rest was his responsibility. And that's where the ladder came in.

For years, Vanderkolk wanted to do a backflip dunk off a huge ladder, but never quite knew if he could do it successfully or if he'd ever have the proper motivation.

"I wasn't sure I was going to do it," he said. "I remember driving to the game that day knowing I needed to do a skit that night but not knowing what to do."

When Vanderkolk arrived at the arena with the huge ladder, he knew he had about an hour to make sure he could actually execute the dunk. He started at a lower level on the ladder to start figuring out the distance and trajectory of his backflip. Knowing full well he could execute the backflip, he tried to get everything else just right.

"Just getting comfortable with it on the crash pad," he said. "The backflip wasn't the concern. It was getting comfortable doing it from that height."

After an hour of practice, Vanderkolk felt ready to do it, despite not executing the trick from the very top of the 16-foot ladder, and told his supervisor he was going forward with the trick during Game 4.

The Bucks took their first lead of the game following a 20-foot jumper from Luke Ridnour with 3:00 left in the first quarter. With fans excited about the 18–17 lead and a turnover from Hawks forward Josh Smith, Bucks coach Scott Skiles took a timeout. The stage was set for Vanderkolk's big moment.

The in-game host let fans know that Bango would be trying a new dunk as the ladder was brought out on the floor. Bango made his way to the top of the ladder slowly, imploring the crowd to make more noise as he took each step up the ladder. Finally, the crowd got quiet as Bango balanced atop the ladder for a moment before bending his knees and jumping off.

And just like that, it was done. One of the best mascot tricks ever completed. A backflip dunk off a ladder in a playoff game.

"I think it probably had the biggest impact of anything I did," he said.

Vanderkolk would never do the ladder dunk again because, as he revealed in a Reddit Q&A in 2013, he was prohibited from doing it a second time because the organization found it just a little too dangerous. At 36 years old, Vanderkolk retired from his role as Bango in 2014 to move on to other things, but to this day, many Bucks fans still remember the dunk and talk about it fondly when mentioning their favorite mascot.

# 94 Bob Weinhauer

As the Houston Rockets shuffled their front office in the summer of 1996, it became clear that Bob Weinhauer's role may be changing, despite serving as the general manager of back-to-back NBA title teams in 1994 and 1995. So, Weinhauer decided to make a move and joined Chris Ford's coaching staff in Milwaukee as the Bucks' lead assistant coach. Though stability might have been what Weinhauer was seeking, he instead found opportunity.

Just one year later, Bucks general manager Mike Dunleavy resigned and then became the head coach of the Portland Trail Blazers. Bucks owner Herb Kohl turned to Weinhauer to fill the opening at the top of the Bucks' organizational chart and Weinhauer jumped at the opportunity to again manage an NBA front office.

Weinhauer started in college basketball as a coach leading the Penn Quakers to a Final Four in 1979 before heading to Arizona State and then eventually to pro basketball with the Detroit Spirits of the Continental Basketball Association in 1985. He hopped over to the NBA as a scout and then assistant coach with the Philadelphia 76ers before moving to a front office role as assistant GM for the 1990–91 season. After that, Weinhauer served as an assistant coach again with the Hawks and Timberwolves before taking the front office role with the Rockets on April 29, 1994. It was a good time to take over in Houston, as the Rockets went on to win the next two NBA titles. When Kohl tabbed Weinhauer, it was difficult to question the hiring of someone who'd served in just about every NBA role.

Weinhauer had a quiet summer after taking over at the start of July 1997, but made a trade that shaped the start of a new era on September 25, as he shipped Vin Baker to Seattle and Sherman Douglas to the Cleveland Cavaliers for point guard Terrell Brandon, power forward Tyrone Hill, and a first-round pick. Brandon and Hill would ultimately not be the players Weinhauer was remembered for, but rather the players he would move to help shape the playoff teams in Milwaukee during the Big Three era.

Unfortunately, one of the moves Weinhauer would be remembered for was one he didn't technically make. When you look through the 1998 NBA Draft, you will see the Bucks traded Dirk

Nowitzki and Pat Garrity for Robert "Tractor" Traylor. Though the transaction record is correct, it is somewhat incomplete as the Bucks never really had Nowitzki. Weinhauer wanted Traylor and made a deal with the Mavericks to take him at No. 6 in exchange for the ninth and 19th picks of the draft. Once Traylor made it to six and the Mavericks selected him, they were responsible for selecting Nowitzki.

At the following season's trade deadline, Weinhauer made two moves that would shape one of the franchise's most memorable teams. With a lockout shortening the 1998–99 season, the Bucks were in an awkward spot at the trade deadline. The team was 12–5 and 6–0 in March when the trade deadline hit on March 13, 1999, but they needed to make some moves. Brandon refused to discuss a contract extension but his deal expired at the end of the season, so Weinhauer sent Brandon to the Timberwolves and guard Elliot Perry to the New Jersey Nets in a three-team deal. In return, the Bucks received Chris Gatling and Sam Cassell, a player Weinhauer knew quite well. Cassell played 20 minutes a game as the backup point guard during the Rockets' title runs in his first and second years in the league when Weinhauer was with the team.

Before Brandon was traded, Hill told Weinhauer he would prefer to be traded if the Bucks' point guard was ultimately moved out of Milwaukee, so the Bucks granted him his request and sent him to Philadelphia for Tim Thomas, the 20-year-old forward and seventh pick of the 1998 NBA Draft, plus veteran forward Scott Williams.

The Bucks struggled slightly after the trade as they adjusted to their new roster and Cassell missed nearly the entire season with an ankle injury, but they still grabbed the seventh seed with a 28–22 record. They would fall at the hands of the Pacers in a three-game sweep, but could still view the season as a positive as they made the playoffs for the first time since 1991.

During the season, Bucks coach George Karl impressed Kohl and started to take on a larger role in personnel decisions. By the end of the season, Kohl decided they no longer needed Weinhauer and opted to find a general manager to work hand-in-hand with Karl instead of above him. And thus, despite the success, the Bucks opted to not renew Weinhauer's contract. As had happened to him in Houston, Weinhauer quickly became the odd man out, despite helping put the team on the road to success.

# 95 Try the Sikma

On July 1, 1986, the Milwaukee Bucks traded center Alton Lister and two first-round picks to the Seattle Supersonics for Jack Sikma.

"I've tried to win with a small team for a few years now and couldn't do it," Nelson told *Sports Illustrated*. "For us to compete with the other good teams, we have got to be comfortable with our big lineup in there."

Seattle's veteran center demanded a trade after the Sonics put together a second consecutive 31–51 season. Before that season, Sikma had been voted to seven consecutive All-Star Games, yet people rarely think about that when discussing one of the best big men of the 1980s.

Instead, they remember one of two things: his hair or his move.

Sikma's blonde hair came to be one of his trademarks. His flowing curls were unmistakable.

"My reception in Seattle was pretty much on the order of 'Jack Who?'" Sikma later told *Sports Illustrated* about being drafted there. "There were a lot of players out there who had been on TV a lot more than some skinny guy from Illinois Wesleyan with a Dutch-boy haircut."

Sikma's hairstyle might have stuck out in the NBA, but not in his hometown of Kankakee, Illinois. He was largely nondescript there until a growth spurt before his senior year in high school sprouted him up to 6-foot-10 and helped him draw the attention of most major colleges in the area. Instead, Sikma opted for Illinois Wesleyan, an NAIA school, where he could grow into his body.

In college, Sikma struggled as he adjusted to playing against elite athletes and other players of a similar size, which led to his coach thinking up a new way to help him deal with the size and pressure of his opponents. Because he had played guard just a few years earlier, Wesleyan coach Dennie Bridges leveraged Sikma's footwork and impressive touch from the midrange and beyond.

Eventually, they decided on an inside pivot, which is unlike most pivots used in basketball. For example, Bucks fans can likely imagine any number of Skyhooks from Kareem Abdul-Jabbar. Typically, the legendary Bucks center would set up on the right block and when he'd catch the ball, he'd plant his left foot and rise up for the Skyhook with his shoulder perpendicular to the defender.

Sikma would instead execute an unnatural movement by planting on his left foot like Abdul-Jabbar and swing his right foot and shoulder toward the defender while ripping the ball right in front of the defense. Sikma typically punctuated the move with a jump shot and in one fluid and unusual motion, he would have a bucket. As he started to use the move more, he also started to release his shot from further and further behind his head. When Sikma reached the NBA, the shot was nearly unblockable and nearly unstoppable. Since no one else had really ever used the move before, it came to be known as "The Sikma" by the time he got to Milwaukee in his 10th NBA season.

Despite performing well during his time in Milwaukee, Sikma would never find what he was looking for in demanding a trade: another championship. In his first season in Milwaukee, the Bucks dropped an excruciating Game 7 in Don Nelson's final season as head coach before the franchise moved on to Del Harris. Sikma put together four more solid seasons for the Bucks, averaging 13 points, eight rebounds, and three assists per game in five seasons, often helped out by his patented move and hair. (Sadly, Sikma opted for a shorter hairdo in his final few seasons in Milwaukee. Some theorize there was some Samsonesque power derived from Sikma's glorious locks, but it was never proven.)

So, the next time you're out on the court, try adding the Sikma to your repertoire to properly remember his time in Milwaukee. Getting a perm and rocking Sikma's hairstyle, though, is a decision you'll need to make on your own.

# 96 The 1977 NBA All-Star Game

As the Western Conference All-Stars prepared for the 1977 NBA All-Star Game, Milwaukee Bucks fans saw something they thought they would never see again. There, laying on the floor stretching, was Kareem Abdul-Jabbar in a Bucks warmup jacket.

The Bucks had traded him two years earlier, yet Abdul-Jabbar was repping the hometown team during warmups. He was asked about it after the game. Surely, it must have been a symbol of his appreciation or a nod to all of the great fans in Milwaukee. Right?

"I forgot my own warmups," Abdul-Jabbar told reporters after the game. "The people here have always been kind to me when I've come back. I wish I could take them back to Los Angeles with me."

Milwaukeeans would surely be happy to see Abdul-Jabbar in green and red, as well as the Bucks-themed jerseys, but the game itself would be what people would remember for years to come.

It was the first All-Star Game after the ABA-NBA merger. Any number of hypothetical arguments could finally be decided on the court. Were ABA lifers like Dan Issel and Julius Erving really going to be able to put up numbers in the NBA like they had in the ABA?

Was David Thompson really as athletic as ABA folks claimed he was? Nine of the players from the Western Conference squad had either come from the ABA the previous season or spent time in the ABA previously.

It was the ultimate mix of great players and styles, as well as a group of players who just hadn't really ever been given the chance to exhibit their skills in the same game before. In 1972, Erving tried to sign with the Atlanta Hawks before a legal battle sent him back to the ABA, robbing the world of Erving running fast breaks with "Pistol" Pete Maravich.

In the 1977 NBA All-Star Game, the pair finally got to play together and put on a show. There was a baseball pass outlet from Erving to a streaking Maravich, a couple of connections in the half-court, and a beautiful up-and-under and-one finish from Erving on a backcut with an assist from Maravich.

The game went down to the wire. The Eastern Conference, led by Erving and Bob McAdoo, appeared to be in control in the second half, but the West rattled off a 9–0 run behind a couple of steals and hustle plays in the third quarter from the Indiana Pacers' Don Buse in his only NBA All-Star Game. Like many of the players participating, he had played in the ABA All-Star Game the previous season. With his energy, the West took the lead and Paul Westphal of the Phoenix Suns helped keep it into the fourth quarter with his strong play.

After a Phil Smith free throw broke up a 122–122 tie, Maravich brought the ball down the court with 52 seconds left and a chance for his East team to take a lead. He drove to the lane on the left side and got swatted by Bobby Jones. Rick Barry dove on the floor for the loose ball. It got tossed ahead to Westphal, who finished it for a dunk and a 125–122 West lead. McAdoo quickly pushed the ball up the floor and drew a shooting foul. He hit both free throws to make it a one-point deficit at 125–124.

The West brought the ball down and took a timeout with just under 30 seconds left. After inbounding the ball, Westphal tried to enter the ball to Abdul-Jabbar in the post and McAdoo stole it. With the shot clock off, the East had a chance to win the game. Maravich brought the ball up the floor to the left wing. A double-screen brought him across the floor to the right side where he attempted to pull up for a jumper, but Westphal stripped him, corralled the ball, and then tossed it over his head to Barry, who kept it until the clock expired. The West won, 125–124.

After the game, Erving was named MVP and the fans booed him mercilessly. They believed Westphal, who made a number of big defensive plays late in the game for the West and scored 20 points, deserved the honor. Unfortunately, the vote had been taken in the first few minutes of the fourth quarter, so voters overwhelmingly voted for Erving, who had 30 points on the night and happened to be leading the East when the votes were cast.

Somehow, one of the greatest All-Star Games of all time managed to get outdone by events both before and after the game, and it all happened in Milwaukee.

# 97 Find an Original Copy of "Green and Growing"

In 1977, the Bucks were experiencing something they hadn't really been through as a franchise: rebuilding.

The franchise was created in 1968, so the first time they had to go through the process of shaping a roster, it wasn't rebuilding; it was simply building. Starting from the bottom, they found the first pick of the 1969 NBA Draft through a coin flip and drafted Lew Alcindor. Things got much better after that as the Bucks became one of the league's best franchises for the next half decade.

Things started to fall apart in the 1974–75 season as Alcindor, then Kareem Abdul-Jabbar, informed the organization he no longer wanted to be in Milwaukee and preferred a trade. He did so privately, but the Bucks fell apart publicly. They went from the 1974 NBA Finals to the middle of the pack in one season, as both the offense and defense fell apart and they no longer had one of their leaders, Oscar Robertson. After the season, Abdul-Jabbar was traded to the Los Angeles Lakers.

The Bucks held it together for one more season with Bobby Dandridge leading the way to a surprise playoff appearance, but when Dandridge moved to Washington as a free agent the following summer, the Bucks' rebuild began in earnest. It started with the roster but spread to the coaching staff as Larry Costello decided to move on after the Bucks won just three of their first 18 games and he handed the reins over to assistant Don Nelson.

Nelson got through his first season, but the Bucks started making moves with him at the helm to build up a small fortune of draft picks in the coming years. In the 1977 NBA Draft alone, the Bucks had the first, third, and 11th picks. They would use those picks on center Kent Benson, small forward Marques Johnson, and shooting guard Ernie Grunfeld.

When all was said and done and the 1977–78 season began, the Bucks' most experienced player was John Gianelli, a center entering his sixth NBA season. During the season, the Bucks played two players entering their fourth NBA seasons (Brian Winters and Kevin Restani), two players entering their third NBA seasons (Junior Bridgeman and Dave Meyers), four players entering their second NBA seasons (Quinn Buckner, Alex English, Scott Lloyd, and Lloyd Walton), and four rookies (Benson, Grunfeld, Johnson, and Rich Laurel). In January, they signed nine-year veteran center Jim Eakins as a free agent.

The Bucks were a totally changed team that also happened to be a very young team, so the organization decided to run with it and launch a new marketing campaign. It was titled "Green and Growing" and it hoped to capture the essence of the team they were building. They had a first-time head coach with a roster full of young players, which could undoubtedly be described as green, and they would hopefully get better, which took care of the growing part. (Note the Bucks also had green in their jerseys! It works perfectly!)

As part of the campaign, the team commissioned a song to be titled, what else, "Green and Growing." The song was incredibly simple. Produced by Kevin Gavin and Otis Conner Jr. and performed by The Green Music Machine, it used just 12 total words:

"The Bucks don't stop here! / Milwaukee Bucks! / Green and growing! / Better each year! / Green and growing! / The Bucks don't stop here!"

Now, that stanza is arranged and re-arranged a few different ways, but that is it for the lyrics. The beat is peppy and quite catchy, which explains why "Green and Growing" was used for years to open Bucks basketball broadcasts.

So, go out and find the original record. At this point, it may be at a garage sale or maybe a secondhand store, but go find it and play it as loud as possible to remind yourself of the good times. Remember that the "Green and Growing" squad surprised the basketball world by winning 44 games and a playoff series that season. Green and growing indeed!

# 98 Rep a Deer Jersey

In the 1990s, NBA teams were willing to experiment with some new ideas on their jerseys. Some were cartoonish. Some were colorful. Some had pinstripes. Overwhelmingly, 1990s NBA jerseys were weird, which meant the Bucks' alternate jerseys for four seasons from 1995 to 1999 fit right in.

Let's start with the colors. Before the 1993–94 season, president of basketball operations Mike Dunleavy decided to take red out of the Bucks' color scheme and instead pair purple and silver with Bucks green. With home whites and road purples, the Bucks decided to use green as the base color for their third set of jerseys.

The trim on the arm and neck holes featured a small white stripe sandwiched between black and purple halves. It was the only piece of the jersey that featured black. The players' names on the back of the jerseys were spelled out in white. The numbers on the back and the front of the jersey were white with a strip of green, then white, and then purple surrounding the number. The numbers on the back of the jersey were placed where you'd expect while the numbers on the front were…not. Explaining exactly where the numbers on the front of the jersey were takes a little bit of work.

The word BUCKS adorned the front of the jersey in the exact same all-caps font used on the home white and road purple jerseys. The trim used on the letters was the same green/white/purple pattern used on the numbers on the back of the jersey, but the Bucks opted for a different fill than white on the front letters. They used a gradient that started white on the top of the letters before transitioning to purple at the bottom. Instead of being centered directly below BUCKS, the numbers were bumped to the right side.

And there, on the left side of the jersey, was a deer. The head of the deer took up most of that side, but the deer's body went all over the rest of the jersey. Part of the deer's eight-point rack wrapped up and over the top of BUCKS above it. The neck and lower body took up the remainder of the jersey's top all the way down to where it tucked into the shorts. The deer was multi-colored, with green, purple, and white all intermingling to create a strange, psychedelic version of a deer.

Combine the deer with the gradient letters and the offset numbers on a green jersey and you have one of the strangest looks in NBA history. And a jersey that you absolutely need to find and wear to Bradford Beach or your next summer cookout.

And, if the green deer jersey doesn't pique your interest because it's just too weird for you, there is another Bucks jersey with a deer on it. The black Bucks "Fear the Deer" jerseys unveiled in 2015 also feature a deer prominently on the front of the jersey. While the 1990s version decided to go with a nearly full body version of a deer, the 2015 version opted for the sternum and head. Much simpler and centered on the front of the jersey, it may be more your style.

# 99 Michael Redd and His Jump Shot

"Guards in the NBA need to have a body, and they have to be able to make threes," George Karl told Michael Redd. "Until you've got all that, I'll be ignoring you."

Redd was selected 43$^{rd}$ overall in the 2000 NBA Draft and Bucks head coach George Karl made sure he knew exactly what he thought of him in his rookie year. The rookie guard appeared in just six games in his rookie year, but his help wasn't really needed as the Bucks went to the Eastern Conference Finals.

As a rookie, Redd struggled greatly to meet either of Karl's criteria for an NBA guard. Ray Allen used to tell the rookie he had an "old man body," which was code for the extra weight Redd had on his frame and his 14 percent body fat. And he was definitely not shooting threes. Part of the reason Redd went in the second round as opposed to the first was his inability to hit jumpers consistently.

The rookie took Karl's words to heart and made it his mission to force his coach to play him the following season. After the Bucks were eliminated from the playoffs, Redd retreated to his hometown of Columbus, Ohio, and spent the entire summer in a local rec center with his father, James, and his high school coach, Keith Neal. Redd spent every day getting up shots in that gym, as well running sprints and lifting weights. By the end of the summer, he had trimmed his body fat down to just eight percent and grown considerably more confident in his jump shot.

Those improvements showed immediately in Redd's second season. He would play in just 67 games, but he'd receive significant playing time in those games, finishing the season averaging more than 20 minutes per game and 44 percent shooting from behind the three-point line.

By the time Redd made it to the 2004 All-Star Game and put up 13 points in 15 minutes, there was no doubt about his abilities as a shooter. Sam Cassell, one of his teammates during his rookie season, called him "easily one of the best shooters in the league."

"He'll stand out there and make 'em like Pop-a-Shots all night long," Cassell told *Sports Illustrated*.

(Fun fact: NBA All-Star Chris Bosh claims Redd and future Hall of Famer Kobe Bryant went head-to-head in a sweaty Pop-a-Shot battle in the 2008 Olympic Village for hours. Teammates couldn't pull them away from the machine.)

Redd became one of the league's deadliest shooters from deep. By bringing the ball over and then partially behind his head, defenders could never touch his shot, which turned him into a menace in every situation. He could whip around a screen without his feet set. He could pull up off the dribble. He could hit one with a hand in his face. It didn't much matter. He was going to get his shot off and it was going to go in.

From 2003 to 2009, few players in the league filled it up quite like Redd. Across those six seasons, the Bucks' lefty averaged 23

*Though his career was cut short by injuries, few Bucks fans will ever forget the beauty of Michael Redd's jump shot.*

points on 37 percent shooting from deep and 49 percent shooting from the field. Along with his 2004 All-Star honor, he was also named to the gold-medal-winning 2008 United States Olympic Team.

Unfortunately, Redd didn't get to have as long of a career as you'd expect for such a talented shooter because of knee injuries that started popping up in his seventh season. In 2006–07, he missed 29 games with a left knee injury. After missing just 10 games in the next season, it looked like the injury might have just been a blip on Redd's injury radar, but then it popped up again in the 2008–09 season. It made him miss nearly a month in November and then got much worse at the end of January, when the Bucks announced Redd had torn his left ACL and MCL.

Redd played just 79 games over the next three seasons, 51 of which came with the Phoenix Suns in the 2011–12 season, before retiring at just 32 years old. With his career shortened due to injuries, Bucks fans would be forced to wonder what Redd's career could have been with different knees.

# 100 Test Your Knowledge of Bucks Trivia

If you've read through this entire book, the following trivia questions should be no problem for you—every single answer is contained in the pages you've just finished reading. If, for some reason, you prefer reading books back to front, let's have some fun and see how much you know about the Milwaukee Bucks!

1. Which Buck battled Kobe Bryant in Pop-a-Shot for hours at the 2008 Olympics?

2. Name the Bucks' career leader in steals.

3. Which three Bucks head coaches were at the Milwaukee Arena for the 1985 NBA Draft?

4. How many consecutive All-NBA teams did Sidney Moncrief make?

5. When the team was created, the organization asked fans for suggestions on the team's name. What nickname was the clear winner of the vote?

6. Name either of the nicknames legendary Bucks announcer Eddie Doucette used to describe the midcourt circle.

7. Who did the Bucks beat in the 1971 NBA Finals, and how many games did it take?

8. In which season did Giannis Antetokounmpo play in his first All-Star Game, and how many points did he score?

9. Name the two Bucks who appeared in the original version of the *NBA Jam* video game.

10. Who is the only Milwaukee Buck to win the NBA's Sixth Man of the Year award?

11. Who's gonna win it?

**Answers:** 1) Michael Redd; 2) Quinn Buckner, 1,042; 3) Don Nelson, Del Harris, and Terry Porter; 4) Five; 5) Robins; 6) Bullseye or Cyclops; 7) Baltimore Bullets, four games; 8) 2017–18, 30 points; 9) Blue Edwards and Brad Lohaus; 10) Ricky Pierce, who did it twice; 11) The Bucks! The Bucks!

# Acknowledgments

It's still sort of crazy to think this book even exists. Writing a book is something I never imagined doing in my career, so I must start by thanking Triumph Books for making it possible. They approached me about writing the book shortly before the 2017–18 NBA season and helped throughout the process to make sure this thing actually came together, despite a crazy Bucks year. A special thanks to my editor, Adam Motin, who made sure it looks like I have some idea of what I'm doing as a writer. That job was incredibly difficult.

To get to a point where someone would even approach me about writing a book, a number of people had to give me opportunities along the way. I started writing about the Bucks while I was at Kansas State University, which is where the long line of thanks before Triumph Books begins. I would have never thought it possible to write a book if Dr. Barb DeSanto hadn't convinced me I could write a thesis and get my master's degree at K-State. I may not be covering the Bucks today without Howie Magner, who listened to me pitch a weekly Bucks column at *Milwaukee Magazine* and actually decidedly to let me publish. My work improved during my time there, as my first editor, Dan Shafer, helped me find my voice and learn to write with more conviction.

When I moved back to Milwaukee in 2015, the folks at ESPN Milwaukee took a chance on me and allowed me to start covering the Bucks for them, which gave me greater exposure and access than I had ever received before. That would not have been possible without Craig Karmazin, Evan Cohen, and Gabe Neitzel believing in me, as well as the help and support I received from Jeremy Marks-Peltz, Pratik Patel, and the rest of my teammates at Good Karma Brands.

I need to thank Charles Gardner from the *Milwaukee Journal-Sentinel* for his kindness from the moment I hit the beat in Milwaukee. Despite being a "competitor" of mine, Charles was incredibly welcoming and showed me the ropes of an NBA beat when he easily could have allowed me to learn a number of difficult lessons on my own. His support helped me become the reporter I am today.

While I'm here, I also need to thank all of the basketball scribes who came before me. It would have been impossible to chronicle anything the Bucks did before my time without the hard work of all of the writers at the *Milwaukee Journal*, the *Milwaukee Sentinel*, the *Milwaukee Journal-Sentinel*, the *Wisconsin State Journal*, *The New York Times*, the *Los Angeles Times*, *Sports Illustrated*, the *Washington Post*, the Associated Press, and United Press International. I spent days looking through all of their work, as well as watching countless hours of games and old footage on ESPN Classic, NBA TV, and Bucks.com.

A huge thanks to my podcast partner on *Locked on Bucks*, Frank Madden, for helping keep me sane throughout the process in our daily chats. And a special shout-out to my Brew Hoop friends Mitchell Maurer and Eric Buenning, who helped me work through a number of ideas, chapters, sentences, and even words as I worked on this book.

I could not end this book without thanking my friends. Writing a book during a crazy NBA season meant a level of hermit-like behavior I've never demonstrated before, which could have been a shock to the system of my friends who had grown accustomed to seeing me on a regular basis. In a relatively short period of time, calls and texts regarding plans for dinner or drinks turned into words of encouragement and check-ins on my progress. And often those messages would be left unanswered or I'd respond to them in a snarky manner, but they kept sending them anyway, which helped immensely during the moments when finishing the book felt impossible.

And finally, a special note to my family. I have not taken a traditional path to where I am today. I have picked an industry that has very little job security, and yet my family has supported me through it all. They may worry constantly, but they never stopped believing in me and what I can do. And that support can come in many different forms. It could be my sister attempting to understand my internal logic and help me plan for the future. Or my brother attempting to get me hooked on coffee and questioning every move the Bucks make. It could be my mom making sure I was actually eating full meals and reading through pages once the book was completed. Or my dad answering my Bucks history questions and making sure he listens and reads everything I create. All of it made this book possible and I could never do what I do without their support.

As a kid, my mom would take us to the Slinger Community Library at least once a week. Each visit, she would insist I grab a book of fiction to read before letting me scour the shelves for books on my favorite teams and athletes. I would read everything I could about them. I was addicted. I've often credited those weekly trips to the library for my love of reading and writing, and now, my book could be one a kid pulls off the shelves on his weekly library trip. That's crazy.

Thank you for reading. Thank you for your support. Let's do this again soon.

# Sources

**The 1971 NBA Championship:** *Wisconsin State Journal*, NBA TV

**Game 6 of the 1974 NBA Finals:** OnMilwaukee.com, Fox Sports Wisconsin

**The Lew Alcindor Coin Flip:** *Los Angeles Times, Sports Illustrated, Wisconsin State Journal*

**Herb Kohl Purchases the Bucks:** *The New York Times, Milwaukee Journal Sentinel*, OnMilwaukee.com, *Milwaukee Journal*

**The Big Three:** *Chicago Tribune, Sports Illustrated*

**Wayne Embry:** *Sports Business Journal*, Fox Sports Wisconsin, NBA.com

**Nellie's Last Game:** *Chicago Tribune, Philadelphia Inquirer, Sports Illustrated*, ESPN.com

**Drafting Giannis Antetokounmpo:** OnMilwaukee.com, *The Vertical, The New York Times*, NBA.com

**Retired Jerseys: Kareem Abdul-Jabbar's No. 33:** The Los Angeles Lakers Broadcasting Network, *Sports Illustrated*, OnMilwaukee.com

**Retired Jerseys: Oscar Robertson's No. 1:** *Sports Illustrated*, NBA.com

**Larry Costello:** PBS Milwaukee, ESPN.com, *Sports Illustrated, Chicago Tribune*, NBA.com

**Edens and Lasry Buy the Bucks:** *Milwaukee Journal Sentinel, Forbes, Milwaukee Business Journal*

**Retired Jerseys: Sidney Moncrief's No. 4:** *Sports Illustrated, The New York Times*

**The Creation of the Bucks:** PBS Milwaukee, *Sports Illustrated*, Milwaukee Bucks. *Milwaukee Bucks 50ᵗʰ Anniversary Book.* Milwaukee: Fox Printing, 2017.

**Game 6 of the 2001 Eastern Conference Finals:** None

**Bucks Finally Beat Sixers:** *Sports Illustrated, Los Angeles Times, The New York Times*

**The Bradley Center:** *The New York Times, Milwaukee BizTimes*, Rockwell Automation, OnMilwaukee.com

**Jim and Jon:** NBA.com

**Redd's 57-Point Night:** None

**Jennings' Double Nickel:** *Milwaukee Journal Sentinel*

**The Big Dog:** NBA.com, *Washington Post, The New York Times*

**Allen Hits 10 Threes in One Game:** None

**Abdul-Jabbar's Punch:** *Milwaukee Sentinel, Sports Illustrated*

**Bucks Win 2005 NBA Draft Lottery:** NBA.com

**Bayless' Buzzer Beater:** *Milwaukee Journal Sentinel*

**Kohl Doesn't Sell to Jordan:** ESPN.com, *Chicago Tribune, Milwaukee Journal Sentinel*

**Bucks in Six:** *Milwaukee Journal Sentinel, Sports Illustrated*

**Monroe Chooses Milwaukee:** ESPN.com, *Sports Illustrated*

**Jabari Parker's Journey:** *Washington Post*, ESPN.com, *Milwaukee Journal Sentinel*

**24–1:** *Washington Post*

**Antetokounmpo's First All-Star Game:** Bucks.com

**Dr. J in Milwaukee?:** woelfelspressbox.com, *The New York Times*

Pluto, Terry. *Loose Balls: The Short, Wild Life of the American Basketball Association.* New York: Simon and Schuster Paperbacks, 1990.

**Trading for Oscar Robertson:** NBA.com, NBA TV, *Sports Illustrated*

**The 1974 NBA Finals Disappointment:** *Sports Illustrated*, OnMilwaukee.com

**Retired Jerseys: Bob Dandridge's No. 10:** OnMilwaukee.com, ESPN.com, *Washington Post*

**The 20-Game Win Streak:** *Sports Illustrated*, NBA.com

**Retired Jerseys: Jon McGlocklin's No. 14:** Bucks.com, *Milwaukee Journal Sentinel*

**Squad 6/Clutch Crew:** *Milwaukee Journal Sentinel*, OnMilwaukee.com, ESPN.com

**Bucks Trade Abdul-Jabbar to L.A.:** *Sports Business Journal, Los Angeles Times, The New York Times, New York Post*

**Retired Jerseys: Brian Winters' No. 32:** *Sports Illustrated*, NBA.com, *Milwaukee Bucks 50ᵗʰ Anniversary Book.* Milwaukee: Fox Printing, 2017.

**NellieBall:** ESPN.com, The Players Tribune

**Bucks Sweep Bird and the Celtics:** NBA.com, *Sports Illustrated, Washington Post, The New York Times*

**Bucks and Spurs Combine for 337 Points:** NBA.com, *The New York Times, San Antonio Express-News, Chicago Tribune*

**Terry Cummings:** *The New York Times*, NBA.com, *Los Angeles Times*

**Retired Jerseys: Bob Lanier's No. 16:** *The New York Times, Sports Illustrated*, ESPN.com

**Saving the MECCA Floor:** *The New York Times, Milwaukee Journal Sentinel*, ESPN.com

**Eddie Doucette:** NBA.com, EddieDoucette.com

**Don Nelson:** The Players Tribune, ESPN.com, CBSSports.com, *Milwaukee Journal Sentinel, Los Angeles Times*

**The Inaugural McDonald's Open:** *Sports Illustrated*

**Paul Pressey:** *The New York Times, Oklahoman*

**Alvin Robertson's Playoff Performance:** Bleacher Report

**Retired Jerseys: Junior Bridgeman's No. 2:** *The New York Times, Fortune*

**The Ray Allen Trade:** *Milwaukee Journal Sentinel, USA Today*, ESPN.com

**The 2017 Comeback That Almost Was:** None

**The Rest of the Big Three Bucks:** *USA Today*

**The 2001 Eastern Conference Finals Conspiracy Theory:** ESPN.com

**George Karl:** *Sports Illustrated*, ESPN.com

**Robert Indiana's MECCA Floor:** ESPN.com, *Milwaukee Sentinel, The New York Times*

**Listen to "Light It Up!":** None

**Vin Baker:** *Sports Illustrated*, WBUR.org

**Del Harris:** *Chicago Tribune*, United Press International

**Mike Dunleavy:** *Sun-Sentinel*

**The MACC Fund:** MACCFund.org, OnMilwaukee.com

**Ricky Pierce:** *Sports Illustrated*

**Chris Ford:** *Sports Illustrated*

**Terry Porter:** *Shawano Leader, Sports Illustrated*

**Terry Stotts:** Associated Press

**Larry Krystkowiak:** Associated Press

**Marques Johnson:** CBSSports.com, *Sports Illustrated*, United Press International, *The New York Times, Milwaukee Journal Sentinel*

**The MECCA:** UWMilwaukeePantherArena.com, CBSSports.com, NBA.com

**The Wisconsin Entertainment and Sports Center:** The Post Game, *Milwaukee Journal Sentinel*

**Bango:** NBA.com, *Milwaukee Bucks 50ᵗʰ Anniversary Book*. Milwaukee: Fox Printing, 2017.

**Bogut Goes Down:** None

**Scott Skiles:** ESPN.com, *Boston Globe*

**Larry Drew:** *Milwaukee Journal Sentinel*

**Jason Kidd:** None

**John Erickson:** NBA.com, *Kansas City Star*

**John Hammond:** *The Sporting News*

**The "Fear the Deer" Court:** ESPN.com

**Bucks in the Olympics:** None

**Shoot a Skyhook:** Yahoo Sports, *Milwaukee Journal Sentinel*, ESPN.com

**Larry Harris:** Associated Press

**Mo Williams' Game-Winner:** ESPN.com

**The Game That Just Wouldn't End:** VICE Sports

**Quinn Buckner:** *Sports Illustrated*

**Jon Horst:** None

**Ernie Grunfeld:** The *Milwaukee Journal Sentinel*

**Play as the Bucks on *NBA Jam*:** None

**Take a Trip to the Basketball Hall of Fame:** None

**Alton Lister:** United Press International

**Get to Know Mike Budenholzer:** None

**A Stop in Milwaukee for Moses Malone:** *Washington Post, Houston Chronicle*

**Bango's Backflip:** *Milwaukee Journal Sentinel*, NBA Reddit

**Bob Weinhauer:** None

**Try the Sikma:** *Sports Illustrated*

**The 1977 NBA All-Star Game:** *San Antonio Express-News*

**Find an Original Copy of "Green and Growing":** None

**Rep a Deer Jersey:** None

**Michael Redd and His Jump Shot:** *Sports Illustrated*

**Test Your Knowledge of Bucks Trivia:** None